*Mac '59 Alumni
Congratulations on the Occasion of
Your Fiftieth Anniversary*

*Alun Joseph, Dean
College of Social and Applied Human Sciences
June 20, 2009*

Macdonald Institute

MACDONALD INSTITUTE

Remembering the Past, Embracing the Future

James G. Snell

THE DUNDURN GROUP
TORONTO · OXFORD

Copy-Editor: Jennifer Bergeron
Design: Jennifer Scott
Printer: University of Toronto Press

National Library of Canada Cataloguing in Publication Data

Snell, James G.
    Macdonald Institute : remembering the past, embracing the future / James Snell.

ISBN 1-55002-445-0

1. Macdonald Institute — History. 2. Rural women — Education--Ontario — Guelph--History. 3. Women — Education--Ontario--Guelph--History. I. Title.

LE4.G83S63 2003   378.713'43   C2003-900346-9

1   2   3   4   5   07   06   05   04   03

THE CANADA COUNCIL | LE CONSEIL DES ARTS
FOR THE ARTS | DU CANADA
SINCE 1957 | DEPUIS 1957

ONTARIO ARTS COUNCIL
CONSEIL DES ARTS DE L'ONTARIO

We acknowledge the support of the **Canada Council for the Arts** and the **Ontario Arts Council** for our publishing program. We also acknowledge the financial support of the **Government of Canada** through the **Book Publishing Industry Development Program** and **The Association for the Export of Canadian Books**, and the **Government of Ontario** through the **Ontario Book Publishers Tax Credit** program, and the **Ontario Media Development Corporation's Ontario Book Initiative**.

Printed and bound in Canada.⊛
Printed on recycled paper.

www.dundurn.com

Dundurn Press
8 Market Street
Suite 200
Toronto, Ontario, Canada
M5E 1M6

Dundurn Press
73 Lime Walk
Headington, Oxford,
England
OX3 7AD

Dundurn Press
2250 Military Road
Tonawanda NY
U.S.A. 14150

Macdonald Institute

ACKNOWLEDGEMENTS

I owe particular thanks to many people who assisted in various ways in the preparation of this book. Rosemary Wagner and Erin-Marie Legacey ably assisted the research. A number of people shared their recollections of the more recent history of Macdonald Institute/FACS when the archival records surprisingly become very slight: Richard Barham, Kathleen Brown, Alun Joseph, Elizabeth Miles, Griffith Morgan, Michael Nightingale, Joseph Tindale, Richard Vosburgh, Marjorie Wall, Janet Wardlaw, Trevor Watts, and Donna Woolcott. The research and writing were supported by a research grant from the College of Social and Applied Human Sciences. The actual production of the book was assisted by Laurie Malleau, Kathryn Virgin, and Phil McGreevy. The Mac-FACS alumni were supportive of the enterprise throughout, as was the UGAA (University of Guelph Alumni Association), which donated funds for the procurement of the pictures found in this text. Thank you to both of these organizations.

TABLE OF CONTENTS

INTRODUCTION

Macdonald Institute is intimately connected with the history of women and the history of rural society in twentieth-century Canada. Founded in 1903, "Mac" quickly reached its target audience of under-educated women in rural Canadian society. Through a succession of courses and programs over the following years, Macdonald Institute became a vehicle for young and middle-aged women to advance themselves. Women from across Canada, but particularly from southern Ontario, took advantage of the programs at Mac to enhance their own position within Canadian society — whether that meant returning to a domestic environment with greater expertise and self-confidence, or putting their new-found learning to more direct use in the workplace.

At the turn of the twentieth century there was considerable concern about the decline of rural Canadian society, which had previously been the backbone of the country. Considerable rural depopulation in Central Canada and rural out-migration to the cities, led by the movement of young women, threatened to create a gender imbalance in the countryside. What was more, considerable concern arose that young women in the urban environment would enter the workforce in large numbers and consequently lose womanly skills. Combined with a new enthusiasm for and awareness of women's social and economic potential, these concerns formed the basis for new ideas about educating women to bring new educational ideas into the countryside. Educated women could bring more sophisticated ideas and new knowledge into rural homes and society through the newly formed Women's Institute movement, or by developing courses in domestic science in the schools of rural and urban Canada. This new-found knowledge would enhance the quality of the domestic sphere in rural Canada (and less directly in urban Canada) and would directly attack some of the primary social concerns of the day.

To cap this movement for a more knowledgeable womanhood a school was needed, where women could absorb the most up-to-date knowledge and ideas about society and the domestic environment and where they could be trained with the necessary skills and knowledge. Through the initiative of Adelaide Hoodless and others, these concerns were developed and focused in Macdonald Institute. Located on the campus of the Ontario Agricultural College in Guelph and placed under the jurisdiction of the Ontario Department of Agriculture, Macdonald Institute received significant start-up funding from tobacco magnate Sir William Macdonald of Montreal.

Macdonald Institute was part of a complex of state and quasi-state institutions and processes designed to shape the lives and ideas of rural women in early twentieth-century Canada. This reshaping was aimed at improving agricultural efficiency and modernizing rural society. It was accompanied by Women's Institutes and by a range of initiatives undertaken by departments of agriculture.[1] Over the years Macdonald Institute evolved into something quite different: a modern educational and research institution addressing some of the complex needs of a modern consumer society and its families.

The resulting Macdonald Institute was tremendously successful over the years. By the 1950s it had become the largest degree-granting home economics program in Canada and had secured for itself a central place in rural society and among young women striving for post-secondary education.

But pressure to change and adapt to the new circumstances and environment of the 1960s pushed the leaders of Macdonald Institute to initiate fundamental changes to the content of the curriculum and to the ways in which students were exposed to that curriculum. Also under pressure was the idea of an institution with a special mandate to assist both the young people of rural society and the young women of Canadian society. The distinct mandate to rural Canadians disappeared and the institutional segregation of young women ended with the new attitudes towards women and gender in the decades following the Second World War. What remained was an institution with a strong educational thrust, intent on training women and men in a variety of applied subjects loosely associated with the old home economics program. Macdonald Institute reinvented itself in the 1960s and

1970s, undergoing fundamental changes as it adapted to the new social and educational environment following the social turmoil of the late 1960s. Everywhere in North America home economics programs faced fundamental decisions about their future. Macdonald Institute is an example of one such program that took account of contemporary social and intellectual pressures and fundamentally adjusted the content of its teaching and research programs. In doing so, it became an integral part of a modern university. Its claims to social and intellectual importance then rested on the quality of its teaching and research, and no longer on its ability to address the immediate needs of its two founding constituents — rural society and women.

In doing so Macdonald Institute lost the institutional support derived from its original rural focus — the support of the Ontario Department of Agriculture. This was replaced with a different set of institutional supports, that of a modern state-supported university.

I

THE EARLY YEARS,
TO 1915

Macdonald Institute was born in an age of both fear and optimism. The fear was that the traditional "strengths" of society and the individual were being lost to the evils of Mammon: the greed and uncontrolled growth of many forms of capitalism; industrialization and urbanization; rampant immigration and migration; disease; destruction of the environment. The optimism was that meaningful and substantial response to these threats was genuinely possible — indeed, society could probably have the benefits of the changes inherent in what was feared while retaining the traditional strengths of society. But to accomplish this would take a great deal of effort on the part of individuals, especially those who were members of the middle class and had the "right" racial/ethnic character — that is, those persons who shared the "best" values and who had the social and political capital to make reform effective. The women and men who led these reform movements knew that they could and must guide their society through the various obstacles (represented by the widespread fears) to a better society. Macdonald Institute, in its own modest way, was born of this impulse.

Among the powerful impulses at the turn of the century was a new-found concern for hygienic conditions and the healthful results that good hygiene could produce. Germ theory had flourished in the Western world since the early 1880s, when it was proved that a specific bac-

terium caused tuberculosis. Good hygiene promised substantially improved health for all who practised it, but first, knowledge of effective hygienic practices must be brought to all households. This could be accomplished in a variety of ways, from more effective house design (the fear of bad air from indoor toilets and central heating was considerable)[2] to antiseptic washing and cooking. It was essential to get this information into the hands of those who could make most effective use of it: those who ran the households in which so much daily time was spent.

More than that, the impulse to respond to the horrendous results of disease, malnutrition, and the high rates of maternal and infant mortality provoked a wide range of concerns. These concerns were met by various responses: inoculation projects (not infrequently met by avoidance or even rioting), safe-milk schemes, sewer and water developments in urban centres, and the public health movement. More broadly, the general public had to be made appreciative of the need for these responses and willing to co-operate with them so as to make them effective. The domestic science movement promised to meet some of these needs.

Women's desire to take a more meaningful role in the changing environment of turn-of-the-century society was a strong impulse for many. Women were challenging the overt and covert barriers to political participation, occupational freedom, educational opportunity, and economic security. Yet for many women these challenges were motivated by a conservative impulse, aiming to make the existing social order more effective. For such people the domestic science movement was attractive since it gave women an enhanced role and status but did not directly challenge the predominant gendered paradigm; in the domestic science movement women were not so much challenging the gendered order but rather working to enhance their role within that order. Women were stepping forward as leaders of the field, as experts whose speeches and writings claimed authority; women led the educational programs that were so central to domestic science. And not least importantly, there was a strong belief that domestic science promised significant and substantial improvement to women's lives — working-class and middle-class, urban and rural — much less the lives of all those nurtured by women — the young, the elderly, the sick, and men. As A.B. McKillop comments, turn-of-the-century women "had provided the institutional mechanisms by which the Victorian cult of female domesticity could essentially be perpetuated, in a more subtle form, for the age of science, industry and 'the new woman.'"[3]

Education was upheld in North American society as one of the primary means by which social problems could be solved and societal and economic change could be controlled and shaped. In the face of industrialization, for example, schools ought to be preparing young people for the adult world of work. For young women and men, particularly for those outside the middle class, this tended to mean the opening up of practical vocational and technical education so that the future work force (paid in the case of men, paid or unpaid in the case of women) would bring to their labour the knowledge, skills, and behaviour most needed. The new education movement emphasized practical schooling for both sexes, and this manifested itself in a significant turn-of-the-century expansion in vocational and technical education, which coincided and overlapped with the domestic science movement. This sort of applied education, instrumentalist in its function, promised particular benefits for girls by giving them in easily accessible form the mental discipline they would need as adults.

The idea of domestic science had broad appeal. First, it openly confirmed the gendered order of contemporary society, suggesting that "modern" women were *not* out to change the world, but simply to improve it and that within their own "sphere." For many, such a program would direct the attention and involvement of young women towards the home, where their "natural" abilities and interests lay.[4] Domestic science also prepared women for the paid workplace. As well, expanded women's opportunities for public activity and leadership tended to be acceptable because those opportunities could be understood within the hegemonic gendered order.

Second, domestic science offered new opportunities to women, where women would be the acknowledged experts, unchallenged by men. Domestic science promised to raise to a new level of prestige the traditional household work of women, by recognizing the complexities of the tasks involved and by subjecting those tasks to scientific scrutiny and understanding (and few words carried more prestige in the twentieth century than "scientific"). At the turn of the century, the term "science" was synonymous with the notion of "efficiency," which helps to explain the appeal of the idea as applied to the home and family. While the domestic science movement certainly worked within a gendered notion of women's work and abilities (and is thus referred to by some historians as anti-feminist), the movement also helped to infuse some women's work with a professionalized status and to give some women a vehicle for upward economic and social mobility.

The broad appeal went even further. Third, domestic science employed credibly the rhetoric of home and family so near and dear to the hearts and minds of vast numbers of North Americans as part of the traditional "strengths" to be preserved. In 1905, for

The Macdonald Girl

Queenly, fair and blooming lassie
Garbed in gown of sky blue hue,
Stately mien, and pose triumphant,
Embryo queen of rare menu.

Goddess of spoon and platter,
Mistress of man's ways and means;
Fairy nymph of kitchen clatter
Caterer of pork and beans.

Enemy of germs dyspeptic,
Mistress of all household arts;
Minister of domestic comforts,
Soft'ner of hardened hearts.

Like a sunbeam 'cross the campus
Trips she fair as thistle down,
Pure as sparkles on the grass blades,
In her light-blue college gown.

Men shall falter at thy footstool,
For thy hand kings deign to sue;
Peerless, bright Canadian lassie,
Queen of the Macdonald blue.

Sound your "slogan," clan Macdonald,
Sound it far with thrilling skirl;
Tell all people and all nations
Know the sweet Macdonald girl.

Kerry O'Byrne

example, the annual meeting of the domestic science movement declared that home economics stood for:

- The ideal home life for today unhampered by the traditions of the past.
- The utilization of all the resources of modern science to improve the home life.
- The freedom of the home the domination of things and their due subordination to ideals.
- The simplicity in material surroundings which will most free the spirit for the more important and permanent interests of the home and of society.[5]

Such language, which was echoed by Adelaide Hoodless and countless others, promised that domestic science offered controlled change and at the same time a confirmation of traditional ideals and values in the face of the crassness and grasping materialism of modern industrial, commercial, urban society. This counterweight to the more repugnant features of capitalism helps to explain domestic science's continuing stress (albeit minor) on aesthetics, bringing to the home and family an appreciation of "the finer things in life." As well, there was in the domestic science movement a strong element of class bias, a sense that the urban middle class would bring to the working class and the less educated of both urban and rural society the values and behaviour of the urban middle class. This would preserve middle-class hegemony in the face of wide-scale migration, urbanization, and industrialization. The teachers and purveyors of domestic science would noticeably be middle-class women. To carry out these multiple purposes the domestic science curriculum mixed science work and housecraft in imprecise proportions, but it was part of a broad process rapidly expanding the number of facilities and the range of choices of subjects available to the young people of the day.[6]

Finally, the primary vehicle for the domestic science movement was a typical one for turn-of-the-century reform movements: the state and its agencies. Reformers like Adelaide Hoodless and others set out to alter the public policy agenda so as to "get the government onside," to gain access to government funding support, and to make use of that most powerful of state agencies, the school. Through the school and the education of generations of girls and young women, families and home life would be transformed and the members of those families would be saved. So it was that at the turn of the century a number of new initiatives began almost simultaneously across the country: at the Hamilton Normal School of Domestic Science and Art, at the University of Toronto, at Mount Allison University, at the Truro School of Domestic Science, and at Acadia University.[7]

Adelaide Hoodless and the Domestic Science Movement in Canada

Mrs. Adelaide Hunter Hoodless.

The most prominent figure in the early years of the domestic science movement in Canada was Adelaide Hunter Hoodless of Hamilton. Hoodless shared with a growing number of middle-class women a desire to make the local and national society a better place in which to live. What was more, she had an increasing sense that she herself had the ideas and personal attributes to carry out meaningful social change. Among her causes, most important here was Hoodless's growing conviction that the school system was not providing the education most needed by girls and young women. Convinced of the need for domestic science in the school curriculum, Hoodless carried on a campaign locally, provincially, and nationally to gain support for this position. She spoke widely on the issue and lobbied both the local school board and the provincial Ministry of Education to adopt domestic science, slowly succeeding. She published an early textbook in domestic science in 1895 and gained provincial support for a training school for domestic science teachers, the Hamilton Normal School in Domestic Art and Science, of which she became president. Hoodless carried this belief in education further when she played a major role in founding the Women's Institutes, a vehicle for making up-to-date knowledge accessible to rural women. Thus began Hoodless's later career fighting for the spread of domestic science education, a fight for what one historian has called "spreading the 'gospel of homemaking.'"[8]

It is unclear just when the idea first arose to link some of these domestic science efforts with the Ontario Agricultural College (OAC) in Guelph. Since 1890 agricultural colleges in the United States had been leading the movement to establish home economics programs, and this American example may well have suggested the idea to OAC officials. As well, agricultural colleges tended to have lower admission standards than more traditional universities, making programs on agricultural campuses more accessible, particularly to rural females; agricultural programs shared with domestic science an emphasis on vocational training, an approach to education that was becoming increasingly popular among educators at the turn of the century.[10] A college focusing on educating farmers' daughters was an answer to "the rural problem" in a very direct way. Paraphrasing one OAC professor, the best way to keep the boys on the farm was to keep the girls there. A domestic science program at Guelph offered a way of introducing an educated group of eligible young women to the OAC students, who, it was hoped, would soon be heading back to rural areas.[11]

As early as 1896 Hoodless gave a talk on the Guelph campus about the benefits of domestic science to rural society, and by 1900 the president of the OAC, Dr. James Mills, had discussed with her the idea of establishing a domestic science program at the Guelph campus. A letter of March 9, 1900, suggests that the idea was originally Mills's and he solicited Hoodless's support; the idea of a domestic science program seems to have been a product of an expansionist program at the OAC.[12] She did more than merely give her support. Hoodless had an extensive network of contacts in government and society, having already persuaded Lord Strathcona to support some of her causes. She was also aware that Sir

Dr. James Mills, president of the OAC from 1890 to 1904.

William Macdonald, a wealthy tobacco manufacturer, had interests in education reform and might be persuaded to support a domestic science program. With the encouragement of Mills and the support of the Ontario government, Hoodless approached Macdonald while Mills contacted J.W. Robertson, a close friend and education consultant of Macdonald and whose support for the project was solicited.[13]

Hoodless and Mills needed from Macdonald funds sufficient to construct and equip a building for the domestic science program. By late fall of 1901, Macdonald had pledged $125,000 for this purpose and in return he had extracted a promise that the government would provide the operating funds for the program. The government's handling of the project was somewhat cavalier; the premier simply wrote Macdonald thanking him for the gift, which would be applied to "the training of teachers in the elements of agriculture and of young women in domestic science." The hard-nosed industrialist would have none of such vague statements. Fearing withdrawal of the money, the government hastily put the agreement in the

Adelaide Hunter Hoodless

Born and raised on a farm outside Hamilton, Adelaide Hunter had a family that was well enough off to be able to send her to Ontario Ladies College for her last period of schooling. She married the son of a well-to-do Hamilton furniture manufacturer in 1881 and over the next seven years gave birth to four children, one of whom died in infancy. Typical of upper-middle-class (particularly Protestant) women of her time, Hoodless was interested in a public role for herself. Such women might not have the vote in most instances, but they shared their husbands' tendency to believe that society needed to change and that reform would have positive, beneficial effects.

Hoodless balanced her commitment to her family and household duties with a growing commitment to a number of social movements. She gained prominence in a number of local and national women's organizations, helping to found a local branch of the YWCA and of the Victorian Order of Nurses. She was a national and international figure in these movements as well as in the domestic science movement. Hoodless was able to persuade the Ontario government not simply to support the domestic science movement but also to pay her as a consultant and advisor in the field. She used this status and government funds to visit American campuses and to obtain the latest information as to what domestic science educators there were doing, making this information available to Ontario educators. By the time of the founding of Macdonald Institute, Hoodless's public role was fading, but when she died in 1910 she was still an active, if less influential, figure.

Adelaide Hoodless was a tireless worker in her chosen social causes. She obviously enjoyed the status and influence that she gained, and later, as her husband's business suffered, she appreciated the opportunities that various government assignments gave her to contribute to the household income. She did not generate new ideas or approaches, but she had ability as a publicizer and advocate of ideas, and she proved herself capable of shrewd lobbying and facilitating.[9]

form of an Order-in-Council. Later, when the government seemed to be bent on using the funds to purchase and clear the site, Macdonald again pushed the government to a different course: the total donation rose to $175,000 to be used for a classroom building (Macdonald Institute) and a residence for women (Macdonald Hall); in return, the government pledged to purchase and clear the site, to share instructors from the OAC for some of the courses and to hire new instructors for others, and to provide the operating funds for the buildings and equipment.[15]

Sir William Macdonald.

One last piece of the Macdonald Institute puzzle remained to be put in place. Hoodless had continued to have considerable difficulty securing the ongoing funding and stability of the Hamilton Normal School of Domestic Science and Art. The new Guelph program seemed to offer a nearby opportunity to secure the place of the Hamilton Normal School in the training of domestic science teachers. It also gave Hoodless greater influence over the character and design of Macdonald Institute, of which the male educators and politicians seemed quickly to have taken control. By moving the Hamilton Normal School to Guelph and folding it into Macdonald Institute, the new program would have a ready-made faculty (hired by Hoodless in her capacity as president of the school) and curriculum. This seemed to be acceptable to all concerned, so the move was set for the summer of 1903, when the buildings were expected to be ready. To make doubly sure of her ongoing influence, Hoodless gained the agreement of the president of the OAC and the minister of agriculture that she could draw up the curriculum for the Institute (though Mills was careful to make it clear that others would be contributing to this process as well).[16]

Coming to the agreement to begin the program turned out to be easier than actually getting Macdonald Institute underway. The government quickly acquired the site for the building on the north edge of the existing campus, clearing three cottages from the location. Labour difficulties, however, delayed construction. When the first girls arrived in September 1903 neither Macdonald Institute nor Macdonald Hall was ready for occupation. Various buildings were used as temporary classrooms, particularly Massey Library, and the girls had to board in town. The result was a less-than-stable learning environment. Nevertheless, when

Sir William C. Macdonald

Sir William C. Macdonald was born and raised in rural Prince Edward Island in 1831. The son of a prominent local landowner, he took readily to a career in commerce in various cities before settling in Montréal. There his firm came to specialize in tobacco manufacturing, at which Macdonald was remarkably successful, eventually earning a fortune.

Unmarried and without direct heirs, he cultivated his role as philanthropist. Macdonald began to donate his wealth to causes he favoured, focusing particularly on education and rural society. He donated more than $13 million to McGill University, in his hometown of Montréal, and he also supported the National Council of Women. His concern for improving the lot of rural Canadians was manifested in a variety of ways: supporting crop improvements; founding the Macdonald Manual Training Fund to encourage practical, applied education; contributing to the consolidated school movement, whereby more "progressive" schooling was brought to the rural countryside by amalgamating small rural schools into single, larger schools with more sophisticated equipment and programs. Macdonald funded the establishment of one such consolidated school in each of Ontario, Quebec, Nova Scotia, New Brunswick, and Prince Edward Island; the Ontario school was built in Guelph on the edge of the OAC campus.

After the establishment of Macdonald Institute, Sir William conceived of and funded the provision in Quebec of a college similar to the OAC — focusing on domestic science, agriculture, and teacher training — Macdonald College. Macdonald was knighted in 1898 and died in 1917. His estate was the basis of what became the Macdonald Stewart Foundation, which continued to contribute to various projects on the Guelph campus over the succeeding century.[14]

a Toronto *Globe* correspondent visited the Macdonald program in that first fall, she remarked upon the "extraordinary" level of "mental exercise" taking place in the classrooms, as if the readers needed to be reassured that these were serious students. These first twenty-five to thirty students did have the advantage of seeing the buildings going up, perhaps taking a greater sense of "ownership" of the process.[17]

With the buildings finally erected, the OAC attempted to place the program on even firmer ground by seeking further funds from Sir William Macdonald. President Mills contacted the benefactor and arranged for Hoodless to visit him once again. Mills was seeking to place Macdonald Institute on a sound fiscal base so that it would not be dependent on continuing government funding. He wanted an enormous sum of money — up to $350,000 — to endow a large number of small scholarships in domestic science and in nature study and to build a small hospital, as well as to provide for the operation of Macdonald Institute.[18] The entire approach was unfair to Macdonald, since it violated his earlier agreement with the government and suggested that Mills was developing serious concerns about the level of the

Macdonald Institute at completion in 1904.

Macdonald Hall, 1904.

government's commitment to Macdonald Institute.[19] The approach resulted in no further contribution from Macdonald. The Institute was left to rely on government support, which would cause serious problems in the near future.

In the meantime, Macdonald Institute needed to get on with the tasks at hand, which were twofold. The first was functional: to teach domestic science with a particular view to training young women who could become teachers in the various educational forums of the nation. The second spoke to a "market" focus: to have special concern for the women of rural Canada, bringing to them the most useful and up-to-date knowledge and practice available.

This second task had been articulated throughout the process of forming Mac, but once in place on the OAC campus the rural interest gained even stronger focus. As originally articulated, the task simply drew attention to the idea that women of rural Canada needed educational support as much as women elsewhere. But on the Guelph campus the domestic science program that in Hamilton had fallen under the jurisdiction of the Ministry of Education now reported to the Ministry of Agriculture. The government saw no need for separate legislation establishing Macdonald Institute (in contrast to the OAC and later the Ontario Veterinary College, Mac's sister colleges at Guelph). Instead, the women's college was subordinated to the OAC, reporting to its president. In part this was undoubtedly because faculty members in the OAC would be providing important instruction to Mac students, but this subordination was also because in 1903 it was difficult (for men at least) to

Mary Urie Watson.

conceive of a post-secondary institution led by anyone but men. Indeed, when a dean of Macdonald Institute was first named, it was a man, Dr. W.H. Muldrew, who was professor of Nature Study. Only when Muldrew died in 1904, having had a very limited impact on Macdonald Institute, was a woman placed in charge. Mary Watson, who had been principal of the Hamilton Normal School and had moved to Guelph with the school, was named director, significantly being denied the more academic title of dean.

Mary Watson would play a significant role in the formation of Macdonald Institute, remaining as the academic leader until the summer of 1920. Watson lacked a university

Mary Urie Watson

Born in 1866 and raised in Ayr, Ontario, Mary Watson was the daughter of an agricultural implements manufacturer. She attended school in Ayr and Toronto before turning to the United States because of Canada's lack of domestic science schools at the time. Watson spent less than one year at the Philadelphia Cooking School before returning to Hamilton to attend Hoodless's recently opened Normal School in Domestic Science and Art.

After earning her teaching certification there, Watson taught domestic science at YWCA branches and in public schools for a brief period before attending the Teachers' College of Columbia University, New York City, where she earned a diploma in domestic art and passed her New York State teaching exams. Watson taught briefly in New York and Missouri before returning to Hamilton in 1901 as principal of the Hamilton Normal School.

When Macdonald Institute absorbed the Hamilton Normal School in 1903, Watson moved to the Guelph campus as the director of Macdonald Institute, reporting to Dean Muldrew. After Muldrew's death in 1904, Watson took over the leadership of Mac as principal. Watson played a leading role in the early years of the American Home Economics Association, and was the only woman member of the Canadian Food Board during the First World War. She developed a close relationship with Mac students, keeping in touch with many in the years following their graduation and organizing the first Mac reunion in 1920. Watson spent a good deal of her administrative time linking Mac graduates with various employment opportunities that came to her attention.

Watson retired from Macdonald Institute in August 1920, returning to her home in Ayr (to which she had travelled most weekends while at Guelph). She died in 1950.[20]

degree, though she had completed post-secondary education in domestic science at the Philadelphia Cooking School and in teaching at Columbia University in New York City. This academic status reflected the applied character of domestic science and the early tendency of advanced domestic science programs to exist outside a university setting. Watson nevertheless reflected the developing professionalization of domestic science. She had advanced training in the subject, had devoted her career to teaching domestic science, and was regarded as an expert in the field. In this she stood in contrast to Adelaide Hoodless, who was soon reduced to a peripheral role at Mac. Hoodless taught a course on ethics and the home to the students, but the course exposed her weaknesses. It consisted largely of platitudes about the role of women and morality in the home life of the nation and lacked serious substance; as well, Hoodless was not a trained teacher and her classroom conduct reflected this. Before long, Hoodless was removed from the classroom. After some conflict and after her protegé, Mary Watson, took over as director, Hoodless was allowed to resume her course (one hour a week), but it was never a central part of the curriculum and was removed as soon as she died. Her advice was still sought in equipping the new buildings, but her long-term influence was curtailed almost completely.[21] Hoodless retained her contacts with Mac, but her involvement was largely social or formal in the future, assisting at teas or attending graduation ceremonies.

THE GUELPH SETTING AND PROGRAM

The delayed opening of the Macdonald buildings (Institute, Hall, and Consolidated School) officially took place on December 17, 1904, with considerable ceremony. Formal invitations to the ceremonies were issued, and a small number of favoured individuals attended an "informal luncheon with the young ladies" in the Macdonald Hall dining room prior to the ceremonies.[22]

Macdonald Institute was an attractive red-brick building with an imposing columned portico at its front entrance. With its beaux arts style, Macdonald Institute rose above the utilitarian character of the campus's other structures to become the most beautiful building at Guelph. By January 1904 the first classrooms (in the eastern wing) were occupied and by the following September most of the building was ready for use. The three-storey centre block was balanced by two-storey side wings in matching style and generously decorated with brick and stone motifs. The domestic science programs occupied the second floor of the building at first, gradually extending to the rest of Macdonald Institute as the other programs (Nature Study and Manual Training) moved out. The second floor contained two classroom kitchens, one

Above: *Long view of the Macdonald Institute buildings, 1904.*

Left: *Macdonald Hall, 1904.*

Close-up view of the horse-drawn wagons used to bring the rural students into Macdonald Consolidated School in 1904.

Macdonald Consolidated School, circa 1904.

Advertisement in the OAC Review announcing the opening of Macdonald Institute.

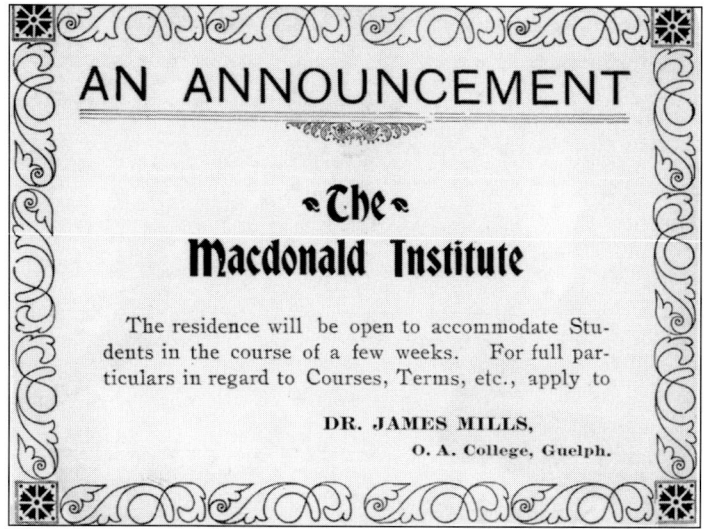

A double room in Macdonald Hall.

Macdonald Hall dining room, 1904.

practice kitchen, a class dining room, a dress-making room, a sewing room, a fitting room, a laundry classroom, one large lecture room, various storage rooms, and a small apartment (two bedrooms, a bathroom, living room, pantry, storeroom, and kitchen). All programs in the building shared an assembly hall, a reception room, a reading room, and a reference library.[23]

The Macdonald Hall residence opened in time for the Fall 1904 semester with space for one hundred women students. Less impressive architecturally both inside and outside, the red-brick building beside Macdonald Institute was a multi-functional facility designed to meet virtually all of the physical and social needs of the residents. It was designed by the same architect used for Macdonald Institute, and the same contractor built both buildings, helping to ensure a complementarity in design and function. On the ground floor were a library, a dining room (for women students only), a kitchen, a drawing room for socializing, offices and an apartment for the matron, a post office (mail arrived three times a day), and a number of residence rooms for students. On the floor above was a gymnasium, matching the size and location of the dining room and sufficiently equipped that the girls could attend twice-weekly exercise classes and have games without needing access to the men's facilities. The gym served as the site for Sunday evening prayer services and for social events and was, in Watson's words, "the constant playground of the women's residence." A sitting room had a number of chairs and tables for socializing and writing, as well as a piano. There was a small number of single-residence rooms along with a larger number of double rooms. On the top floor was a hospital, and this is likely where the staff (mostly maids) had their rooms.[24]

Within this physical setting, Macdonald Institute struggled somewhat to find its educational niche. The OAC president, James Mills, announced as early as 1903 that plans were underway to offer a four-year degree course (the degree would be from the University of Toronto, which conferred the BSA degree for the OAC's agriculture graduates),[25] but these plans would not reach fruition for almost half a century. Instead the Mac programs focused on more immediate goals. Programs in Nature Study and Manual Training were originally housed in Macdonald Institute and were part of the initial emphasis on teacher training in the expectation that these programs, as well as domestic science, would have a major role to play in Ontario's schools. Both programs shared with domestic science an educational philosophy that emphasized the benefits of an applied, hands-on approach to learning. It was because of these links that W.H. Muldrew, who was in charge of the Nature Study program, was named the first dean of Macdonald Institute. Both programs soon moved away from Macdonald Institute and faded in importance on the Guelph campus.[26] What remained was domestic science.

Domestic science had several advantages in determining Mac's survival. First, it appealed to a new educational market — women, who were otherwise scarce on the Guelph campus.[27]

Second, the Ministry of Education had, through the Hamilton Normal School, given its imprimatur to the training of domestic science teachers at Mac. Third, there was a strong sense of mission to make the knowledge encompassed within domestic science available to the young women of early twentieth-century Canada, particularly those residing in rural districts who had less access to the educational institutions and processes that were becoming so influential in contemporary society. The strength of this new idea for women's education is shown by the contemporary founding of a degree-granting domestic science program at the University of Toronto.[28]

The domestic science programs changed frequently as various options were tested and as faculty honed the program content to best reflect the standards of the discipline, societal demands, and the needs of the students. The flagship program — the Normal program — was a two-year teacher training course in domestic science, focusing on pedagogy and on chemistry, foods and cooking (including bacteriology), economics, English, the house, hygiene and health (including biology), and laundry. Students for this program had to be at least eighteen years of age and to have completed the equivalent of junior matriculation in Ontario; applicants with a general teaching certificate could be admitted directly to the senior year of the program, creating *de facto* a one-year teacher training program. Most students in this teacher training program attended for two years and they formed the core of the student body, giving it continuity and scholarly leadership. In the first years of this program, students who wished to proceed to a degree (Mac offered only a diploma) could do so by attending the University of Toronto, where the Macdonald courses were credited towards the Toronto degree program. But by the mid-1910s this transfer of credits had become problematic and Watson tended to advise students to look to American campuses (such as her alma mater, Columbia) where the transfer of credits was apparently much easier.[29] Students in this program carried out their teaching observations and their practice teaching at the Macdonald Consolidated School (now the Macdonald Stewart Art Gallery), just across the field from the Institute. Macdonald Institute and the OAC tried offering summer courses for teacher training in the campus specializations and for a time these were well attended, but the summer courses did not continue. Graduates of the teaching program could expect to earn about $50 a month when they started out, according to Watson, but often waited many years to move beyond that salary.[30]

In keeping with its mandate, the Macdonald Institute teacher training program aimed particularly to furnish domestic science teachers for rural areas — either for schools or for local Women's Institutes. Such teaching was particularly problematic because most rural schools (much less rural homes) lacked modern technology — running water, electricity, refrigerators, washing machines. It was a major challenge for Mac faculty and graduates to develop effective teaching techniques in such an environment and to equip their students to bring hygienic and nutritious practices into such homes. Macdonald Institute faculty developed or found simple, portable equipment — trestle tables, boxes of utensils, kerosene stoves — to deal with this problem and to enhance accessibility to rural areas. More generally, however, teaching at Mac featured the hollow-in-the-square industrial education approach.[31]

Beyond teacher training, Macdonald Institute developed several programs offering diplomas in domestic science. From the start, a two-year Housekeeping program awarded successful students with a Macdonald Institute Housekeeping Certificate. The fundamental thrust of this program does not seem to have changed in these years. It aimed to train "professional and skilled housekeepers" who were interested in a professional career as an institutional manager (a matron of a hospital or residential institution, for example). The program's professional character was emphasized by the encouragement of "mature" students and by the bias in favour of older (aged twenty-five or more) applicants. Courses focused on foods and food chemistry, housekeeping practices, textiles and sewing, laundry, and household sanitation and hygiene, as well as English, dairy work, and horticulture. Graduates who went on to complete "six months successful housekeeping in an institution" were granted a Professional Housekeeper's Certificate, but it is unclear to what extent Macdonald Institute supervised this practical work or what criteria were used to judge "successful."[32] Watson herself was convinced by the 1910s that there was a considerable demand for professional housekeepers and encouraged applicants to consider the program; graduates, she estimated, could earn a good living — salaries usually

Gardening was an important part of the practical education at Mac. The extent of the gardens can be seen in this picture from the early years.

A postcard printed before 1910.

The extensive gardens. The house in the background is still part of the university, one of many in use on Gordon Street.

Here the Macdonald Girls are joined by the students from Macdonald Consolidated School, circa 1908.

started from $35 to $40 a month (and were as high as $900 annually) plus room and board.[33] The number of Mac grads in institutional housekeeping positions across North America suggests that Watson was correct. In the spring of 1914 the Mac program was described in the United States as the only one that "trains housekeepers scientifically" and the "skilled young women" graduates of the program were essential for operating modern hospitals.[34]

In 1903 a two-year non-professional Housekeeping program began but it proved unpopular and was dropped. In 1912, however, Watson was convinced that a demand for such a program had developed, especially for girls "desirous of preparing for life in the country," and the Associate program commenced. The first year of the program essentially shared courses with the first-year Housekeeping program, but the second year emphasized applied learning: while the senior-year Housekeeping students focused on the problems and characteristics of institutions, Associate students focused on the home.[35] The minimum age for entrance was seventeen, and Watson often suggested this course as an alternative to applicants too young to enter the teacher training program. Successful applicants needed at least two years of high school education and one year of housework experience.

For young women who could afford to spend fewer resources — time or money — at Macdonald, there was a Homemaker course (after 1905). In that year the one-year Homemaker program replaced the earlier (1903) Housekeeper program. Here, young women of at least

An early cooking class. The manual training movement championed practical education.

A 1904 cooking class in the newly opened Macdonald Institute.

seventeen years of age with high school entrance qualifications or a good elementary education could obtain a basic grounding in domestic science. The program emphasized courses in "plain cooking" and foods, sewing, laundry, home management, and sanitation, as well as brief exposure to child study, home nursing, ethics, and aesthetics in the home; electives varied from English to millinery to home dairying. The calendar proclaimed that students in this program and the Associate program would gain "a goodly measure of mental training" as well as practical study.[36] Beginning in 1910 this program explicitly focused on rural women, usually defined as "farmers' daughters" so as to distinguish between these young women and the daughters of rural professionals or merchants. This emphasis was real. Up until sixty days before the course commenced each year, only applications from farmers' daughters were accepted; once the sixty-day point passed, the waiting list was opened up and other young women took whatever open places remained. After 1910 Director Watson found herself frequently writing to young women and their families explaining that the spaces in the popular program had all or almost all been taken by farmers' daughters, to the exclusion of other applicants.[37]

The practical classroom experience. Here the Mac girls learn the art of butter-making in 1905.

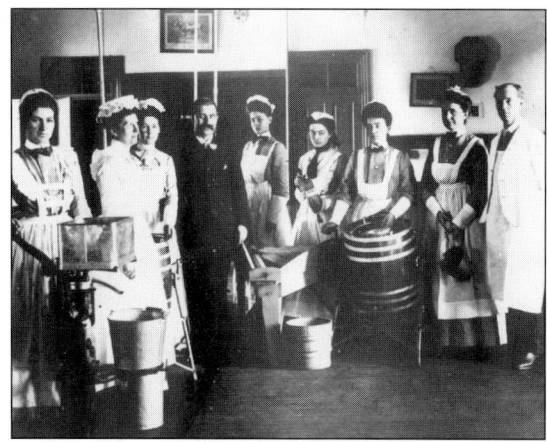

Miss Howland's classroom in 1908, part of a three-month short course.

Finally, Macdonald Institute offered its so-called "short courses," three-month courses offered in the fall, winter, and summer semesters (foretelling the future three-semester system of the University of Guelph). These courses had two quite different groups of students in mind. For a brief while, there was a short course for teacher training in the summer. More central to Macdonald Institute's rural mission were the short courses aimed at girls from the

The important first step before they learned to make butter.

countryside, which provided practical education for young women who expected to spend their lives in rural Canada. There was a sense in these courses of exposing the students to the "better" elements of life in "modern" society in the hopes that the countryside would be incrementally improved by these young women taking their knowledge back to their farms. There was also a sense that girls ought no longer to rely solely on learning household skills from their mothers and female relatives; experts, as the source of the most up-to-date research and theories, needed to involve themselves in the instruction.[38] These short courses

focused on "plain" cooking, "plain" sewing, care of the house and home management, and
home nursing. These students, as well as those in the Homemaker course, heard Adelaide
Hoodless's ethics lectures. The short-course students also had a chance to develop their
interests by selecting electives from a wide range of possible courses. The impression left is a
three-month program that exposed rural young women to a form of urban and community life away from the farm, where their minds might be stimulated and where more likely
they simply matured. Here too the minimum age was seventeen, and students needed to have
completed their elementary school education to be admitted.[39] These short courses were very
popular in this period, usually being filled almost entirely by farmers' daughters; the administration frequently turned urban applicants away as there was no space available for them.[40]

Throughout the first twelve years at Macdonald Institute there was a clear tendency
towards making the curriculum more demanding and more intellectual. The applied and
practical character of the programs was constant. But the inclusion after a few years' experience of more academic subjects suggests a growing sophistication (or an attempt to coun-
teract the stigma associated with such applied programs).[41] For example, English and then
physics were added to the teacher training program; biology, bacteriology, and physics were

added to the Housekeeping program. The location of Macdonald Institute on a campus with a growing interest in degree programs influenced the reshaping of the Mac curriculum in a more academic and scholarly direction.

Macdonald Institute had one last educational program that in this case offered no diploma or certification. This was the college's link with the Women's Institutes (WI). Adelaide Hoodless had played a major role in founding the WI movement, which provided a venue for rural women in particular to gain access to knowledge and ideas and a forum in which they could begin to develop their own self-help skills. Founded in the mid-1890s, the link to Macdonald Institute began with the creation of the latter. Mac was the site of the WI annual conventions from 1903 to 1910, at which point attendance at the meetings outgrew Mac's capacity, although the WI conventions returned occasionally to Guelph in celebration of the historic connection.[42] More important than this physical connection was a philosophical one: both sought to bring knowledge and skills to women of rural Canadian society and both idealized education. Finally there was a fiscal connection. The state, through the Ontario Ministry of Agriculture, accepted a supervisory and financial responsibility for the institutes

The Women's Institute members, on campus for outreach programs, lining up in front of Creelman Hall in 1915.

through its Institutes Branch. This branch was initially responsible for the Farmers' Institutes and simply expanded to include the Women's Institutes as they expanded across the province.[43] This was important because it gave Macdonald Institute, through its link with the OAC, access to an additional stream of state funding.

The Macdonald Institute's connections with the Women's Institutes were fundamentally encouraged by OAC President Creelman's interest in promoting the OAC to the Ontario government through extension work. The advent of county agricultural representatives in 1907 had been conceived by Creelman as a further means to employ OAC degree graduates, and now the links to the Women's Institutes offered parallel opportunities for the graduates of Macdonald Institute's programs.

Historian Terry Crowley has criticized the early education at Macdonald Institute "as training rather than as higher learning." Young women received some instruction in the scientific basis of cooking, but most of the teaching emphasis was on proper procedures and mechanical repetition. Much of the learning stressed the same sort of elementary skills acquisition that occurred at the OAC:

> The perfect hand stitch was greatly admired but its acquisition overlooked learning about the effects of textile machines on domestic production. Repetition, rote memory work, and exact duplication based on manual dexterity were highly valued … Laundry and cooking, for instance, were taught in a "hollow-in-the-round" configuration. An instructor standing in the middle gave the commands and the students responded under careful scrutiny as they executed each separate step. Such methods reinforced ideas at the college that confounded knowledge with method and that prized the immediate product rather than the critical intelligence needed to survive in a rapidly changing world.[44]

This was an educational philosophy with which Mary Watson was quite comfortable. It was this philosophy that allowed Manual Training and Nature Study to share accommodations with the domestic science programs in the early stages of Macdonald Institute.

The initial expectation had been that the benefits of further schooling and of domestic science were so obvious that the young women of rural Canada would flock to Macdonald Institute as soon as it opened its doors. But this did not happen. The numbers of rural women, though reasonably impressive, were lower than expected for a number of reasons. Many rural families were cash poor; the expenditure of scarce financial resources on a

Bird's-eye view illustration of OAC and Mac in 1904.

daughter's schooling was not necessarily viewed as a good investment; and the benefits of advanced schooling, though accepted by most urban, middle-class people, had not yet been recognized by much of rural society, and as a result many of the aspiring applicants lacked the basic educational qualifications to enter the desired Mac program.[45]

When this trend became apparent, Mary Watson retained the overall strategy of Mac's role in rural Canada and developed a set of tactics to attain that aim. Beginning in 1907 she attended the WI annual conventions, speaking as more than simply the head of the host institution. Watson reached out to the WI and offered the use of Macdonald Institute's resources. Watson and her staff developed an innovative "clippings file" on a wide range of domestic science issues and containing articles and reports on various relevant topics. These files were available on loan for a two-week period, free of charge to any WI members who were preparing talks for their local groups. Later the loan service opened to the public. A 1908 advertisement by Mac officials in a national women's magazine offered to make these materials available through the mail to any WI member upon request. The response was rapid and extensive, amounting to some 350 requests for information in the first year. An initial collection of some fifteen hundred files gradually expanded to more than five thousand by 1916. The OAC administration was so impressed with the popularity of this outreach program that President Creelman asked Watson's staff to co-operate with a decision to create a parallel program through the Massey Library at the OAC.[46] Such a program meshed nicely with the OAC's existing emphasis on extension work within the broader rural community.

Mac also developed an outreach program by which some of the short courses were offered in small rural communities, facilitating local involvement in the courses and easing the social and economic disruption otherwise caused by the absence of an often vital member of the household economy. These courses, by no means incidentally, offered employment to Mac grads, who began to tap Ministry of Agriculture funds in a parallel role to the male "ag reps" who carried new knowledge and ideas in agriculture across rural counties. These tactics showed a flexibility that was effective in entrenching Mac's role and reputation across rural society and would reap benefits in the years to come, and in the short run these tactics worked well. The domestic science crusade reached broader numbers of women; the idea and the role of education in rural society flourished; and Mac's connections with state processes strengthened. Macdonald Institute's outreach to the rural communities of Ontario played, in the judgement of Linda Ambrose, an "invaluable" role in reshaping rural society for women.[47]

In the long term, however, the link between Mac and the WI became increasingly tenuous as the needs of the WI and of Macdonald Institute slowly diverged. WI members expanded their horizons beyond the issues raised by domestic science to include broader political and social problems, while Mac became increasingly an institution of "higher learning" seeking to emphasize the academic features of domestic science and the intellectual rigour of post-secondary education. But while this connection with the WI lasted, it played a vital role in entrenching Macdonald Institute in Canadian society.

The links with the WI movement emphasized further the applied character of the intellectual interests at Macdonald Institute. Watson herself described Mac as "a technical school" without much time for the arts, English, or mathematics. Nevertheless the school shared with other educational institutions of the age a rising faith in empiricism and a new interest in analyzing society.[48]

Annie Ross, MD.

Carrying out these programs was a staff led by Mary Urie Watson. The early faculty members at Mac all had post-secondary education, though few had gone beyond an initial degree or diploma. W.H. Muldrew, the first dean, had a doctorate in pedagogy and this was likely an important factor in his being named dean. Watson herself had graduated from Columbia University's diploma program in teaching and from an American cooking school. Most of the other Mac staff had studied in similar programs, though there were occasional master's-level degrees represented.[49] Annie Ross, a long-time instructor in home nursing and child study, was unusual both for her medical degree and for the fact that she remained at Mac until the late 1930s (with one brief leave). The high rate of staff turnover must have weakened the teaching and the sense of community at Mac. The number of domestic science staff, who were all female, increased from three in 1903, levelling off at nine by 1910. By then the turnover was slowing so that there were only two new instructors in 1911 and a relatively stable staff environment had been gained; 1914 was the first year in which there were no new instructors at Mac. The median period of employment for the total of twenty-three faculty members in the years 1903–1915 was just three academic years.[50] All of these instructors were given the academic title of instructor, lecturer, or demonstrator. None of the Mac faculty members were professors; although some of the OAC professors had no higher academic training, the professoriate was reserved for men. All of the women instructors appear to have been unmarried, it being typically quite difficult for women in most professional occupations to combine paid work with married life. The OAC faculty members played an important role in teaching many of the students, and a small number seemed to enjoy joining in the broader task of mentoring these young women.

Mary Watson was the leading scholarly figure among the Mac faculty members. In 1905 she published *Public School Household Science*, which was a revised edition of Adelaide Hoodless's 1898 textbook. Watson reorganized the textbook, removed the material aimed at high school students and teachers, and focused simply on elementary students. The new edition was more concise and more authoritatively written, and had greater coverage of such topics as assessing and buying, preparing and cooking various foods. After the American Home Economics Association was founded in 1908, Watson was elected third vice-president, the sole Canadian on the executive; in 1915 she was named to the council. During the First World War, the Canada Food Board in Ottawa made use of Watson's expertise in the national cause.[51]

Through its array of courses and overlapping programs Macdonald Institute carried out an educational mission that gave substance to the domestic science crusade of Adelaide Hoodless and others. Fighting the stigma of being a mere "cooking school," a Mac spokesperson commented that the purpose of domestic science went far beyond teaching girls how to cook, sew, and clean a house:

> The aim is to help girls "make a home" rather than "keep a house" — to establish at an early age respect for and an intelligent idea of the home as the most important factor of civilization; to teach respect for and pride in the performance of duties in the home; to secure greater co-operation between the home and school; to secure better food and sanitary conditions; to understand the principles of economics as applied to household manage-

ment and in the relation of the home to the state; and to apply theories acquired in this and other departments of school and college work.[52]

The tensions produced by this somewhat romantic desire to enhance home and family life, on the one hand, and the perceived need to provide practical training and skills on the other were a constant problem. So too were the tensions between both of these aims and the slowly growing wish to problematize and make more academic the domestic science curriculum. On the more personal side, a Mac education also produced tensions at home when students returned from school and sought to institute their new knowledge and approaches in a more traditional environment.[53]

Watson certainly presented herself publicly as confident of the quality of the Mac program and students. In a response to an American enquiry, she described the program and admission process:

> With us everything is a part of the home economics work. Our whole effort is toward helping the students who come to us to make the most of their time. We do our best to help a girl choose the right course and the one she is able to carry, before she enters; then if she fails to make the required standing in her first examination and is reported as a loafer, or mentally unready for the course, we either recommend her to drop out or insist upon her doing so. We are greatly assisted in holding to our standard, by the fact that we have always more applicants for admission than we can accept.[54]

To be fair, this assessment was reflected in the graduates themselves. They were getting jobs in a variety of occupations across the continent and appear to have thought well of the education received at Macdonald Institute.[55]

STUDENT LIFE

Macdonald Hall was the focus of much student life since so many of the young women lived in residence while in Guelph. The regular day began with a 6:45 gong to signal that breakfast would be served in forty-five minutes. At 8:30 students assembled at Macdonald Institute for a brief prayer meeting and roll call before beginning classes at 8:45. Classes ended at 12:05 and recommenced at 1:30, after lunch ("dinner" in those days). When classes ended at 4:00, stu-

Mac 1908, a photograph from Zoe Elizabeth Vallier's scrapbook.

The Mac girls taking a spin with the Aggies in 1910.

dents were free to run errands or get some fresh air until dinner at 6:00. A gong sounded the beginning of "study hour" at 7:30, which lasted until 9:30. Students then had one hour before lights were required to be out and the students in bed. There were, of course, variations to this regimen. On Mondays and Thursdays "study hour" began a half-hour earlier to allow a one-hour exercise class to begin at 9:00. Friday nights and weekends were much less organized and

Left: *The entire cast of an entertainment night doing "blackface" in 1910.*

Right: *Life at Mac was not all study. There were many extracurricular activities, and frequently they involved the students at Macdonald Consolidated School. This "tug of war" took place in 1910.*

Left: *The Mac baseball team in their uniforms, circa 1911.*

Right: *Macdonald girls baseball team on the steps of Macdonald Hall, circa 1911.*

A typical winter outing: Mac girls enjoying their snowshoes.

regulated. Anyone venturing outside in the evening required an acceptable chaperone, and Mac girls were forbidden to attend dances in downtown Guelph.[56]

Initiation was a central feature of residence life and in Mac's case a frequent one, since new students arrived three times a year. By the standards of the OAC and other male-dominated colleges, Mac's initiations were undoubtedly tame events. Seniors clothed in authoritative dress (often in mock court setting) put the new students through mildly humiliating actions — singing songs, offering obeisance to the seniors, cleaning seniors' shoes, eating silly foods, being treated in childlike fashion — designed to make them feel part of Mac in general and members of their own cohort within Mac in particular.[57] The result was a sense of community and the growth of individual attachments, evidenced in these days by the creation of various Mac "cheers," school colours, class pins, and the planting of a tree by the graduating class.[58] It needs to be said, however, that the characteristics of student life inevitably developed less among the large number of short-course students passing through Macdonald Hall. As well, the constant turnover of students inhibited a fuller development of a sense of community.[59]

The regulation dress codes likely also contributed to that sense of community. Mac girls wore a standard blue uniform, over which they placed various protective garb — aprons for cooking, coveralls for the laundry, protective dress for chemistry labs, and a gym outfit. The uniformity, while creating a sense of community, must have also stimulated a longing for individual expression.

Central to the student environment was its overwhelmingly female character. Only women were accepted into the domestic science programs,[60] and Macdonald Hall allowed only limited access to males. For almost all of the Mac students this all-female environment would have been a unique experience in their lives to that date, as would living in a large community. Women filled the administrative and authoritative roles, and it is interesting to contemplate the effect of these older women as role models for the students. The young women students learned to interact with large numbers of other young women and could and did take on responsibilities and roles that might well have gone to their male counterparts outside the Mac environment. The Mac students created for themselves a governance structure[61] with four major leaders — the presidents of the athletic association, the literary society, the YWCA, and the house president — and their own set of clubs, operated by Mac students for Mac students: a literary society (featuring both literary and musical elements, and eventually including debating), an athletic association, and a branch of the Young Women's Christian Association. As well, Mac students put on a number of local entertainments across the school year, often featuring music (in which the matron, Mrs. Katherine Fuller, frequently played the piano). There was empowerment in this, as well as the acquisition of important life skills. Mac students themselves took the initiative in setting up a system of monitors and mentoring. Students also organized a number of women's sports teams and events in these early years — baseball, gymnastics, swimming, field hockey, ice hockey, snowshoeing, tobogganing, skating, tennis, field days, a walking club — though the only evidence of a competitive character was occasional games with local city teams. Life in an all-female environment such as Macdonald Hall facilitated the students' development of perspective and knowledge about themselves as women, relatively separated from the male-dominated outside world.[62]

In the almost self-contained atmosphere of Macdonald Hall,[63] the occupants created for themselves an environment in which they had the potential to mature, to acquire new skills and develop old ones further, to create lifelong friendships, and to understand better their own lives and characters as women. Many of these students, especially those from the rural countryside, were likely away from home for the first time in their lives, certainly for the first time for such an extended period of time (whether for three months or two nine-month sessions). The potential for personal growth and maturing that this made possible was considerable, and many young women undoubtedly took full advantage.

Likely too of importance was the fact that there was a minimum age for admission to Mac. Students had to be at least seventeen years of age, and there was a bias in the admission process towards accepting older applicants with otherwise similar credentials. The likelihood of greater maturity was built into the Macdonald regime. Watson commented to one enquiry: "We do not take girls under seventeen, and at that age expect them to be largely responsible for their own conduct. As you will see the girls are granted a fair share of liberty. This liberty is seldom abused."[64]

Realistically most Mac students could expect to return eventually to a full-time career as homemaker, wife, and mother. In the meantime many would use the skills, knowledge, and personal maturing to advantage by entering the world of work. Many teaching grads took up work as domestic science teachers in schools or for the WI. Others frequently took up jobs as: institutional dietitians or managers (such as matrons), especially in hospitals, usually after a short, additional period of apprenticeship; social workers in some form, particularly in association with YWCA branches or settlement houses where domestic science programs reached out to inner-city girls; food laboratory technicians; or operators of domestic science programs for companies' factory workers.[65] Still others returned to their homes or soon married and took their knowledge and skills into their own homes. But virtually all would have brought to their future life experience the maturing and the personal and intellectual growth that are particularly aided by college life.

Outside of Macdonald Hall the young women added a vital new element to life on the Guelph campus. It is unclear whether they shared some classes, such as English or chemistry, with their counterparts from the OAC. But they quickly came to share extracurricular life with these young men.[66] Indeed Mac girls soon took the lead in campus social life, in spite of the physical segregation of the Mac campus and perhaps because their stricter residence rules gave them the leverage to set the tone for much of the heterosexual activities on campus.[67] As well, Mac Hall with its large rooms (dining hall and gymnasium) could host well-attended social events. The fact that the men considerably outnumbered the women on campus also added to the men's attraction to Mac. There was an annual round of campus events, slowly changing over these early years and including: the Hallowe'en Ball in costume;[68] sleighing parties; the annual At-Home, sponsored by the OAC and Mac literary societies; Winter Carnival in January;[69] the February Conversazione (the social highlight of the year);[70] monthly meetings of the Mac Literary Society, which at first often entertained faculty and students from the OAC and evolved through joint programs with the OAC Literary Society to become the Union Literary Society; and finally the May Day Fête. There were also a few shared organizations: the philharmonic club, with equal membership on the executive between Mac and the OAC; *The OAC Review*, where one or two young women reported on activities in Mac; the yearbook, where a higher proportion of Mac students gave women a stronger voice; a choral club; a drama club; the cosmopolitan club; a book club. By 1913 the YWCA began to hold its meetings with the campus YMCA, usually in Massey Hall.[71] Some of these events could be very large — concerts of seven hundred, conversaziones of one thousand — and the college authorities' attempts to restrict mixing of the sexes gradually weakened; the dances, for example, evolved from promenades in the early years to mixed dancing by 1911. In 1912 the Christmastime festivities "got a little beyond regulations," enough that the president of the OAC curtailed the number of dances for the winter term.[72]

The Mac Hall girls in 1905.

On the steps enjoying the sunshine in 1913.

Perhaps underscoring the inherent campus tensions between the sexes were the irregular athletic challenges (usually hockey or baseball) between the Mac girls and some of the OAC students or faculty. The tone of these contests was almost always one of jocularity, and there is little doubt that most participants and observers had fun, but the tensions were there. Female inequality and weakness were explicitly emphasized: the men would demonstrably give themselves some form of handicap (such as one hand tied behind their backs); the refereeing would often favour the "weaker sex," as women were known in those days; the men would often wear some elements of female apparel (such as skirts). One account, for example, congratulated the men on "the marvellous dexterity" with which they managed their skirts and went on to say:

A word of praise must be given here to those of the O.A.C. team who trimmed their merry widow hats with such exquisite taste. So beautifully were the hideous colors of red, purple and pink blended together that one might think that millinery was included in the course of studies at O.A.C. Also the dainty hosiery, twinkling now and then from beneath the rustling draperies, showed off to perfection the young "ferry boats" which so elegantly completed the effect.[73]

This particular game ended when the men "allowed" the women to score the winning goal. By such language and behaviour was sexual difference underscored and the relatively frivolous and weak nature of women (their attire, the Mac curriculum) confirmed. These sexual tensions and the gendered hierarchy were addressed more directly and critically in these years in various campus forums by the frequent discussion of women's suffrage.[74]

The famous Mac versus OAC hockey game of 1907.

Mac students participated and in doing so legitimized these gendered processes. The May Day Fête is a useful example. This ceremony began in 1910 when the Mac girls themselves chose it as a fitting representation of their values on graduation. Prior to decorating the maypole, the Mac students selected a May queen, chosen in one example for her "kindly gracious manner and dignified mien" as well as for her general popularity. Late in the afternoon the Mac students, dressed in "dainty white frocks," paraded to the site — twenty girls carried shepherd's crooks and buttercup flowers, while others brought blossom-covered

May convocation, 1910.

Left: *Convocation 1911. Mary Urie Watson in black robes.*

Right: *Convocation ceremonies included the May Day Court and the maypole dance. May 1910.*

boughs and wildflowers; the maypole bearers brought the pole. Two "dainty little flower girls" cast blossoms along the path of the May queen and her attendants on their way to the crowning of the queen by Director Watson. The maypole itself was then decorated and "several dainty dances" were completed around it before the girls proceeded to a garden party tea (served by students from the Housekeeping program), followed by an evening concert and fireworks.[75] With this sort of behaviour, Mac girls reflected the hegemonic character of gender, and yet it was the Mac students who controlled the ceremony, who filled the various roles, and who elected the queen: the event was also empowering.

Yet within a decade of the founding an important pattern had already been set. Young adults, thrown together in a shared environment, found that they had much in common. Many of the young women "paired off" with men from the OAC, so much so that by the early 1910s the Mac programs, particularly the short program, had already earned the famous nickname, the "diamond ring" course.[76]

The 1915 "Blow"

Macdonald Institute had done well in its first decade or so. It had attracted significant numbers of students to a variety of programs; its graduates were staffing significant positions in all regions of the country and in the United States as domestic science teachers, dietitians, and institutional managers. Students came from all across the country and from foreign countries, and the demand for entry into most programs exceeded the capacity of the college, especially in residence. There is every indication that the students themselves felt that they were learning a lot. In short, the Macdonald programs were meeting a need and the college had already acquired an enviable reputation in the post-secondary education of women.

But in 1915 a crushing blow was delivered to the Institute: the Ontario Ministry of Education withdrew its accreditation for the teacher training in domestic science program, shifting its accreditation to the University of Toronto, which reported to that ministry.[77] The one-year teacher training program, for those with existing teacher certification, had been particularly popular, at times having three times the number of applicants as there were spaces (just ten).[78] There is no evidence that the Ministry was dissatisfied with the performance of Mac itself or with the quality of its graduates. But the OAC was under the jurisdiction of the Ministry of Agriculture, thus limiting the direct influence of the Ministry of Education. Macdonald Institute began to pay a price for its ties to the OAC.

The links to the OAC were a source of both considerable strength and weakness to Mac. Through the OAC the ties to the rural community had been secured, and the rapid rise in Mac's reputation was undoubtedly connected to the well-established status of the OAC across rural Canada. The OAC had served its rural constituency well for half a century already, and Mac benefited greatly from that. The OAC faculty played a significant role in the educational programs of Mac and added some scholarly status to its educational programs. Through the OAC the ties to the Women's Institutes and the state funding supporting them had been accessed, helping Macdonald Institute to meet its responsibilities in rural communities. The Macdonald faculty members' scholarly interests in food and nutrition meshed well with those of the OAC, and various OAC reports and publications took advantage of the Mac faculty members' expertise.

But at the same time the OAC placed some very real limits on the kind of potential that Mac might realize. The OAC link further encouraged Macdonald Institute to focus on its role in rural society, limiting somewhat the market potential of Mac's programs. Association with the OAC provided a structural process by which women were subordinated and were seen to be subordinated, placing a "glass ceiling" on the aspirations of the faculty and students of Macdonald Institute. Rather than hiring their own qualified women chemistry professors, for example, the women faculty members were restricted to the domestic science programs. And there was some stigma entailed in Mac's association with the OAC as a technical school. Finally, by cutting Macdonald Institute off from the Ministry of Education the connection with the OAC led directly to the loss of Ontario accreditation for the teacher training program and indirectly to the slow progress made towards acquiring degree programs.

The 1915 loss of the teacher training accreditation was a serious blow to Macdonald Institute. But Mac had a number of achievements to that date that might well be relied on for the future. Young women continued to come from all parts of Ontario, from British Columbia and the Prairies, from the Maritimes, and from outside the country (United States, Great Britain, South Africa). Some of these broader links were assisted by the diversion of some of Sir William Macdonald's money to provide scholarships for students from Quebec and the Maritimes. Macdonald Institute attracted attention quickly, receiving a formal visit from the governor general, for example, in December 1905. As the first distinct post-secondary institution for women in Central Canada, Macdonald Institute offered young women and their families an alternative to the male-dominated campuses of the universities. Mac was acquiring a reputation for successfully meeting the social and educational needs of an important sector of the young adult population. Indeed, graduates of such programs had to meet high social expectations; in this respect, joked one Mac grad, domestic science training "is not an unmixed blessing" and it is "rather wearing to live up to the reputation."[79] There was solid substance and achievement on which to build for the future.

THE KEMP FAMILY ALBUM

The following pictures are the personal photographs of Jean (Kemp) MacDonald, DHE 1915 (Macdonald Institute), and her brother, E. Lew Kemp, OAC 1914, portraying student and campus life in 1914–1915. The photographs were donated by Jean's daughter, Mary Porteous, mother of two FACS graduates (Sharrie Porteous Woodley, FACS '79, and Mary Anne Porteous Baker, FACS '87). We gratefully acknowledge this contribution to our book.

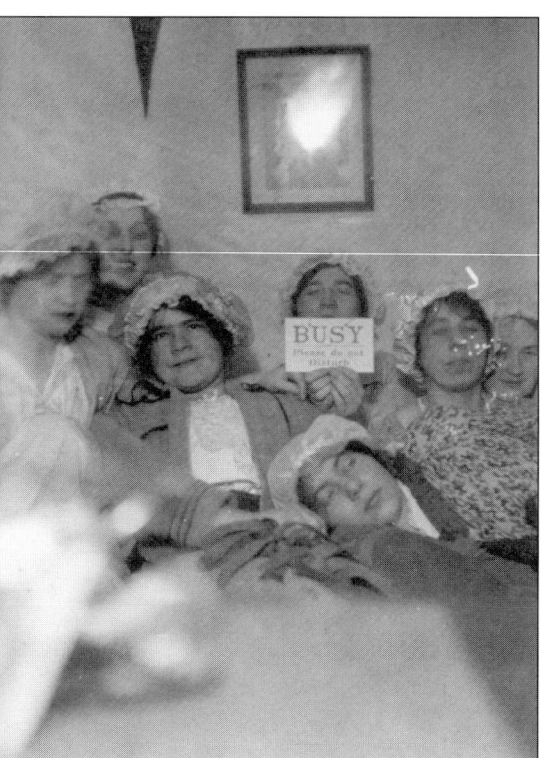

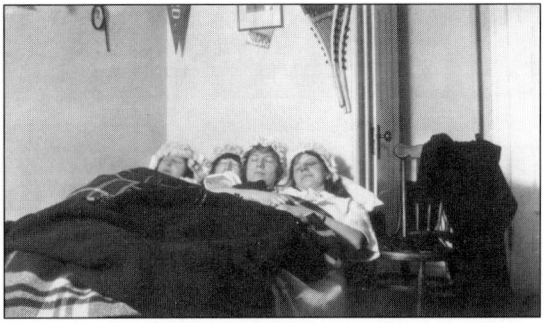

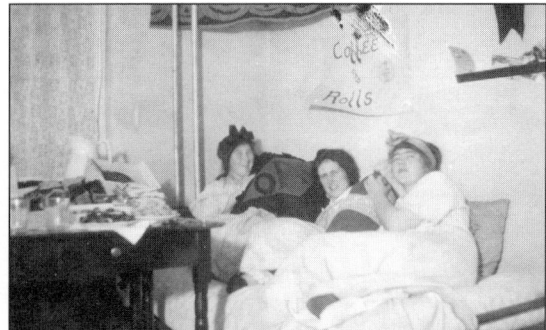

II

Establishing a Niche, 1915–1929

The decade and a half following the start of the First World War were of fundamental importance in the history of Macdonald Institute. A new director took over the leadership of Mac, giving the programs some new elements and seeking new academic features to enhance the status and quality of the programs. The role and place of Macdonald Institute in the academic life of Canadian women became entrenched. Students played a central role in this process, focusing their interest on particular programs and giving renewed character to the campus life.

The Wartime Environment

Mary Watson's last five years at Macdonald Institute were dominated by the wartime environment. The First World War affected every element of life at Macdonald Institute. Mac students and graduates prepared goods to send for overseas relief or to assist Canadian soldiers. Macdonald Institute staff, particularly Watson, contributed to some of the bulletins issued by the Federal Food Controller and recommended cookbooks for use overseas. A

Macdonald Institute and Macdonald Hall from OAC, circa 1917.

Left: *Macdonald Hall, circa 1917.*

Right: *Macdonald Institute, circa 1917.*

Left: *Massey Hall and Library, circa 1917.*

Right: *Long view of Macdonald Institute, circa 1915.*

Food Conservation Bulletin Board was set up in the students' reading room for the posting of official and unofficial literature on the subject. The home nursing sections of the curriculum were converted to St. John's Ambulance courses, and the girls were encouraged to secure the St. John's certification. Mac girls established a Red Cross branch, where they raised funds and prepared bandages and knitted goods for the soldiers at the front. Macdonald graduates felt that they were setting a national example in food conservation in their own homes and in co-operation with Food Economy Committees in their own communities.[80]

The war permeated the Mac environment, but never disrupted it. When initiation was held in the fall of 1914, it was called "mobilization" and a poem commemorated the event:

> Come ye freshies, one and all —
> Who this year enter Macdonald Hall,
> Britannia, the Great, demands of you
> A mobilization, strong and true.
> Your hair you must wear in three big cones
> And a newspaper uniform to cover your bones.
> No shoes on your feet, but rubbers instead —
> And a Napoleon hat placed firm on your head.
> In full kit, thus arrayed and in stockings of white
> We hope you will come prepared for a fight.[81]

Fundraisers were held on campus for wartime causes, and rationing affected student life and cooking classes. The smaller number of boys on campus gave the Mac girls greater opportunities to shape campus life and to have their voices heard in campus organizations. And yet "life went on." As Watson herself commented, the war had not altered attendance at Mac and the staff remained busy with their teaching duties. The students maintained their traditional spectrum of activities, occasionally giving them a veneer of the wartime environment.

It was the graduates of Mac who gave full expression to the national and social urgency represented by the war. Several found work as nurses or dietitians in military hospitals. Others went overseas, usually as volunteers and often joining the Voluntary Aid Detachment (VAD) and serving in or in support of military hospitals.[82]

Immediately on the end of the war, the Spanish Influenza pandemic swept across Canada. Mac was not spared. Early and rapid response helped to mitigate the worst effects of the disease. Signs of the disease appeared early in October 1918; classes were cancelled for nine days, all social activities ceased, and Mac placed itself under quarantine. Of the over fifty cases only

The 1919 visit of the Prince of Wales was a highlight of the year for these students.

Mrs. K. Fuller and the Prince of Wales on the steps of Macdonald Hall.

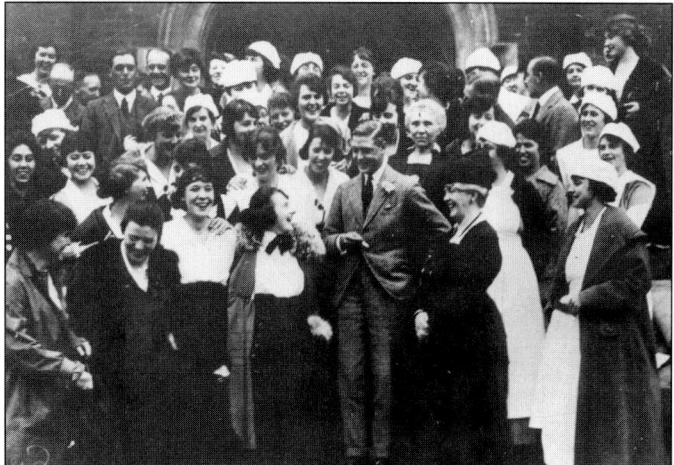

two students had to be sent to the city hospital and all who fell ill recovered nicely. Mac students responded to the general crisis by volunteering their labour in the kitchens of the Guelph General and Isolation hospitals in late October. Watson was somewhat overly optimistic about Mac's recovery from the disease, however, when she announced on November 26 that "we are quite clear of it now." A few weeks later there was a further outbreak in Guelph. Exams were postponed and the Institute closed early for the Christmas holidays. This caused some anxiety among those scheduled to arrive for the new term in a few weeks.[83] When a further, "pretty hard" outbreak occurred in January 1920, two large rooms in Macdonald Hall were converted into a hospital and a nurse was engaged to look after the students; three students were transferred to the city hospital for treatment and all recovered after some anxious moments. Several students and staff members were forced to leave Mac and return home to aid their families.[84] The ripple effects of the influenza continued for some time. Students who had been ill received special consideration for weak marks and concerned parents asked for special accommodation for their daughters.[85]

The social highlight of these years was the visit of the Prince of Wales in October 1919. For a society raised on the nationalist rhetoric of wartime Great Britain this was a pre-eminent event, and not the less for the fact that the young Prince Edward was a bachelor among all these eligible young women.

NEW INITIATIVES

Constantly in search of new sources of students and securing an academic niche for Macdonald Institute, Watson showed considerable initiative regarding recruitment. In the immediate aftermath of the First World War, for example, she contacted several Ottawa and London, England agencies regarding her plan to take part in an assisted immigration scheme. Young British women would be sent out to Canada where they would first enrol at Macdonald Institute for training; there they would "begin their Canadian life with our Short Course in Domestic Science." Any immigrants with greater access to capital might wish to consider taking a longer course of training. It was unclear whether this would be a way of making the young women more eligible on the marriage market or for employment as domestics — probably both — but the college would gain some additional students and raise its profile with the federal government.[86] When implemented, this scheme was a disappointment. The young British women simply used the plan to gain assisted transport to Canada; once at Mac, they reneged on the agreement (performing student work in return for free education and board) and moved into mainstream society.[87]

Similarly, with returning soldiers bringing home war brides, Watson saw an opportunity to ease the young women's transition into Canadian domesticity by offering a special short course. Here, for "just" $30, the war brides and young Canadian women marrying veterans would be assisted in the transition to married life by receiving lessons in plain cooking, laundry, housekeeping, gardening, and home nursing. It was a good idea, but after Watson promoted the project with the Canadian Patriotic Fund and the Great War Veterans' Association, there was only one applicant and the scheme died a natural death.[88]

A constant source of new students remained the Ontario countryside. If rural young women would not come to Mac in sufficient numbers, then Mac would go to them. Watson began to offer the short program, with its limited demand for facilities and student preparation, in outlying communities. In a speech in 1917 Watson referred to this as a travelling Macdonald Institute. In the fall of 1915, for example, a short program was taught in Ayr. Some twenty-two young women, mostly from the countryside, took the course five days a week over a twelve-week period. But these courses met with limited response, possibly because the $15 fee remained high for rural pocketbooks, and the experiment was quietly dropped.[89] But the outreach remained, especially in the loan collection, which continued to expand and to reach into the heart of the Ontario countryside. By 1916 the number of files had expanded from an early fifteen hundred to more than five thousand, and these were steadily reviewed and edited to bring them up to date. The most popular topics fell into

Creelman Hall, originally the dining hall only for OAC, was later used by the Mac girls.

Prior to the conversion of Macdonald Hall dining room into more residence rooms, the girls enjoyed eating in style. Circa 1915.

several categories: social service; cookery and foods; home or family.[90] The records for this sort of outreach experience are voluminous and must have been very time-consuming. Macdonald Institute faculty members spent a great deal of time corresponding with individual women, mostly from Ontario, regarding a wide variety of topics: from providing a recipe for black currant jelly, discussing the building of fireplaces, planning meals and menus, to analyzing the problems of youth.[91]

Watson was also interested in expanding the opportunities for student workers. Macdonald Institute employed just two such workers in the early years, but the opening of Creelman Hall as a men's dining hall (in 1914) offered expanded work since the administration seemed to link women with the serving of food and waiting on men. By modern standards, this remained a restricted work scheme. School authorities were so intent on maintaining the idea of full-time education that student workers at this time performed their work for a full year in advance of becoming a subsidized student, but relatively few applicants (three or four a year) showed any interest in taking this route.[92] There was also a college loan fund, operated by the administration, that offered interest-free loans to needy students entering their second year of a program; repayment terms were very generous.[93]

Watson's interest in outreach was fundamental to the philosophy behind Macdonald Institute. Mac was on a mission to take the "gospel of homemaking" to the women and men of Canadian society, particularly those of the rural countryside, and many policies aimed to implement this project. This outlook was maintained by Olive Cruikshank after she became the new director in the summer of 1920. By 1926 Cruikshank had initiated a new tactic designed to take Mac's knowledge to the young women of Ontario. This tactic used Mac's long-time link with the Women's Institutes to draw in the next generation. Teenage girls from across Ontario came to Guelph for a four-day conference at which they were exposed to the ideas and information dispensed by Mac. This brief time away from home was likely the first time many of these girls had been away from their home communities and from their parents. In the first year some 240 girls came to Guelph, attending sessions on farm work, girls' health, and citizenship and participating in singsongs, plays, and physical education.[94] While the adult branches of the Women's Institutes had become increasingly separate from Mac, here was a project on which both co-operated.

It is striking that Mac's rural mission had an unpredicted impact on Mac graduates. In a study of Mac grads at the end of the war, 62 percent reported living in a city and a further 30 percent reported living in the Prairies or Atlantic Canada. Few had returned to the Ontario countryside, following a pattern of rural-to-urban migration common within Canadian society at large. It was almost as if rural young women were using an education at Macdonald Institute as a means to geographical mobility, a way of escaping rural society, though it may well be that one of the effects of Mac and the exposure to more modern (that is, urban) domestic ideals was to attract these young women to urban areas. This is further suggested by the fact that between 73 and 85 percent of Mac students had come from southern Ontario, yet fully 30 percent now lived in other provinces and 13 percent lived in the United States.[95]

Another innovation that began near the end of the war was to reward winners of contests run by the Department of Agriculture in co-operation with local Junior Women's Institutes. The prize was a tuition-free short program at Macdonald Institute, though often the prize was still too costly to be accepted, since the winner still had to pay for accommodation.[96]

TEACHING

A steady turnover in staff continued, though to a much lesser extent than during the first decade. Watson continued to rely on her network in the United States, particularly at Columbia University Teachers College. She did complain, however, that Canadian regulations made it difficult to hire Americans.[97] In part, the turnover was an inevitable characteristic of an all-female staff within the gendered social order of the day. Married women could not work in such occupations as teaching. Any staff member getting married was expected

Left: *Mayme C. Kay, MA.*

Right: *Winnifred A. Schenck, BS.*

Left: *Katharine B. Doughty, BS.*

Right: *Mrs. K.T. Fuller.*

to resign and usually did so without fuss or complaint; this was simply "the way things were." But there was also a solid core of instructors who formed a stable nucleus for the teaching staff in these years — Dr. Annie Ross, Jean Roddick, Katharine Doughty, Winnifred Schenck (who arrived in 1924), and Mayme Kay (who arrived in 1926 and was soon Olive Cruikshank's able lieutenant). By the mid-1920s almost all faculty had a university degree, and Mayme Kay had a master's degree. Several of those instructors who left did so to take up a more senior appointment elsewhere, as when Frances McNally left to become director of home economics at Acadia University. The Macdonald staff were generally as qualified as those in the OAC, though no Mac staff member was ever given the title of professor in these days. Yet this too was simply another manifestation of the gendered social order, and not a cause of any overt resentment.[98]

Miss Jean Bradley offers a useful example of the type of faculty members at Mac in these years. After attending Sarnia Collegiate, Bradley took the Mac short course program in 1909. Four years later she returned to Guelph to take the two-year Normal course. After graduating, she taught home economics for two years and then attended Johns Hopkins Hospital in Baltimore, Maryland, where she spent two years as a student dietitian and then as an assistant dietitian. With this training she took a job as dietitian in a Winnipeg hospital before joining the Mac staff in the fall of 1919 as an instructor in laundry and household administration. In 1922–23 she took a leave of absence to gain her BSc in household science from Columbia University, returning to Mac as instructor in foods and cooking until her untimely death in 1928. By modern standards her post-secondary education was limited, but her career demonstrates a constant striving to improve her credentials and to expand her education and experience.[99] Macdonald Institute offered a means to improvement and upward social and economic mobility for ambitious, intelligent women. The increasingly qualified staff suggests an increasingly academic environment at Mac.

Miss Jean Bradley.

Teaching remained the pre-eminent task for these instructors, and yet the content of some of the courses varied little across time. The sewing notes of a student in 1920 are almost identical to those of a student in 1904; even some of the fabric being used for specific demonstration pieces was the same.[100]

Cruikshank began to consult the faculty members more extensively. Faculty meetings were held at the end of term to consider the fate of problematic students at least as early as 1921. Also striking about the faculty members was that they frequently used their summer months or took a leave of absence to upgrade their qualifications. Cruikshank herself, for example, spent several weeks at the Montreal General Hospital in 1924 studying special diets, so as to improve her teaching in that subject area.[101] In the late 1920s, during a debate about a new class schedule, one faculty member responded by emphasizing the desire to maintain her research, fearing that the schedule would take up more time:

> If we kept to our present schedule and were given moderate [teaching] programs I, for one, would be able to spend more time on experimental work, study, planning of work etc. I think a teacher of cookery should have more time for such things if she expects to improve her course and keep up to date. *Our present program does not spell progress in that line as we have not*

the time nor the energy to do as much as we should like to after hours. Why,
Miss Cruikshank, we should have as good a cookery department as there is
in Canada — but the fact is that now I have to spend many of the evenings
in just "keeping up" with my classes.[102]

This professionalism carried over into faculty attendance at professional conferences,
such as those of the American Dietetic Association or the Ontario Dietetic Association, as
often as finances permitted.[103]

CRUIKSHANK'S INITIATIVES

Miss Olive Cruikshank.

In the summer of 1920 Mary Urie Watson
retired and was replaced by Olive
Cruikshank from the Manitoba Agricultural
College. The arrival of a new director of
Macdonald Institute in the summer of 1920
brought some important changes, though
continuity remained the overriding characteristic. Cruikshank's commitment to home
economics was of long standing and she was
ambitious for Macdonald Institute to take
its "rightful" place at the national forefront
of domestic science programs. "Home
Economics," she wrote, "is a subject that
centres around the problems of the home.
… It includes a study of foods, shelter and
clothing viewed from the standpoint of
hygiene, economics and art, and a study of the relations of the members of the family to
each other and society."[104] The most immediate change to students' daily lives was the
closing of the Macdonald Hall dining room and the adoption of Creelman as the central
dining facility for all students on the Guelph campus. The freed-up space in Macdonald
Hall was converted to additional bedrooms, extending the total accommodation capacity
to almost 160 students.[105]

Olive Cruikshank (1858–1948)

Born in 1858 in southwestern Ontario, Olive Cruikshank received her BA in Household Science in 1914 from the University of Toronto and embarked immediately on an academic career. In 1914 Cruikshank joined the University of Toronto as matron of a girls' residence. Within a year she moved west, joining the Faculty of Household Science first at Regina College and then at the University of Manitoba, where she developed a reputation as a strong teacher with leadership abilities. After J.B. Reynolds moved from the University of Manitoba in 1920 to become the new president of the OAC, he contacted Cruikshank and brought her to Guelph to succeed Mary Watson as director of Macdonald Institute. She taught two classes a week at Mac, most of her time being taken up with administration.[106]

Cruikshank worked tirelessly on behalf of Mac. She frequently went off during the summer months to upgrade her knowledge in foods and dietetics, but devoted more attention to constantly seeking to upgrade Mac. She facilitated research development and was aggressive in her pursuit of a degree program for Macdonald Institute. During her tenure, the curriculum was reformed, contacts with the Women's Institutes were renewed, and new residential space opened to allow the Mac population to grow. She led the move to completely renovate the food labs at Mac in the late 1930s and the result was a model for such labs for several years to come.

"Cruikie," as she was known by her friends, came from Wingham, Ontario. Living in close proximity with one another, the staff inevitably had somewhat close and usually friendly personal relations, as evidenced by the letters and cards Cruikshank received from staff members while they were on vacation. She was able to remain a friend while maintaining the distance necessary to carry out her tasks as director of the programs at Mac.

After the 1941 closure of Macdonald Institute, Cruikshank remained on the Guelph campus, becoming quite active in war work for such organizations as the Farm Service Corps and the advisory committee of the War Time Prices and Trade Board. In 1943 she left Guelph to become the first administrator of Laurentian Terrace in Montreal, a residence for lower-salaried women in government war work.

Cruikshank herself anticipated important changes in the curriculum soon after her arrival, sharing with Canadians at large a sense that the country was entering a new era.[107] Cruikshank sought expansion and innovation much more than had Mary Watson. Many of those changes were connected to the University of Toronto with which relations were competitive and at first unco-operative. Enquiries from those interested in taking the first two years of study at Mac and the final two years in Toronto's degree program were initially discouraged. Watson wrote that Toronto's "arrangement of classes differs so greatly from ours that they do not fit well" together; nor was there any desire within Mac to alter the curriculum to facilitate such cooperation.[108] By 1924, however, educational standards had changed sufficiently that more Mac graduates were seeking opportunities to acquire a degree. The Macdonald Institute officials reached an agreement with the University of Toronto, allowing graduates of a two-year program at Mac who had also passed high school matriculation to study for one or two more years at Toronto for a non-specialist or specialist BHSc, so the curriculum differences between the two programs could not have been too dissimilar after all. Discussions in 1922–23 had attempted to go further. Would the University of Toronto facilitate the development of a degree program at Mac by conferring degrees on four-year Mac graduates, in much the same way that Toronto's degree-granting powers were used for graduates of the OAC and the Ontario

Veterinary College, which had recently migrated to the Guelph campus? Toronto declined to co-operate and instead revamped its own program to meet the Guelph challenge. Mac officials went so far as to place a paragraph in the 1921 course calendar anticipating a degree program, but by 1925 the paragraph was removed.[109] Macdonald Institute was a pawn to the superior powers at the University of Toronto. Lacking strong support from the OAC leadership or the Ministry of Agriculture in its dreams of a degree program, Mac was vulnerable to the caprice of those who were *de facto* its Toronto masters.

Still, Cruikshank did not give up easily. In 1928 she explained to the deputy minister of agriculture just why a degree program at Mac made sense. It was true, she admitted, that Toronto already offered such a program and that Mac grads could gain credit standing at Toronto, "but so far it [Toronto] is attracting very few. It seems to me if there were two institutions offering degrees in Home Economics in Ontario, the competition would be good for both institutions and more Canadian girls would take their training in Canada." At the same time Cruikshank fought against becoming simply a junior college to the University of Toronto's program. Even if qualified, she argued, students who had failed their first year at Toronto ought not to be allowed to transfer to the Guelph program; "in my opinion, we do not want them," no matter what Toronto officials recommended.[110] Mac's academic niche did not include subordination to the University of Toronto, in Cruikshank's mind.

The programs at Macdonald Institute slowly evolved. Officials gradually improved the standards and expectations in the programs. One of the first to benefit was the popular two-year Associate program. In 1917 the course calendar announced that especially successful associates would be offered the opportunity to stay on for a third year where they could take both senior Normal and senior Homemaker classes aimed at giving the students a particularly good base for dietetics, but few students took this option.[111] Dietetics remained a popular career choice, but almost all graduates opted for field placement in a major institutional setting to complete their qualifications, rather than remaining at Guelph.

In 1922, the age requirement of seventeen was formally dropped, though likely informally encouraged, and there was no longer a requirement for one year's household experience or for letters from high school principals; instead, the main requirement was academic: the Ontario Junior Matriculation Certificate or its equivalent. This was in line with the higher standards brought to the OAC by President Reynolds. At the same time the Mac curriculum was altered "considerably in order to make it worth while for the applicant with the higher academic standing." The yearbook correctly credited this raise in standards to the popularity of the program and to the efforts of Miss Cruikshank, who was clearly proud of the changes. This was the program that Cruikshank envisioned building into a four-year degree program. "For the girl who is young

Left: *Early set-up of the kitchens for class activities.*

Right: *Details of the kitchen set up for classes at Mac, circa 1915.*

Left: *The ladies ready for another lesson.*

Right: *Sample lesson card from Miss Geddes, 1915.*

and who has a good high school education, the Associate Course is a course which keeps her reasonably busy, which stimulates her mentally, which gives her some standing if she wishes to use her work professionally and which gives her an intelligent appreciation of the problems of housekeeping and we hope of homemaking as well," summarized Cruikshank.[112]

The Housekeeper program lacked the popularity of the Associate program. In an attempt to increase its appeal, superficial changes were made in 1921 after the arrival of Olive Cruikshank. The program name was changed to Institutional Management, in hopes of making its career expectations more explicit. The minimum age was lowered from twenty-five to twenty-four, and the curriculum altered. Students moved through a wide range of courses (from colour and design, psychology, and textiles to bacteriology, English, and physics) but the bulk of their time was spent on cookery, chemistry, dietetics, and institutional methods, none of which represented any major change from the earlier curriculum. Applicants needed at least two years of high school education or its equivalent. This was a program designed for slightly older students interested in returning to school to improve their employment prospects. The program's negative image is suggested by a comment in the 1926 yearbook: "When most of us entered the Institutional Management class in September 1924, it was for the one and only reason that we were barred from entrance to any other class [program] by not having the necessary matriculation certificate." The following year the students in Institutional Management described themselves as "more or less a joke around here."[113]

The Normal program continued to train teachers in home economics. In the face of the loss of the Department of Education's approval for the Normal program, Mac immediately dropped its one-year course in 1915 but maintained its two-year course with continuing success. Although the two-year diploma was no longer recognized by the Ontario Department of Education, the certifi-

Horticulture continued to be a course offered at Mac. Here the ladies are touring the OAC greenhouses, circa 1920.

The "Mac-ites" inside the greenhouses, circa 1920.

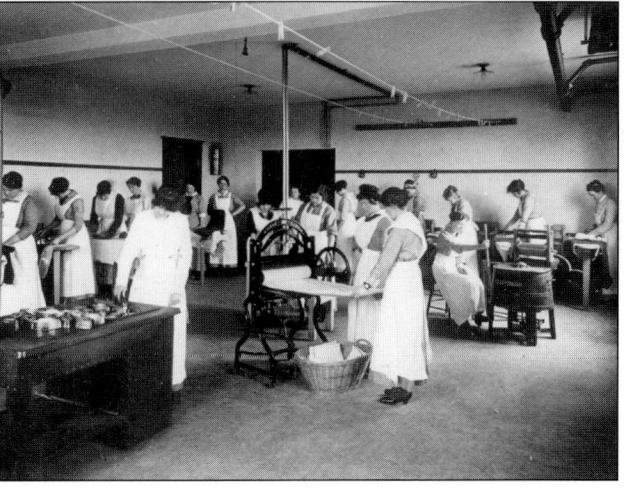

A 1920 class learning proper laundry techniques at Macdonald Institute.

cate remained valid in all other provinces.[114] The stature of a Mac diploma remained high across Canada. Students from both the Truro (Nova Scotia) School of Household Science and the Alberta Provincial School of Agriculture made arrangements to pursue a second year of study at Mac.[115] By 1922 Cruikshank had regained Ontario accreditation for the program, so that graduates could use their certificate in Ontario as well as in other provinces.[116] A number of minor changes were made to the Normal curriculum, but the character of the program was not significantly altered. Gradually the Normal program's place of pre-eminence among Mac programs was giving way to the Associate program.

Inside Massey Library reading room, OAC campus, 1917.

As a way of giving the students additional practice in teaching, the senior Normal students taught girls from Guelph schools and student nurses from St. Joseph's Hospital on occasion. Nothing emphasizes more effectively the essentially conventional character of the home economics program at Mac than the course drawn up by the senior Normals for elementary school students. The students would spend the first two weeks preparing salads and desserts, furnishing the living room, and planning a hope chest. The second two weeks were devoted to supper dishes, food for the sick, and diabetic cookery. Finally, three weeks were spent on meal planning and serving, followed by kitchen planning and selection of utensils.[117] The confirmation of marriage, of the subordinated and service role of women in the home, and of the material character of women's aspirations stands out.

The one-year Homemaker program continued relatively unchanged. It remained a good option for those girls unable to get a good high school education and "quite a number take the One Year Course preparatory to taking nurse's training," according to Cruikshank.[118]

In all of the programs the emphasis remained, as it had in the beginning, on an applied training. Cruikshank estimated that two-thirds of all classroom time was "spent on practical work." The practice apartment, commonly known by some as "Westin," played a prominent role in applied training. Each student spent six days in the apartment: three days in planning meals, cooking, and doing dietetic work; and three days in housework and serving meals. The meals were served to at least six persons, including the director and three other staff members who paid for the meals as board. In the 1930s the work was reorganized so that students rotated through a series of duties — guest, host, housemaid, maid, housekeeper, and cook — over a two-week period.[119] Another indication of the applied character of the programs is Cruikshank's comment that students were expected to buy few textbooks; $15 for books and stationery in a year was very generous.[120] The quality of this applied training is perhaps suggested by a summer employment program of the Canadian Pacific hotels. In 1924 the company hired thirteen Mac girls to work at its western summer resorts; this was so successful that the following year the number hired was doubled. Other resorts and hotels, such as Bigwin Inn in Haliburton, Ontario, made similar hiring targets of Mac students.[121]

By the end of the 1920s there were various signs of an enriched program. Institutional Management students began in the fall of 1920 to take occasional trips to Toronto to visit major institutional kitchens and accommodations, including the Hospital for Sick Children, the Toronto General Hospital, the Simpson's Arcadian Court and cafeteria, Eaton's College Street, and Muirhead's new cafeteria. Students examined major social policy issues — sweatshop labour, divorce, women's employment, housing — and were put in touch with social leaders who agreed to offer advice and comment regarding the students' research.[122]

Under Olive Cruikshank's leadership, the students gradually took greater responsibility for their own program, albeit in relatively minor ways. In 1922 the students submitted a petition suggesting the sort of graduation program they wished. A number of the suggestions were accepted by Cruikshank and incorporated into the planned ceremony: the speaker would come from a list proposed by the students, the valedictorian would be chosen by the students, the graduating students would put on a pageant and could host a dance at the end of the ceremony. In 1924 the students' council successfully petitioned for a change in the timing of the study hours so as to facilitate interaction with the men's residences. In later years student petitions asked that classes be rearranged (not cancelled) to facilitate long weekends.[123] What is important here is that the students felt sufficiently empowered to draw up petitions.

PROBLEMS UNRESOLVED, CHARACTERISTICS MAINTAINED

Mac continued to appeal to a variety of young women and their families. Education at Mac met many purposes. Some sought to learn the skills needed by most adult women in the home. Others sought personal growth or simply some limited independence. For many Mac was at least a way to open the door to advantageous future employment. Parents found the Guelph program an attractive prospect, but so too did many young women. When his daughters' applications had been rejected, one father wrote Watson of his disappointment:

> This is the course I want my daughter[s] to take. I want them to be home-mak-
> ers. It appeal[s] to me more than any other school for girls. I have been look-
> ing forward to sending my girls to you ever since they were little children.[124]

In other cases, the motivation came largely from the students. "Margaret is anxious to do something and be something," wrote one mother, "and we want to give her a chance." Another explained: "I have just come over from Scotland to join my brothers both of whom are farming. I have very little knowledge of housekeeping & I am very anxious to learn the Canadian ways that I may be able to make my brothers comfortable."[125] These young women had expanding horizons, and Macdonald Institute offered a means to opening up opportunities.

Macdonald Institute offered an opportunity to leave home and establish some personal independence. But at least a few students were sent by their parents because the parents had decided the Mac experience and discipline would be a good thing, a strategy that did not always work successfully. In 1916, for example, Watson corresponded with a Toronto merchant who had left strict instructions that his two daughters were not allowed to go home to Toronto without his written consent or while he was away. One daughter's response to this enforced discipline was straightforward refusal to sit her exams, daring the school to enforce its rules. Watson reacted quickly and decisively:

Top Left: *Inside Mac Hall where the girls forged new friendships and gained invaluable life experiences.*

Right: *From the scrapbook of Bessie Bigelow (far left), circa 1916.*

Centre Left: *Informal cross-country ski trip in 1923.*

The girls from Mac in 1922.

Some traditions are time-less: Mac girls with the beloved University cannon, early 1920s.

Class picnic on the second floor of Macdonald Hall, 1923.

At our Faculty Meeting just held, every one of our teachers agreed, under no circumstances should she be allowed to return, and as I quite agree with them, your daughter will not be allowed to attend this school any longer. …

As for the other daughter:

We are not running a school where the discipline of a jail or a convent is required or enforced, so that our teachers are again unanimous in deciding that your daughter's application for another term be refused.[126]

Nor was Macdonald Institute willing to accept other than healthy, hearty young women. This was expressed frequently to enquiries from persons claiming some health problem. When a father wrote from New Brunswick to explain that his daughter was ill and would be several weeks late in arriving for the start of the term, Watson reminded him that the daughter required a health certificate to begin the program. Furthermore, she went on:

I would point out that this school is not a satisfactory place for a delicate girl, as the work, between the practical work and the lectures, is fairly heavy, and delicate girls receive no special consideration. I would not [want to] be unduly discouraging, but New Brunswick is a long way from

Guelph, and I think you should consider the matter carefully if your daughter is not strong and well.[127]

The college was intent on keeping its educational focus in the forefront and its standards high.

The young women themselves often had trouble meeting the college's standards in the face of various outside obstacles and demands, particularly family demands. Young women were regularly part of any family's "reserve labour force," and had to be available to meet new or emergency domestic demands. In the fall of 1918, for example, one student explained her demanding circumstances. The primary male breadwinner in her family was in France, and her brother and sister-in-law had contracted the dreaded and often deadly Spanish Influenza. The student had been trying to work on her demonstration for Mac but this was proving difficult in the face of family nursing needs. Her nursing of the family was endless and exhausting and would undoubtedly delay her return to Mac in January, but would officials make a special exception and allow her to write her exams for the fall term if she could manage to come to Guelph for the day?[128]

Mac offered a relatively inexpensive alternative to a university education, which in time and money remained beyond many families' capacity. It also offered a social space in which women felt relatively safe and welcome, a somewhat protected female environment, in contrast to university campuses elsewhere. For those interested, and many young women were, at least for the short term, education at Mac offered a practical basis for a future career. In an era when the idea of social utility was gaining pre-eminence, the Mac programs gave young women a largely practical and applied education that could be put to use reasonably quickly in the job market. Macdonald Institute was not a finishing school, at least in its own self-image, but rather a cog in the social apparatus contributing directly to industry and commerce.[129] Last, and by no means least, Macdonald Institute provided these young women access to a group of young men who had above-average education and "prospects." No one was ever crass enough to admit to any marital aspirations as a motivation for attending Mac, but its "diamond ring" character was well known.

The arrival of foreign students added to the broadening experience of Mac. In the mid-1920s single students came from Japan, and in the aftermath of the war a group of four young women came from South Africa and others thereafter.[130] Students from across Canada also attended, often co-ordinating their travel plans so as to have companionship for the long train ride from the West or the Maritimes.

Across the 1920s pressure was building, particularly from middle-class, urban society, for access to Mac. "We are being besieged by overly anxious applicants and very concerned parents," complained Cruikshank in 1926. In that year a large number of eligible applicants had been turned away — twenty for the Normal course, fifty for the Associate course, nine for the Institutional Management course, fifty-one for the Homemaker course, and seven for the short course; more had been turned away than had been accepted into the junior year. Urban applicants tended to outnumber rural ones by a two-to-one margin.[131] The continuing preference given to farmers' daughters denied access to many urban young women; this frustrated the families involved, leading them to try various tactics to circumvent the rural preference. Simply asking to be placed on the waiting list for next year did not solve the problem because by then more rural women had applied. In 1927–28, fully 48 percent of the student body were farmer's daughters or came from Ontario towns and villages with populations of less than five thousand.[132] By 1921 the appeal of Macdonald Institute was such that the Ontario Department of Agriculture began to offer a short program in domestic science at the Kemptville Agricultural College, hoping that the overflow from Mac would accept placement in Kemptville. However, this alternative could not match the cachet or location of the Guelph campus.[133]

Over the years various officials — the president of the OAC, the minister and the deputy minister of agriculture — tended to interfere in the Mac admissions decisions, suggesting the level of attraction in admission to Mac. For these officials there were political issues at stake. How could they justify rejecting someone from Ontario when applicants from other provinces or even foreign countries were being accepted? Cruikshank struggled against any temptation to disadvantage those from outside Ontario. Not only were there educational advantages to having students with varied backgrounds, but any disqualification of outside applicants might jeopardize the standing of Mac certificates in those jurisdictions — Mac graduates would eventually pay the price in reduced job opportunities.[134] No such rule was instituted, but public officials did insist on a few favoured applicants "jumping the queue," and Cruikshank acquiesced.

Once the students had graduated, Macdonald Institute staff went a considerable distance in helping to place Mac grads. Indeed, the director's office resembled an employment agency not infrequently. The director fielded many enquiries about the employment potential for various occupations, with particular and sustained interest pointing towards dietetics. The director kept track of grads, where they were located, what further training or experience they had gained, and whether they were looking for work. Institutions, particularly hospitals, YWCAs, and public health departments from all corners of North America contacted Macdonald Institute officials regarding possible placement of graduates.[135] Linked to this continuing contact with grads was Mary Watson's decision to host, in June 1920, an "old girls' reunion," the first concrete evidence of the beginnings of an alumnae association, though grads living in Toronto had established in 1917 a Macdonald Institute club, which brought the grads together to socialize (often playing bridge) and do charitable work. One of the club's accomplishments was to draw up a plan of thrifty, nutritious meals for Canadian families. Thereafter Mac alumnae began to meet regularly in June of each year. Holding the reunions on campus had the added advantage of bringing the graduates back while the students were still present, so that the event operated in part as a careers night for the students.[136]

STUDENTS

Student numbers remained high throughout the entire period of 1915–29, but the distribution of students among the various programs shifted over time. In 1929 Mac reported the following distribution of students: 27 in the two-year Normal program, 104 in the two-year Associate program, 24 in the two-year Institutional Management program, 34 in the one-year Homemaker program, and 10 in the three-month short course.[137] What was more, there was almost always a significant waiting list each year, especially from urban families seeking admission for their daughters. The limitation on taking these additional students was often not teaching space but residential space. There were two relatively simple possible solutions. One was to have students board off-campus, but this was not popular and there was difficulty finding sufficient and suitable boarding houses. The second was to have more residential space, but apart from the new space in Macdonald Hall (resulting from the adoption of Creelman for meals) no new space became available immediately. In the meantime, it is obvious that the students were defining the Mac curriculum by "voting with their feet." Several of the programs were proving significantly less popular than others and there was a redistribution of resources. Particularly noticeable was the reduction in the short program. After two decades in which the short program had been offered three times a year, there was much less need for such a program, given the rise of home economics courses in schools and through local branches of the Women's Institutes. Macdonald Institute was moving beyond such introductory programs to emphasize a more academically demanding curriculum.

Student life slowly changed to reflect the contemporary social environment. Most of the pre-war student groups and activities remained — the literary society, the YWCA (soon replaced by the Student Christian Movement), the philharmonic society, and various sports groups and teams. Mac competed externally in basketball from 1923, playing teams from

beyond Guelph, and an art club was formed a few years later. Initiation continued to play a significant role in creating a spirit of class solidarity until such ceremonies were banned in 1928.[138] The annual At-Home Dance organized by the Union Literary Society took place in Macdonald Hall as usual, but by 1920 a difference was noticeable: the dance had evolved from a "dry old prom" to something more "snappy."[139] The OAC boys continued to face the Mac girls in athletic contests, with the boys ostentatiously adopting some form of physical handicap for the event. Most notably, Conversat changed from a general social event with the demonstration of various skills and talents to a major and usually quite elaborate formal dance. By the mid-1920s Conversat had become the highlight of the social season and an almost exclusively student event, alumni now being generally excluded. In 1921 an estimated twelve hundred people attended Conversat, reflecting its new importance in the campus social life.[140]

Restriction and protection remained key characteristics of the Mac residential and campus environment. Miss Watson had a reputation for objecting to the noise made by high-heeled shoes tapping on the hardwood floors, so there were regulations about that. Students of the modern era would be struck by the fact that at this time attendance was taken in every class and attendance reports were sent to the director. More generally the residence regulations attempted to ensure that the women residents would conduct themselves with decorum — "in a ladylike fashion," as officials would undoubtedly have put it. The regulations are worth quoting for the environment that they tried to create:

Regulations Governing Macdonald Hall [1921]

These regulations are designed to protect resident students, and to assure parents and guardians that Macdonald Hall is a wholesome place for girls to live in.

Residents are expected to govern themselves, and the Student Council, which is appointed by the students themselves, is charged with the responsibility of seeing that these regulations are respected and observed. When it is necessary for the Student Council to impose penalties for breach of discipline, the Council shall have the support of the Superintendent and of the President.

1. Study hours are from 8 to 10 p.m. and must be observed according to the directions given by the Student Council.
2. Lights go out at 10:30 p.m. At 11 p.m. there must be quietness.
3. Calling or talking from the windows is forbidden.
4. Residents before accepting outside invitations must obtain permission from the Superintendent, and before leaving must "sign out" in the book provided for the purpose in the Superintendent's office, and give particulars required. Such permission does not cover absence from classes.
5. Residents under twenty-one years of age are permitted to accept outside engagements only upon written instruction or telegraphed request of parent or guardian. Such requests must be addressed to the Superintendent, and must specify destination.
6. Friday evening is usually reserved as "free night" for college functions. Occasionally the Student Council may change "free night" to some other evening.
7. Each resident is allowed one evening each week off the campus and must return to the Hall not later than 10:15 p.m. With this exception, residents are required to be within the bounds of the campus after 6 p.m. No one is allowed out on Saturday evening or Sunday evening.
8. Residents are not allowed to walk from town after night[fall] except with a chaperon.
9. Certain privileges respecting visits to town are allowed to senior students, at the discretion of the Superintendent.
10. Boating and skating on the river are prohibited.
11. Chaperonage may be required, at the discretion of the Superintendent, for all outside engagements.
12. The fashion of evening dresses worn at social functions must be approved by the Superintendent, and extreme fashions will not be permitted.
13. Residents may attend church in Guelph on Sunday, in the morning only — and are expected to attend College Chapel service on Sunday afternoon.[141]

Students entering or leaving Mac Hall had to sign out in a large book kept by the matron, and sign back in on return.[142] This atmosphere of supervision, common to all women's university residences at this time, was furthered by the close proximity of most faculty members. Most of the instructors lived in residence at Macdonald Institute and took board at a nearby home.[143]

The residence regulations make it clear that there was ongoing concern to restrain heterosexual contact. The 1920 yearbook depicted Macdonald Hall as "No Man's Land" in reference to the restricted access. In 1929 alarms were attached to the outside doors of Mac Hall, set to ring if the doors were used after curfew at 10:45. In May of each year, after classes had concluded at the OAC, Mac regulations were relaxed noticeably: "Macites have all sorts of privileges now that the men have gone. They are allowed to go walking until dusk on the campus, to go to church in the evening — but then as one of the Homemakers remarked wearily: 'What's the use?'"[144] Female-male socializing remained a central part of campus social life, dominating the social calendar and the cultural environment.

The men from the OAC and OVC often prided themselves on their social exploits with Mac girls. Men interested in women were known as "fussers" (a complimentary term) and the pre-eminent fussers were noted in the pages of the yearbook. One young man in 1915, for example, earned "the honorary degree of Master of Scientific Fussing and the envy of his admiring class mates." Another in 1928 was known as a real fusser whose "motto at the Hall" was "love 'em and leave 'em." The Mac girls were potential trophies for many of the male students, but there were also comments that the girls (with their "silvery voices and twinkling feet") were distractions to the boys.[145]

The Guelph campus as a whole remained unbalanced and segregated. There were far more men than women on campus, and the Aggies tended to dominate — in addition to their greater numbers, they also tended to be on campus for four years (as opposed to Mac's two at the most), and their college dominated the local political structure. This imbalance was exacerbated when the male-dominated Ontario Veterinary College moved to the Guelph campus in 1922. When combined with the strong regulatory environment associated with women students in these days and with the geographical concentration of the Mac campus, the result was a tendency towards having two separate campuses — one male and Aggie, and the other female and Mac. The two campuses met and mingled regularly for meals at Creelman, though men and women sat at separate tables,[146] and irregularly otherwise. There was a strong assumption that the Guelph campus was primarily for the training of young men. In writing about the various organizations on campus, one OAC student unselfconsciously discussed the benefits for men: to "train men for executive business … and all the other countless experiences which are so necessary to a professional man of today."[147] It was thus not surprising that the major offices in the student organization and campus awards went to men and that the Mac girls tended to be given nothing more than minor representation on what were otherwise men's clubs. *The OAC Review* had for years printed every OAC student's marks at the end of the year, but not until 1929 were Mac students included in this very public process.

Mac students suffered in comparison with the OAC men when it came to athletic endeavours. The athletic facilities, apart from the Mac Hall gymnasium, were considered to be the men's, and women used them only when "allowed" to do so by the men's teams. In 1917, the Mac girls acknowledged the generosity of the men in this regard, limited as the generosity may have been by the standards of 2003: "Through the kindness of the boys, we were allowed two periods a week for hockey practice …" as well as access to the boys' swimming pool on Saturday mornings. A year later the *Libranni* reported that the girls were "allowed" to use the shooting range.[148] This sense of the Mac girls as interlopers, as present in these public spaces on deference, characterized much of the ongoing atmosphere of the campus, reflecting the prevailing gender order across society. Female access to additional facilities and space was a result of reduced wartime pressure on facilities from the boys; after the war, the boys demanded a return to their privileged position. Within the girls' own public space, however, the Mac students and staff were in charge.

The heart of that public space was, of course, Macdonald Institute and Macdonald Hall. Because the girls lived so much of the time at the Hall, it gained a special place in their thoughts, often earning a nickname — such as "the Zoo" in 1915 or "Mt. Misery" in 1916. As well, some cliques within the Hall established their own sobriquets — the "Basket Gang" (1920), the "Safety Pin Society" (1925), and the "Sweat Shirt Gang" (1929–30). The friendships made and the fondness for the place were special.

This space was also the focus of most of the key events in student life at Mac. It was the site of the initiations, the teas and dances, and it was here that the major ceremonies of student life occurred. Each year in June the junior students organized, as a class task, the senior

1925 Macdonald Institute basketball team.

dinner for the graduating class. The dinner was held in the Mac Hall reading room, where the meal, prepared by the junior class, was also served by them. At the end of the dinner the junior students "usually find their seniors" and arranged themselves informally about the room to listen to the speakers.[149] It was a time and place of camaraderie, support, and friendship.

Women's dominance over their own public space was subject to male challenge from time to time — a male flouting of female attempts at control, a demonstration of male "humour" and of the men's ability to go anywhere and do anything. The girls were subject to male "inspection" and remarks daily on the steps of Creelman. Pranks were at the centre of the boys' challenge to the girls. In 1922, for example, at Halloween an animal skeleton and a farm wagon blocked the entrance to Mac Hall. These pranks had, of course, the social function of confirming the fact that this territory was normally "off limits" to the male students. The men's tendency to "ogle" the girls as they left Creelman was another means by which the gendered order was reinforced.[150]

Macdonald Institute was a maturing institution. Its standards and expectations were rising. Its various functions were being sorted out and some older tasks cast aside for new. It had been around long enough that its graduates were making a name for themselves and for the school, as when Roberta McAdams, the first woman elected to the Alberta legislature, returned in 1919 to speak to her alma mater.[151] Indeed Mac witnessed speeches from a large number of successful women speaking to Mac girls about the potential accomplishments by women in modern Canadian society; the speakers were clearly intended to set an example in word and in their own achievements. Mary Watson wrote: "Macdonald Institute has done nothing spectacular and never will. We are just carrying on in our own quiet corner, and hoping our work will count towards the general good."[152] She was speaking of the wartime environment, but her comment serves as an effective characterization of Mac's experience during the 1920s as well. The gospel of homemaking remained strong through the 1920s and played a fundamental role in securing Macdonald Institute's niche in the academic world.

III

Macdonald Faces Decline, 1929–1945

In the years of economic depression and international warfare Macdonald Institute reached its nadir. Indeed its fate was in the balance by 1945. While the Depression years themselves had relatively little impact on Mac, the war years were devastating: Mac was closed down and ceased to function. For a variety of reasons this was a time of considerable change internally at Macdonald Institute. In December 1933 one OAC student complained about the "lack of pep" on campus, which he put down to the quantity of work assigned and to the economic depression. This reflects a more general sense of social quietude in Ontario campuses throughout the 1930s. While the Depression may have "rocked" most Ontario universities, Macdonald Institute survived relatively unscathed, only to be completely closed by the war.[153] The academic initiatives of the early years sustained a relatively vibrant environment, albeit one constrained by scarce resources, but societal demands on the institution eventually exceeded the ability of Mac to respond.

Left: *Macdonald Institute, circa 1930.*

Right: *Macdonald Hall, circa 1930.*

Left: *Front view of Macdonald Hall, circa 1930.*

Right: *Macdonald Hall entrance in the 1930s.*

Left: *Reception areas in the 1930s.*

Right: *Side view, circa 1930.*

Right: *Macdonald Consolidated School, circa 1930.*

Academic Changes and Frustrations

One characteristic of the academic change occurring in the 1930s was growth. Enrolment at Macdonald Institute continued to rise, largely because of expanding residential facilities. By 1929 the total enrolment reached 214 students, rising to 239 in 1935, in contrast to the steady rate of female enrolment at Ontario universities generally. Of the 239 students, 99 were from farms or villages of fewer than 1,000 residents; 42 were from small communities with populations between 1,000 and 10,000; and 93 were from towns and cities of 10,000-plus population. A further 15 students were from provinces other than Ontario.[154] These rising numbers were possible because the number of girls living in private boarding houses near the college was growing. As well, new residential space was being brought into service.

New residential space was crucial in facilitating the growth in student numbers. In 1927 funds were found to purchase "the Springer Residence," a house between Creelman and Johnston halls (presumably the building now known as Drew Hall) that was renovated and converted into residence space for some twenty further students. But this did not relieve the pressure sufficiently. Some thought was also given to taking over space in Johnston Hall. In the place of the Springer Residence a new building was constructed at a cost of $50,000 to house fifty Mac girls. On a site northeast of Macdonald Hall, the new Watson Hall — now International House — opened in September 1931 but was incomplete, and construction continued for several months amid the regular functions of the school.[155] As well, Macdonald Institute expanded to include a new extension housing the central laundry, and kitchenettes

Watson Hall in 1934.

were added to Mac Hall. In its early days Watson Hall had a marked international flavour among its residents, foretelling a feature of its later character.[156] Even with the new accommodation the number of applications considerably exceeded the accommodation limits at Mac. Cruikshank urged disappointed applicants to write the provincial minister of agriculture and other politicians so as to strengthen Macdonald's request for further resources.[157]

But the student numbers were rising at a time when there were limited new financial resources, and the growth placed considerable strain on the teaching resources. New sections of courses had to be created and the pressure on laboratory space and equipment was heavy. The number of instructors expanded from ten in the 1920s to thirteen by the mid-1930s, but even then the strains on the teaching staff were noticeable. When illness occurred among the faculty members, the slack was picked up by the other instructors without additional compensation. As well, female faculty members were expected to take on other gendered roles on campus; when the annual summer school opened the residences to a new set of students, several of the women teachers, including Cruikshank, were expected to act as matrons of the various residence halls.[158] At the same time, many faculty members were attempting to upgrade their credentials by taking summer courses elsewhere or leaves of absence for a full year. The result was a teaching staff that felt a great deal of pressure. As wages for Macdonald faculty members fell behind those for high school teachers, "several of the staff feel very disgruntled" at the working conditions, reported Cruikshank. A faculty petition was sent to OAC President Christie voicing this discontent, focusing on the issue of holidays. The upshot was that Macdonald faculty members were to be treated as civil servants, subject to the rules and expectations of the civil service, rather than as teachers.[159] Yet this did not completely dampen the increasingly academic and scholarly environment.

Growth in a period of limited resources necessitated some serious rethinking of the Mac curriculum. Failure to find funding for the acquisition of a practice house (to replace the practice apartment) led to 1932 proposals to revamp the curriculum and renovate parts of the Macdonald Institute building. Rather than add new space in a time when funds were scarce, the proposal was to convert the living quarters of the various instructors in the northeast wing of the building. Several of the rooms were to be converted to cooking labs and a nursery school with an observation area that could be put into operation by making use of the outside entrance used by the instructors; one bedroom would be converted into a research lab. Perhaps most significant for the future in these proposals was the evidence of growing concern to include the study of children and child care in the program.[160]

This growing interest in child study was further evidenced when Mothercraft was added to the curriculum of most of the Mac programs in 1932. Dr. Annie Ross was responsible for this innovation and classes ranged across a series of topics and issues associated with children, especially infants, and mothering. The Mothercraft Movement was an attempt to bring a more thoughtful and knowledgeable approach to mothering, especially among disadvantaged groups. Macdonald Institute claimed to be the first college in Canada to incorporate Mothercraft into its curriculum. The course itself was designed to prepare the young

Dr. Annie Ross

Annie Ross was a graduate of the Women's Medical College, Trinity University (Toronto) and came to Mac in 1904, the year after it started. In later years she upgraded her teaching qualifications by taking a course in social service at Toronto, in teaching at Columbia, and in physical education in Boston. She acted as school physician at Mac and taught physiology and home nursing; for the period 1909–1920 she also taught physical education. In 1924 she moved to become matron of Johnston Hall.

Dr. Ross was popular with both faculty members and students, and was a mainstay of campus life. When she retired in 1936, *THE OAC REVIEW* commented: "Her insight and kind understanding of youth; her courage of convictions; her sense of humour and ready wit; and her genuine kindness has endeared her to members of the staff and to the student body."[163]

women for more effective mothering themselves and to better understand early childhood. Young mothers came to a round-table conference from time to time to discuss young children and their behaviour problems, and a half-day nursery school — something that Cruikshank had been planning since 1928 — began operation, facilitating observation of the children as well as guidance to the mothers.[161] Another current enthusiasm, eugenics, also made its way into the curriculum.[162] In these initiatives Macdonald Institute was able to respond to changing societal expectations and attitudes regarding childhood and the family, despite the scarcity of new resources.

The strain on resources arising from the growing student numbers finally forced college officials to some major revision of the curriculum. Most significant was the cancellation of the Institutional Management program in 1937. By 1936 only five new students had registered in the program and with these numbers it was not possible to justify the resource allocation demanded by the program. There had been fewer and fewer older women applying for the course, and graduates had been having trouble finding employment; there was also a sense among the students that the girls in the program were somewhat exploited as cheap labour, working on various tasks that regularly required labour — waitressing, ordering in the pantry, and laundry, for example. In the midst of the Depression and of changing educational expectations, the program had outlived its usefulness.[164] The short program too suffered from lower numbers. In this case it began to be offered less frequently, with the fall and spring offerings dropped.

The Normal program, so central to the early vision of Macdonald Institute as a training ground for home economics teachers, carried on, though the numbers had become very low — just five to eight new students joining the program each year. Links were made with the Guelph Board of Education for the students to take practice teaching classes in Guelph Central School; twice a week for ten weeks, the student teachers did lesson assignments, presented lesson plans, and gave lessons to the local students. This new arrangement replaced one begun in 1920 or earlier whereby the Guelph separate schools had sent a group of thirty to forty students to Macdonald Institute for weekly classes from the student teachers. This complemented the long-standing arrangements with Macdonald Consolidated School (now the Macdonald Stewart Art Centre) to teach home economics to the girls there. Despite the range of training acquired in the Normal program, its graduates continued to be disadvantaged in seeking first-class certification in Ontario.[165] It is not surprising that the program was not renewed when Macdonald Institute reopened in 1946.

In contrast, the two-year Associate program continued its 1920s pattern of steady growth. This program was the major beneficiary of the new accommodations built for Mac girls and of curriculum reform. Students found the program attractive for several reasons, according to Cruikshank. First, it led directly to employment opportunities. Second, there was an increasing appreciation of home economics education and parents realized that this education was a valuable foundation for later life. Third, students in this program could proceed directly to higher training, receiving full credit for the work taken at Mac. In the early 1930s, before the new Watson Hall opened, the demand for enrolment was so strong that more students were being turned away than accepted.[166] The Associate program had become the central program at Macdonald Institute and was the base on which the future degree program would be built.

The one-year Homemaker program continued to receive solid student enrolment. The 1931 Homemakers reflected on what they had learned during the year: "Although our main reason for coming here was no doubt to learn the rudiments of housekeeping — an art which we can always use — there must be no belittling of the value which we derive from our social activities." They had had at least one party of some kind every week, and from such activities had learned "new poise and social alertness" which would be a great value in the outside world.[167] Life at Mac gave the students an opportunity to mature and to learn independent social skills.

The actual learning experience was a positive one. Students were challenged by the standards of the day. For example, intrinsic to the senior-year experience and looked on with considerable foreboding were the "demos." These were forty-minute-long demonstrations on a particular subject before the entire class, based on research and using illustrative materials.[168] Nor were students allowed to "slack off." Attendance was required at 80 percent of classes, on threat of disqualification from examinations, a threat that was only rarely enforced.

Presumably in an attempt to understand better the academic aspirations of the student body, Macdonald authorities conducted a survey of the first-year students in 1937. There were ninety-six respondents, and to some questions more than one answer was given:

Purpose in attending Mac?
- to learn to cook and sew   15
- parental urging   16
- preparation for employment   33
- program is more practical than university work   10
- preparation for a degree   1
- other   39

What will you do after graduating from Mac?
- • teach home economics   5
- • get a university degree (either directly or after a
  period of employment)   47
- • get a job   15
- • further training (mostly in dietetics)   25
- • other   6

What phase of home economics most interests you?
- • cooking   16
- • foods   17
- • dietetics   47
- • textiles and clothing   12
- • other   23

What the authorities found was a diverse student body with a variety of interests and career goals. Interest in foods and nutrition was particularly strong, while interest in child study and the family was not even noted. The questionnaire results are also suggestive of a very positive learning environment. Upon arrival at Mac, only one student already intended to pursue further studies; but within a few months close to a majority now considered the possibility of university education and an overwhelming majority intended to acquire further training and education.[169]

Historian A.B. McKillop suggests that many Canadian women, especially those marginalized by limited education or by poverty, had little opportunity to shape the direction of their lives.[170] But there is a sense among those young women enrolled at Macdonald Institute of empowerment, albeit an empowerment curtailed by the prevailing gendered and social order. Young women from both urban and rural society were consciously choosing various opportunities at Mac to give a particular shape to their future lives and this survey is a useful manifestation of that broader phenomenon. These young women did not even allow the limitations of Mac's academic offerings to limit their intellectual aspirations.

Also on the positive side was the fact that the reallocation of resources was to prove crucial in Macdonald Institute's future. The food labs were redesigned and refurbished with a major reconstruction in 1937–39. The old food labs had been transformed with "gleaming stainless steel" table tops and sinks, new gas and electric stoves, built-in cupboards, a raised platform with a "streamlined" desk, and the latest linoleum. In another food lab unit kitchens of different configurations replaced the old hollow square tables that had been in use since the start. The modern and varied equipment offered students an opportunity to test their food preparation using different cooking techniques. The students were particularly proud of the new, up-to-date environment: "We who are privileged to work in this new kitchen find it ideal for modern efficiency. We know of no other institute, excluding those for experimental purposes only, which can boast of so many modern features."[171] These new labs became a central showpiece for Mac for the displays during Farm and Home Week. The labs not only served well during the coming wartime but played a central role in the new life given to Mac after the war. Indeed the labs acted as a model for such facilities across the country in the years that followed.[172]

There were other ways of enriching the quality of the education offered at Mac. Visiting speakers were brought in to lecture: from Ontario Hydro on electricity and electrical appliances; from the Fruit and Vegetable Branch of the federal Department of Agriculture on the marketing of canned fruits and vegetables; from Consumers' Gas Company on gas and gas appliances. Professors from the University of Toronto began to give specialist lectures on the latest research about various topics, such as diabetes or hormones; a woman lawyer was brought in to speak to issues in family and housing law.[173] And class field trips to various applied facilities in Toronto — such as Harris Abattoir, Weston Biscuits, a Pullman dining car, and several institutional kitchens — expanded the students' learning.

Macdonald Institute was under increasing pressure across the 1930s to offer a degree program. Many girls at Mac developed an interest in pursuing degree work elsewhere, and a poll of the graduating class of 1938 indicated that of ninety-seven respondents more than half contemplated going on to a degree program.[174] Professional standards were rising, and Mac officials conceded that the two-year courses at Mac were "no longer considered adequate for those entering professional work, therefore our graduates must seek further training elsewhere." By 1935–36 there were twenty-three Mac graduates pursuing a BHSc at the University of Toronto, while five others had gone on to American universities.[175]

The direct result was a renewed attempt to acquire a four-year degree program of its own, in co-operation with the University of Toronto. In 1936 a meeting of top-level administrators was held, attended by Cruikshank along with the president of the OAC, the president of the University of Toronto (Dr. Sidney Smith), the University of Toronto registrar, and several Toronto Home Economics Faculty members. The Guelph representatives put forward their arguments in favour of a degree program of their own: the increasing demand from Mac students and alumnae; the difficulties that Mac students had in adjusting to the Toronto environment; the OAC parallel; the costs of a Toronto program (at least double the cost at

Guelph); and the absence of a clothing and textiles option in the Toronto program. The Toronto representatives resisted. Any awarding of the same degree would have to have the same fee structure; there was no demand for a clothing and textiles option; would having duplicate programs create "a dangerous precedent?" Years later the Toronto registrar emphasized the defensive attitude at Toronto: "We were able to stave off the attack by saying that the staff at Guelph would have to become part of the Faculty of Household Science at the University of Toronto, and that the curriculum and examinations would have to be the same as at Toronto."[176] Toronto had no interest in allowing Guelph its own degree program and thus losing a steady stream of students for Toronto's own competing program.

The failure to acquire a degree program must have been very frustrating to Cruikshank and her staff. Without a degree program there were very real limitations to what Macdonald Institute could accomplish, and those limitations were becoming more apparent every year. The rising professionalization of dietetics and other occupations, the growing desire for the status and prestige represented by a degree, and the expanding thirst for increased education all challenged the diploma status of Macdonald Institute. This was a challenge in which Macdonald's "hands were tied." Circumstances would have to change significantly before Macdonald Institute would be able to meet the changing societal expectations of post-secondary education.

Despite Olive Cruikshank's assurances, the Depression job market affected the opportunities available to Mac grads, and this was crucial for an applied program. In the early 1930s most of the graduates moved readily to jobs or to further training, but in the later 1930s it was a different story. "It is increasingly difficult," she wrote one contact in 1938, "for two year graduates to secure suitable openings and only a small percentage to secure suitable employment, so preference is given to those with degrees." And there were more and more young women graduating with degrees in the subject area. Mac grads, who were usually quite young, were increasingly disadvantaged in the marketplace without further university-level training. What was more, the standards for dietitians had been raised. After 1937, in order to qualify for certification one required at least a pass degree in home economics, meaning that Mac grads without a degree began to be denied entry into hospital training programs for dietitians. Cruikshank conceded that for professional work in home economics, a degree was now "essential."[177] Without a degree program, Macdonald Institute faced a future of increasing marginalization. Any doubts about this were confirmed by the growing number of students who were rejecting admission to Guelph in favour of direct admission to a university program.

Yet despite these limitations and frustrations, there were very real signs of academic improvement at Mac, as evidenced in the rising academic standards and professional expectations. One manifestation of this at Mac was the rise in the number of financial prizes awarded. In 1929–30 the students' council of Macdonald Hall endowed a scholarship to be given to the student in a two-year program with the highest standing in her second year. The Mac Alumnae began a long tradition of scholarship support by sponsoring three prizes to the students with the highest graduating average in each of the two-year programs.[178] To receive credit for their year's work students required an average of at least 60 percent over the three terms. Students in danger of not achieving this standard were called in for consultation with Director Cruikshank and letters were sent to their parents, informing them of their daughters' academic problems. The marking standards were high enough that many students — 20 percent in December 1935 — failed to attain the minimum average required.[179]

During this time faculty research increased and began to receive more attention, and more faculty members had graduate degrees to their credit. Several Mac faculty members took leaves of absence to obtain a master's degree — Esther Sommerfield from Iowa State Agricultural College (MSc) in 1931; Mary Clark from Columbia University (MA) in 1932, for example — and Frances Hucks spent two days a week in 1929 at the University of Toronto upgrading her undergraduate degree to honours standing. Others took graduate or special courses during the summer at various universities or hospitals.[180] An undergraduate degree was a prerequisite for new instructors by the 1930s. At the 1933 graduation exercises, three faculty members of Mac received recognition for their foods research, and Mac faculty members regularly gave reports to the Women's Institutes meetings on the latest research in their field. Some faculty members were seconded for significant portions of their time (even full time) to food research projects led by OAC faculty members. Extensive research was carried out on potatoes, on eggs, on the use of honey, on canning, and on the use and storage of leaf lettuce, for example. The results of some of this research appeared in published government bulletins and leaflets designed for popular use. The research carried out by Mac faculty took its cues from the OAC and had the

Left: *Jean Roddick.*

Centre: *M. Frances Hucks, BHSc.*

Right: *Mildred A. McQueen.*

Left: *Esther C. Sommerfield, BSc (HE).*

Right: *Gladys G. Hassard BA.*

advantage of showing the Department of Agriculture that it received good, useful experimental work for its money.[181] Research became an important enough element of work at Macdonald Institute that the annual reports began to devote a page or more to the various projects being carried out at the college. As historian Ruby Heaps points out, the research carried out by home economists in Canada, and by nutritionists in particular, played a leading role in women's contributions to scientific advancement.[182]

The staff continued to reflect the characteristics evident in the 1920s. There was a solid core of continuing instructors who made a full-time career of teaching at Mac, and there were a number of others who, in the circumstances of the day, taught for a short time at Mac and then moved on to better-paying jobs or marriage. By 1929 there were twelve full-time instructors living in accommodation at Mac.[183] Among the mainstays as teachers were Mary Clark, Gladys Hassard, Annie Hicks, Frances Hucks, Mayme Kay (who was named assistant director), Jean Millar, Jean Roddick, and Winnifred Schenck. Most notable among the newcomers was Mabel Sanderson, herself a Mac grad, who would play a central role at Mac until the 1960s. Much was expected of these instructors. Apart from planning and teaching their courses for the various programs, they were assigned publications to write (articles for the popular press or a note for a Ministry of Agriculture bulletin, for example), taught special classes for two-week students or at the Girls' Conferences, and participated in the social life of Mac. Simply being a good teacher was not enough; Cruikshank wanted "team players" and manipulated her salary recommendations to reward those who behaved accordingly. Salaries as a whole remained low (between $1,200 and $1,600) and were allegedly below those of high school teachers or college instructors elsewhere.[184]

Macdonald Institute, however, retained a number of advantages in the contest for survival. The number of applications ensured a steady student population. The program and the campus were attractive to many. One factor attracting students to Guelph in preference to other campuses was the lower costs. In the debates with the University of Toronto in 1936, it was estimated that it cost at least $459 a year to attend the University of Toronto but just

$247 a year at Guelph, not taking into account the higher cost of living in Toronto. Elsewhere Cruikshank estimated the annual costs as somewhat higher:

- fees for three terms
    - $45 for Ontario rural students
    - $75 for Ontario urban students
    - $90 for non-Ontario students

- room and board
    - in a single room ($6 a week) = $216.00
    - or double room ($5.50) = $198.00

- other fees and costs
    - $21.25 [185]

At those rates, choosing Macdonald Institute had some distinct economic advantages that would not be ignored, particularly in the context of the 1930s. Part of the argument in favour of opening a degree program at Mac was that it would allow some students to attain a degree who could not otherwise afford it.

The rural mission that was so fundamental to Macdonald Institute's mandate was maintained throughout the 1930s, thanks in large part to the links with the OAC and the Department of Agriculture, but the application of that mission was weakening. In 1928, the president of the OAC lamented that farmers' daughters were not taking sufficient advantage of the opportunities offered by Macdonald Institute, but at least some of the fault lay with Mac itself and its increasing pursuit of a more academic and scholarly environment. In the early 1930s the explicit preference in favour of farmers' daughters and rural women disappeared from the course calendar, though Mac continued to take in large numbers of such young women; as well, the admission process of holding all spaces open for rural students only until sixty days before opening classes ended. The fee structure itself retained its rural bias, charging just $15 per term for each student who was a farmer's daughter or who lived in a rural (less than one thousand population) community — other Ontario students paid $25 per term, and non-Ontario students paid $30 per term. Given the overall costs of a Guelph education, the rural savings were minimal, but they did send a positive and encouraging message to rural society: Macdonald Institute had rural interests at heart, but not at the cost of its own overall effectiveness when judged by academic standards.[186]

Outreach

Central to the continuing outreach function of Macdonald Institute and a continuing manifestation of its active interest in reaching the rural community were the Girls' Conferences held in association with the Women's Institutes each April or May for four days, beginning in 1925. About 200 to 350 girls (much larger numbers than had been initially hoped for) came to the campus annually to be entertained and educated, meaning that more girls experienced Macdonald Institute through these conferences each year than enrolled in Mac programs. Interestingly, numbers generally rose across the 1930s, peaking at almost 576 in 1936 and 450 in 1939; 200 applicants were allegedly turned away for lack of space in 1938. Conference attendees had to be at least sixteen years old and unmarried, and many were sponsored by their local Women's Institutes branch. The cost of attendance was $4.50 for four nights' room and board, plus the costs of travel to Guelph; those driving in from nearby locales could get meals for fifty cents a day. The young girls were housed in Johnston Hall or Mills Hall after the OAC students had left for the summer. The conference girls ate their meals in Creelman Hall, with a Macdonald instructor assigned to each table as hostess, and Mac girls and conference girls mixed together at each table. Instructions were given as to suitable topics of conversation at the tables.[187]

The program for the girls was drawn up by Macdonald faculty members, but the Mac girls put much of the program into effect, organizing folk dances, putting on pantomimes, and generally taking charge of the entertainment. Classes were generally cancelled during the conference to allow the students to lend their support. Each year the girls arrived on a Tuesday evening. The following morning they sat through an opening ceremony before having a two-hour tour of the various departments of the OAC. On Wednesday afternoon the girls were occupied with a program in War Memorial Hall, consisting of a community singsong and vocal solos interspersed among talks about the functions of the OAC — particularly "What the O.A.C. has to offer to the Farm Women and Girls of Ontario," as the 1927 program put it. The following year this was replaced by demonstrations of various handicrafts. In the evening the girls attended a banquet, with a featured speaker — in 1927 it was Ethel Chapman, editor of the women's section of *Ontario Farmer*; in 1928 Lucy Maude Montgomery, author of *Anne of Green Gables*, spoke to the girls; in 1931 the featured speaker was Miss Marshall Saunders, author of the best-seller *Beautiful Joe*.[188]

After breakfast on Thursday morning the girls met in Macdonald Institute Assembly Hall, this time breaking up for group discussions on such topics as foods, recreation, housing, clothing, and "habits." The groups reported back and a general discussion was held on the topics, followed by a talk on health (presumably with an emphasis on young women's health). In the afternoon, following a discussion of textile processes in various mills, the girls were given their choice of a visit to a local mill or to the Ontario Reformatory, followed by a visit to the Guelph downtown shopping district. That evening there was a community singsong, a debate among some of the conference girls, and a physical education demonstration put on by several Mac girls. Friday was the last full day on campus, and it was spent in the morning on further discussion groups (on personal finance, for example, or budgeting) and then on a series of addresses on such topics as girls' poultry clubs, canning and garden clubs, and farming for girls. The junior Mac girls served an afternoon tea, followed by various Mac girls playing leading roles in another physical education demonstration and a play. Mac students also gave demonstrations on various topics: posture and pep, sprucing up old furniture, diets for nutritional anaemia, efficiency in kitchen planning, meals for young children, and other topics.[189]

The order of events changed from year to year, but the overall content varied only a little. The conference was one more mechanism for carrying the message of the OAC and of Macdonald Institute to the young women of rural Ontario. Given the numbers of girls involved annually and the clear instruction to local Women's Institute branches that attendance should be open to girls who had not before attended, the annual Girls' Conferences were a major vehicle for spreading the "gospel of homemaking" across rural Ontario and for exposing countless homes to the ideas of home economics. There is some indication that the conferences acted as a recruiting device for Macdonald Institute, but there is no evidence that there was any deliberate intention of using the conferences for this purpose. What was intended was to expose further elements of female rural society to the "broadening" ideas of Macdonald Institute. But it was also "a splendid opportunity" for Mac students "to get in touch with girls from many rural districts" and to carry the message of Mac Institute by example.[190]

Linked with the Girls' Conferences were the two-week courses that continued to be offered. Participants were almost always girls from rural communities who had won various competitions through the Junior Women's Institutes and thus came sponsored by the Ministry of Agriculture. Groups of some twenty to forty young teenagers were exposed to home economics and to Macdonald Institute, to say nothing of spending time away from home in what to them must have seemed a big city. The curriculum covered child study and home nursing, household management, laundry, millinery, and physical education. When the numbers were quite low, the girls were simply included in regular classes to give them some exposure to the ideas and mission of home economics. Otherwise the girls were given a number of options within each subject for study and were asked to vote on the topics to be considered.[191] Teaching these girls was one more task added to the regular teaching load of the staff, but represented another way in which Macdonald Institute operated with a notable flexibility in seeking to bring within its purview the largest number of females possible, particularly those from rural areas.

Finally, Macdonald students and staff regularly participated in Farm and Home Week at the OAC every June, beginning in 1932. This was an event aimed at adult women with whom the Macdonald personnel took another opportunity to bring the "gospel of home-making" into the homes of rural Ontario. Displays, lectures, and demonstrations occurred throughout the week as Mac staff and students preached the latest ideas in nutrition, homemaking, and family care.[192]

STUDENT LIFE

Throughout the inter-war period, residence life continued to be dominated by regulation and attempted control. The residence superintendents periodically checked each student's room for tidiness and gave the quality of cleanliness a grade. The grade had no academic impact and it is unclear whether this form of attempted coercion was meaningful among the girls. Other attempts to have the girls conform to a gendered standard were easier to enforce. Mac girls, for example, were allowed to wear gym tunics to Creelman only for breakfast or lunch and only if the attire was covered by a coat; girls were required "to dress" for dinner.[193] Despite the Depression there were signs of rising affluence among the girls. School officials found it necessary to ban radios and gramophones from students' rooms in 1934, and there was some toleration of girls having their own cars (infrequent as this must have been). Overnight guests in residence were explicitly forbidden.

The male authorities, particularly G.I. Christie, president of the OAC, were particularly concerned that the regulatory environment for girls be well maintained. At one point Christie recommended that a bell be rung at various points in the day "in order that the student programme may be carried out in the regular way." At another point he enquired if there was any way in which the girls could be stopped from fraternizing with the boys by strolling and visiting during the noon hour, so that each sex could get on with its school work. In a 1936 letter to Cruikshank, Christie complained that some Mac girls visited the ground floor of Johnston Hall at inappropriate times: "It is not very flattering to have these comments made on the girls who come to the building at these times. I would think a warning would help them see their position."[194] A real concern here was to shape the behaviour of the OAC boys, and to do so indirectly by controlling the Mac girls.

The ladies of Mac 1930 showing some of their amazing spirit (left); outside of Macdonald Hall (right); bundled up for classes in 1929 (lower left); and from their rooms in Mac Hall (lower right).

And they're still smiling, fifty years later at their 1980 reunion.

To reinforce this environment Mac officials co-opted parents in the early 1930s. Questionnaires were distributed to all parents of girls in residence seeking the parents' advice regarding the regulations. In particular, Mac officials tried to solicit co-operation in restricting the number of weekends spent away from residence. "We do not encourage students to spend frequent week ends away from the college, as they miss much of college life, as it has an unsettling influence, and as it is often a physical strain. However, we are anxious to meet the wishes of the parents in this regard." How many weekends may their daughter spend away from Mac, where is she allowed to go, and how may she reach her destination, asked the questionnaire.[195] Punishments for violations of the regulations were usually handed out by the students' council and usually entailed suspension of social privileges on or off campus for a period of time.[196]

Top Left: *Typical residence room in Mac Hall during the 1930s.*

Top Right: *Cooking class in 1937.*

Centre Right: *Macdonald knitting club in the mid-1930s.*

Centre Left, Bottom Left, Bottom Right: *The Macdonald Club picnic in 1941.*

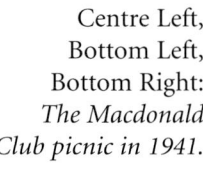

The social environment remained an active one. Indeed, it was necessary to restrict regular student dances to two nights a week — half-hour "hops" on Mondays and Thursdays — while "socials" were held on Tuesdays and Fridays. Beyond that were all the special occasion events, such as the Short Course Reception Dance in January, the Senior Sleigh Ride in January, Conversat in February. The succession of dances meant that the young women required several semi-formal and formal dresses if they were to attend such functions. The regular 10:45 curfew for Mac girls limited the length of the events, but the sheer number of social occasions is striking.[197] Not all dances were held in Macdonald Hall gymnasium as they had been at one time; now Creelman Hall was cleared of its tables to make way for dances as well.[198] Also, the regulations suggest that Mac girls could be found more often in town. By 1932, for example, girls were allowed to walk back from town after dark provided that they were in groups of at least three; otherwise, a chaperone was still needed. Girls were now permitted to attend Sunday evening church, as well as in the morning.[199]

For several years already Conversat had been the social highlight of this very social environment, ranked by some as second in the province only to the Royal Military College's June Ball. The 1930 dance is a good example. It was, of course, a joint Mac-OAC event and had a joint organizing committee, in which the girls were outnumbered eleven to two. Creelman Hall was decorated extensively. The decorations usually reflected some general theme or era; this time the dance had a futuristic theme. Creelman was "lavishly decorated in colorful futuristic design." On the wall behind the orchestra was a huge spreading fan, with black ribs and panels of green, yellow, and orange; scattered across the fan were musical notes suggestive of syncopated music. The chandeliers were covered with large octagonal shades of the same colours and design, and the window coverings continued the colour scheme and design. A bizarre note was struck with silhouettes of medieval figures poised in dance postures. The two main sitting-out rooms, one on the balcony and one on the main floor, were luxuriously decorated. During the fifteenth dance balloons and novelties were released from the ceiling, and "moon dances" were scattered throughout the program for a romantic touch. That year, for the first time, the buffet lunch was set up in Mac Hall so "a covered canopy was built from the Dining Hall to Macdonald Hall to protect the guests from the elements." The receiving line included the OAC president and Miss Cruikshank, and representatives attended from surrounding universities. The students danced for hours to the music of Gilbert Watson and his orchestra, the curfew being lifted for this event. Conversat was judged expensive for the era — over $10 for tickets, corsage, and clothes. The "dance craze" of the early century lived on at Guelph.[200]

Left: *Macdonald Institute gymnastics club, mid-1930s.*

Right: *The shooting club, 1935.*

Left and Right: *Conversat, 1935.*

Conversat, 1939.

Perhaps as an indication of the Depression or of growing ideas of female equality, there was an attempt to start what was called "the Fifty-Fifty Club," promoting the idea that men and women would share equally the costs of an evening. The attempt was short-lived, succumbing to gendered traditions, but it was revived more than once, suggesting some of the underlying tensions.[201] A related innovation in the late 1930s was Sadie Hawkins Week, in which gender roles were reversed and girls took the initiative in asking boys out and paying the costs.[202]

This attempted change parallelled another failed attempt, this time trying to relax the residence rules at Mac. Students of the 1930s found the limitations and

The choral society, 1935.

restrictions of residence rules more unacceptable than in the past. A comparison with the rules at other universities revealed a generally more restrictive environment in Guelph, though the criticisms here came at least as much from the boys on campus.[203]

Beyond the dances were many other events: the initiations each September (traditionally characterized by freshmen girls in green berets), the Junior Prom in September, the Hallowe'en Dance, an all-girl pyjama party in Mac Hall, the debates often staged by the Union Literary Society, the presentations of the philharmonic society (for example, the *Mikado* in March 1930), and the year-end athletic concert. In 1930 Mac and the OAC co-operated to establish regular Sunday afternoon "grabeterias," which featured lunch and a program; their main purpose was to provide an event that facilitated heterosexual socializing much too early for any curfews to be breached. At other times in the second half of the school year, the various years within each program had their own dinners, attended by the students and school officials.[204]

Graduation now had well-established traditions. The two-year graduates wore academic black gowns and caps, while the one-year graduates wore long white dresses. Junior girls wove a daisy chain that had come in the 1920s to replace the May Day Fête, and as a final class project

The daisy chain, mid-1930s.

Left: *The maypole dance (shown here in the 1930s) was an important part of any graduation ceremony.*

Right: *The night before graduation the girls gathered to make the daisy chains for the next day's ceremony.*

Left: *Class of '39 during convocation.*

Right: *Another picture from the graduation ceremonies of 1939.*

for the year, the juniors prepared and served the graduation dinner for the seniors. Graduation services were held in War Memorial Hall and always had a featured dignitary giving a graduation address. The students themselves were represented by a valedictorian each year.[205]

It was not easy for the young women exposed to this range and intensity of social activity to maintain an appropriate balance between socializing and school work. The mother of one young girl responded when her daughter had a number of failures in her December examinations:

> "I do feel that she will catch up, as she realizes what it means to her if she falls down this year. The initiation was such a lark, and in fact, the dances, football games, etc were simply dazzling for her. Her description of all these good times is almost worth recording and … we are particularly happy about her friendship with her roommate."[206]

The social activities ranged across a wide array of interests, both heterosexual and homosocial. But what was new to most girls was the extensive mixing with the boys from the OAC and OVC. As if to celebrate this, the 1934 *Libranni* announced facetiously that a new sorority, the

Spinsters Club, had been inaugurated; its only problem was that there were so few members.[207] The girls may have been less explicit in celebrating heterosexuality than were the boys on campus, but both sexes shared the same hegemonic environment. What was occurring here, as on other Canadian campuses at the same time, was the shaping of a youth culture, separate from that of adolescents and not yet part of the adult world, a culture distinctly the students' own.[208]

Beyond the organized events were the unorganized events, the small parties of various cliques of girls in Mac Hall, held in one room or another. Here is where the friendships were solidified and the confidences exchanged. As one Mac girl recalled:

> These good times among ourselves are centred within parties in the individual rooms. Each one has her own ring of friends, and if Saturday night comes, or any night in fact, with not much to do, you will see stacks of bread, bottles of catsup and everything imaginable, being carefully carried, under our coats and in the open too, from the dining hall to Mac.

Otherwise food could be obtained from the Tuck Shoppe or The Café.[209] These social gatherings were at the heart of the Mac environment and gave the girls a social confidence and meaning that were central to the Mac experience.

Athletics retained their central place in many girls' lives at Guelph. There was a wide range of activities in which participation was possible: basketball, tennis, badminton, hockey, baseball, and swimming. In 1930 a joint OAC-Mac field day was held featuring various track and field events. This was complemented by less formal games such as ping-pong or crokinole in the basement recreation room of Mac Hall. Basketball continued to be the sole sport in which a Mac team competed outside the campus, but this did not stop the girls from forming a number of teams in the various sports.

This socializing itself had a recognized educational function. Students were away from home usually for the first time, in a position of quasi-independence for the first time and with new social responsibilities; the heterosexual social environment broke the tendency towards homosocial activities from which the students had come. The students acquired a new maturity, but this maturing was by no means unique to the Macdonald Institute environment. It was the sort of thing that happened at all post-secondary institutions. Mac girls shared in this phenomenon, and the new sense of self-assurance and self-awareness was forever linked to Mac and the Guelph campus.

The alumnae caught the spirit of this socializing. In 1930 Mac grads in Guelph organized a local branch of the Mac Alumnae and began to hold regular meetings and "socials."[210] They

Mrs. Katherine Fuller

Katherine Fuller, a widow with a daughter of her own, began her career as matron/superintendent of Macdonald Hall in 1904 and remained in that position for twenty-seven years, until 1931. Inevitably in that position as "house mother" she came to know the girls well. She served informally as a "dean of women," counselling and giving advice. In the midst of her career, the *OAC Review* paid tribute to her: "Mrs. Fuller is the perfect House Mother. In her person, natural gifts both physical and mental, education, experience of the world, the joys and cares of a family, the discipline of grief and strong religious convictions have united to produce the very woman who is needed to fill the position."[211]

She joined in the student activities with enthusiasm, often presiding at various functions with her piano playing — either by herself or as accompaniment for others — and was an active supporter of cultural events. Her versatility at the piano, playing music from Chopin to well-known hymns and on occasions varying from group singsongs to convocation processionals, was ideally suited for her to make a significant contribution to the cultural and social life of the campus. Mrs. Fuller was also an active participant in the Mac YWCA and hosted regular Bible study classes on Sunday mornings.

It was a sign of the high regard in which she was held (and of the low pay and pensions at Mac) that a collection was taken up among the students to supplement her pension when she retired in 1931.[212] At that time she was replaced by Mrs. A.E. Barber.

also became an important force on campus, assisting in the honouring of former teacher Jean Bradley on her death and of Katherine Fuller, the first matron, on her retirement. The Mac Alumnae instituted several scholarships to support the academic environment.

One other characteristic of the social environment deserves mention. During the 1920s there had been several Asian students, primarily from Japan, to break the otherwise overwhelmingly "white" character of the staff and students. When approached in 1934 about an application from an African-Canadian girl, Cruikshank advised against the girl's application. No "coloured student" had ever attended Mac, she responded. The classroom work would be of great value,

> but we fear it would be very lonely for her socially. College activities, lectures, philharmonic concerts, dances, etc., play a great part in college life, and we fear that a sensitive girl would have many a lonely hour. So much depends on the applicant herself. One can make the work so time absorbing that the lack of social life will not bother one. Probably the applicant will not wish to live in residence and it might be advisable for her to stay with coloured people in Guelph and come only for classes. We feel that it would be very difficult for her as well as for the other students to have her in residence.[213]

What was of no doubt to Cruikshank was that any person of colour would be denied admission to the social life of Mac. Racism was alive and well throughout Canadian society, and Macdonald Institute was no exception. Such attitudes made for a particular type of social environment at Mac.

THE WAR AND CLOSURE

By the later years of the 1930s Depression, Macdonald Institute was beginning to show signs of decline — or at least of coming up against new barriers that stood in the way of Mac continuing to fulfill its evolving academic niche. Some of its programs had difficulty attracting students; attempts to expand to a degree program were frustrated, and some of the more academic students demonstrated a growing desire to be part of a degree-granting program; and Macdonald graduates had increasing difficulty in finding jobs. Macdonald Institute was not keeping up with the evolving societal demands placed on it. The initiatives of the early and mid-1930s — and these were important in furthering Macdonald Institute's academic niche — were insufficient

Left: *A clipping from the Times (London, England) concerning Macdonald Institute.*

Right: *From* The Globe and Mail, *June 10, 1941.*

STUDENTS INITIATE R.C.A.F. CHEFS INTO CULINARY ART

First Instructors Arrive to Prepare for Opening of Wireless School

Left and Right: *Pictures of our "boys" fighting for the country from the* Libranni *in the 1940s.*

Left: *The classrooms in Macdonald Institute used for the Wireless School during the war years.*

Right: *Military Ball on campus, 1944.*

to overcome these problems. The biggest barrier of all was the Second World War. The public and governmental desire to prosecute the war to the full extent of available resources had an unanticipated result for Mac: the school was completely shut down and turned over to the military for wartime purposes.

The impact of the Second World War, which began in September 1939, was quickly apparent at Mac. Early in 1940 sixteen Air Force chefs arrived for training in quantity cooking. The chefs received training in butchering, menu planning, kitchen hygiene and sanitation, food preparation, and cooking, over a six-week period. This was followed by eleven more six-week courses for other chefs and their assistants. As well, Mac offered a special course for Canadian Red Cross workers in wartime nutrition, foods, and child care. Eventually the RCAF Cookery School, using up to five of the existing Mac instructors and all of the facilities, had a peak enrolment of 576. Other instructors found employment elsewhere, working at a Women's Institute branch, at surrounding universities, and at the Toronto Sick Children's Hospital, among other places.[214]

In the fall of 1940, Miss Cruikshank organized the commencement of a new organization on campus, the Women's Auxiliary for War Services. The WAWS's purpose was to coordinate the war work of the Mac students and to develop some of the suggestions for women's war work in general. The girls would all spend two hours a week on training in such areas as military drill, map and compass reading, gas mask and air raid drill, and rifle shooting. Increased class time was devoted to first aid and home nursing, and girls received instruction in stretcher bearing. The girls took courses that qualified them for the St. John Ambulance First Aid and Home Nursing certificates. As well, the Engineering Department of the OAC offered a popular Motor Mechanics and Ambulance Driving course for women.[215]

Suddenly in the spring of 1941 it was announced that courses at Mac would cease for the duration of the war; current students would transfer to the University of Toronto to complete their programs. Here was a fundamental statement of the perceived marginal character of the contributions being made by Macdonald Institute. It was so unimportant that it could be completely shut down (while the OAC continued to instruct the overwhelmingly male agriculturalists). Was this a statement about the relative importance of women's education, or about home economics, or about Macdonald Institute itself?

A grand total of 6,284 young women had passed through the halls of Macdonald Institute as students since 1903. They had matured there and grown more confident in themselves as young women. They had been given knowledge and skills and the ability to put these to good use. In her last message to alumnae and in the spirit of the wartime emergency, Olive Cruikshank called on Mac graduates to participate in the Mac tradition of responsibility to help society.[216]

The buildings — Macdonald Hall, Macdonald Institute, Watson Hall, Maids' Hall, Mills Hall, War Memorial Hall, and others — were put to good use. Thanks to the generous offer of Ontario Premier Mitch Hepburn, the buildings were made available to the federal government for the war effort. Quickly RCAF Wireless School No. 4 took up the quarters not being used by the RCAF Cookery School, adding "temporary" buildings as well. At the

ONTARIO AGRICULTURAL COLLEGE 1941

All who heard a recent British broadcast were stirred to learn that the slogan I.A.D.O.M. (It All Depends On Me) is above the doorways of many factories in England where hundreds and thousands of young women are employed on war work. We are privileged to live in comparative security on this continent because of the courage, the heroism, the endurance and the suffering of these young women and the thousands of others who serve in the British Empire.

You know from your knowledge of Foods and Nutrition that sailors, soldiers and air men have to be adequately fed for many years before they are called to serve. You realize from your studies in Psychology that mental confusion, that crouching fears, that indecisiveness and that panic are as truly weapons for the enemy as aeroplanes and tanks.

As graduates in Home Economics your greatest responsibilities and your greatest opportunities will be to guard human resources and human welfare. May you accept the challenge I.A.D.O.M.

Olson R. Cruikshank

Wireless School, men and women trained for the war in wireless and radar, primarily. The official handover occurred on May 1, 1941, though the Mac girls were allowed to finish out their year during May (graduating a month early so as to make the remainder of the facilities more quickly available). Cruikshank remained on campus until 1944, handling various administrative tasks as well as being available for foods research.

Staff of Macdonald Institute with autographs, from the 1941 Libranni.

The disruption to Mac was tempered only by some continuity in personnel. Dr. Hugh Branion, who was to play a long-time role in the OAC and the University of Guelph, became head of the RCAF Cookery School (though he joined the armed forces to do so). Among the staff hired by Branion was Louisa Brill, a Mac alumna. Brill taught cooking for the duration of the war and remained on to help return the buildings to their original teaching purposes; she was a central member of the Macdonald teaching staff for the next two decades. Cruikshank continued to work on campus, handling extension work and maintaining a public presence of the idea of Macdonald Institute and its programs. Five of the staff members stayed on to teach in the RCAF Cookery School, while the rest dispersed to other positions off campus. The Macdonald Guelph Club, made up of alumnae living in the Guelph area, played an important role in keeping the spirit of Mac alive on campus during the closure. The club prepared exhibits for College Royal (the annual public demonstration of skills and knowledge on campus), held meetings on campus, and prepared an expanded Mac alumnae section of the *OAC Review*.

In February 1945, with the end of the war in sight, the RCAF returned all the buildings, land, and facilities it had occupied, together with any buildings or improvements added during the occupation. A stipulation of the use of the buildings had been that they be returned in their original condition, but instead the federal government gave money in lieu of the necessary repair work, leaving it to the OAC officials to find scarce contractors to do the work. The remaining staff set to work organizing the restoration of the buildings and retrieving equipment stored elsewhere on campus.[217]

Macdonald Institute could now get on with its work. But 1945 was somewhat of a turning point. Without a degree program Mac had proven to be increasingly unable to meet the demands of its users. The wartime closing had suggested that this was a fundamentally marginal institution of little importance, performing a function of little value to society. What was more, its staff had been dispersed during the war; a new staff would have to be assembled and students recruited. From these perspectives, Macdonald Institute was in serious trouble in 1945.

IV

MACDONALD REINVIGORATED,
1945–1964

With the renewal of academic and social life at Macdonald Institute in the aftermath of the war, new opportunities opened up for Mac. The acquisition of a four-year degree program encouraged Mac administrators and faculty in their academic aspirations and the degree program itself blossomed as an increasing number of young women sought post-secondary education. Soon Macdonald Institute had the largest home economics program in the country, and administrators began to think of expansion of the program. A nursery school became an important addition to Mac facilities, and Dean McCready began to make plans for the teaching of graduate students. Macdonald Institute in the post-war world reverted, as did so many Canadians, to the pre-war world for defining the college's aspirations and parameters. Yet ironically, at the same time that Macdonald Institute became the pre-eminent home economics program in Canada, cracks were beginning to appear in the standardized depiction of women's future. Despite the predominant signs of conformity in the 1950s, there were emerging signs that women were no longer content with the gendered parameters that so restricted women's possible actions and aspirations.

Left: *Macdonald Institute in the late 1950s.*

Right: *Macdonald Institute and Hall, circa late 1940s.*

"The Grand Old Lady" in all her glory.

The famous Macdonald Hall well.

A New Beginning

Despite the somewhat shaky foundations of Macdonald Institute in 1945, there is no evidence that any serious consideration was given to allowing the college to remain closed. Mac was important for the Ontario Agricultural College, broadening its otherwise narrow educational mission, and continued to play a minor, if somewhat diminishing, role in the education of young women in Ontario. Plans were made for the reopening of Macdonald Institute in the fall of 1945 with essentially the same curriculum and aspirations as before the war. When the buildings could not be refurbished in time, the reopening was postponed until the fall of 1946.[218]

The fate of this rather unimaginative new beginning remains unknown because almost immediately an outside force precipitated a dramatic and substantial change in Macdonald Institute's academic position. The home economics program at the University of Toronto was judged to be in some serious trouble and in 1947 the dynamic president of the university, Dr. Sidney Smith, ordered an independent investigation of the program. Dr. Clara Brown Arny of the University of Minnesota was hired to carry out the investigation and to report back to the president. Arny was given several proposals that she might wish to take into account. Included in those proposals was the 1936 request by Olive Cruikshank that Macdonald be allowed to develop a four-year degree program, using the degree-granting powers of the University of Toronto. Smith's reasons for including Macdonald in the Toronto review remain unclear. Macdonald Institute was outside his jurisdiction and there is no indication that he sought permission (at the OAC or elsewhere) to include the Guelph college in this investigation.[219]

Within four months Arny's report was presented to Smith. The American home economist damned the program at the University of Toronto, finding its facilities outdated, some of the teaching weak, the curriculum poorly planned, and the program administration inadequate. Macdonald Institute, on the other hand, received considerable praise. The facilities she saw were reported to be "far better" at Macdonald Institute than at Toronto — the space and equipment for teaching food preparation and meal service and for teaching clothing construction. Clearly the renovated laboratories of the late 1930s and the necessary refurbishing caused by termination of the wartime environment had created an effective teaching environment. What was more, Macdonald Institute represented some of the strong rural traditions associated with home economics. Arny pointed particularly to Macdonald's links with the Women's Institutes as an important indication of the college's links with rural women. "Mac. Inst. could prepare persons for extension work better than the University," Arny judged, "particularly because of its rural setting and the fact that it would attract rural girls who are already familiar with rural life." The net result was a forthright recommendation from Arny that Macdonald Institute be given a four-year degree program, while the diploma program continued separately.[220]

What was more, Arny recommended that all of the 1936 restrictions on any such proposal not be followed. The fees at Macdonald should not be forced to be the same as those at the University of Toronto — Macdonald fees were tied to those at the OAC and those fees and cost of living "are low enough to make college education possible for many who could not afford to attend the University." The Guelph college should not be required to adopt the same courses and curriculum as Toronto — "the two programs should be developed to serve different groups and should not duplicate each other" — nor should the examinations be the same. The staff at Guelph had clearly impressed Arny during her visit that spring. "The final decisions should lie with the group in Guelph" regarding staff selection and courses. The new director, Miss Lindsley, "seemed to have considerable vision for the development of the program."[221]

All in all, the report was everything that Macdonald Institute might have wished. Its Toronto rival was entirely damned and Macdonald's own strengths were recognized and emphasized. Arny's vision for a home economics program meshed with that at Guelph, particularly its rural outreach. It was equally important that President Smith accepted the report. It is unclear whether there was some pressure from the Ontario government to follow through on the report's recommendations, but Smith did refer in later correspondence to a promise that he had given to Ontario Premier George Drew, who was himself a native of Guelph.[222] There is also evidence of pressure from Mac alumnae, from the OAC alumni, and from the Women's Institute in favour of a four-year degree program at Macdonald Institute.[223]

The acquisition of a four-year degree program was a momentous development for Macdonald Institute. This placed Macdonald on a similar footing with the OAC and OVC, both of which also used the University of Toronto's degree-granting powers for their students; this was important for the internal politics on the Guelph campus. More importantly, the decline in Macdonald's attractiveness for Ontario students was reversed. The rising desire for a university degree among young women could now be satisfied within Macdonald Institute itself; no longer would students need to transfer to Toronto to complete the degree program. Macdonald would now have its stronger students for a full four years, rather than just two, making possible a very different social and educational climate on the campus. And finally, Macdonald Institute began to travel down an academic path that had previously been closed to it. Its university-level academic aspirations would be developed and strengthened, leading to important new possibilities in the future.

DOROTHY LINDSLEY, 1946–1949

With the re-establishment of Macdonald Institute planned for 1946, a new director was needed. In August 1946, just before the September classes were to begin, Dorothy Lindsley was hired from the University of Toronto to be the associate director. The late hiring is an indication of how little change was made in the old diploma curriculum. Nevertheless, Lindsley had to scramble to get Mac ready for the new students — the refurbishing and repainting of both Macdonald Hall and Macdonald Institute had not yet been completed. Much of the equipment from the Mac laboratories had been housed in various OAC departments during the war and had to be shipped back across campus. By the end of the renovations the Mac buildings presented a new face to the world, as one alumna reported in 1949:

A tour through Macdonald Hall and the Institute showed many progressive changes since reopening. The girls' residence has lost much of its severity. A kitchenette on each floor with milk and crackers provided suggested some minor social activities. An infirmary with two beds, and an adjoining lounge room for convalescence added to the welfare of the students. A workroom, furnished with sewing machines, desks and tables and a recreation room were also worthwhile changes.[224]

Dorothy M. Lindsley.

By the end of September Lindsley and five faculty members were ready to receive the new students as life began again at Macdonald Institute.

Lindsley was in part responsible for a more relaxed, co-educational environment on campus. The war had created a new tone in social relations and the Guelph campus witnessed some of the results. Many of the old rules and traditions were relaxed. In Creelman Hall, self-serve cafeteria-style eating replaced the formal pre-war environment of waitresses and table service. Residence life at Macdonald Hall was also more relaxed. Although there was still a ten o'clock curfew on regular weeknight, girls could stay out until one-thirty on evenings when there were parties on campus, and students were allowed a limited number of days "off" from these regulations. Lindsley brought with her a new, fresh outlook on Macdonald's future and she readily impressed Dr. Arny on her visit in the spring of 1947 with visions of what a degree program might look like.

After news that the University of Toronto would be amenable to granting degrees — BHSc — to graduates of a four-year program at Mac, Lindsley busied herself planning for the new program. She established an advisory committee, consisting of Mac graduates and experts from the Ontario Department of Agriculture, to work on the task. The new degree would depend on close collaboration with various academic departments in the OAC — English, Chemistry, Botany, Microbiology, and Nutrition. It was also necessary to persuade the various administrative bodies at the University of Toronto, including the senate, that the proposed new program met the standards of the university. The Guelph faculty was placed

Dorothy Lindsley Walden

Dorothy Lindsley received her post-secondary education at the University of Toronto, receiving a BA in Home Economics and an MA in Food Chemistry. Upon her graduation with her MA, she was hired as an instructor in the Food Chemistry Department at the University of Toronto, where she taught for six years. In 1946 advice was sought from the Household Science Faculty at the University of Toronto about a new director, and the leading members of the Toronto faculty recommended Lindsley. At age thirty-three, she was hired away from the University of Toronto by the president of the OAC to become associate director of Macdonald Institute. As associate director she played a crucial role in attracting and developing the new four-year degree program. Her leadership was abruptly cut short in 1949 when she married a chemistry professor at the OAC, requiring her resignation from Macdonald Institute.

In partial recognition of her services to the college, Lindsley (now Mrs. Walden) was appointed to the newly formed board of governors of the now independent University of Guelph in 1965, where she served until 1974.

under scrutiny as were the details of the new four-year program. While the students began the four-year program in September 1948, it was not until the winter of 1949 that formal approval of the program was granted by the Toronto senate.[225]

Lindsley's impressive leadership of Macdonald Institute was abruptly cut short by the kind of event that affected only those institutions dependent on female leaders in this period. Lindsley developed a romantic attachment to Professor Frank Walden, then a member of the OAC Chemistry Department. The couple was seen around campus together rather frequently — too frequently for the liking of OAC President W.R. Reek. He asked Lindsley bluntly what her intentions were, and she made it clear that she would soon be marrying. Lindsley had faced the dilemma shared by many women working in middle-class occupations at this time: she could work or she could marry, but she could not do both. The gendered character of contemporary Canadian society was once again made clear through the history of Macdonald Institute.

Margaret McCready, 1949–1968

With the forced resignation of Dorothy Lindsley, the search began for her replacement. The solution was soon found in the person of Dr. Margaret McCready, who had been director of the Household Science program at Macdonald College, McGill University since 1939. McCready brought with her some outstanding credentials and some long-standing ties to Guelph, where she had been raised. She had considerable experience as a university administrator and teacher; she possessed a PhD, which brought added academic prestige to her new position; she had several scholarly publications to her credit; and she had training and experience in both dietetics and applied human nutrition. McCready had just completed a term, 1946–48, as chair of

Dr. Margaret S. McCready.

the University Education Committee of the Canadian Dietetic Association. Her energy and enthusiasm for the job and her leadership role in Canadian education — she was president of the Canadian Home Economics Association, 1948–1950, and president of the Ontario

Margaret McCready

Raised in Guelph, where her father had been a faculty member on the campus, McCready earned a BA in Household Economics (Toronto) and a PhD (Aberdeen, 1946), writing a dissertation on food survey analysis. McCready had worked as a dietitian in New York City and Toronto, where she had spent some time as dietitian at the St. George's School for Child Study, University of Toronto and studied children's eating habits. She had then become director of visiting housekeeper and nutrition services for the Ontario Red Cross. In 1937 McCready moved to the United Kingdom where she was a diet surveyor for the United Kingdom Carnegie Diet Survey, before joining Macdonald College of McGill University as associate professor of nutrition and director of the School of Household Science.

While director of Macdonald Institute she maintained a high public profile elsewhere through her leadership in the Canadian Home Economics Association, the Ontario Educational Association, the Canadian Council of Nutrition, the Canadian Consumer Association, the Ontario Dietetic Association, the Canadian Save the Children Fund, the Vanier Institute on the Family, and the Canadian Freedom from Hunger Committee. She represented Macdonald Institute as a member of the senate of the University of Toronto. This outside role was paralleled by an equally high profile at Guelph. She was noted for her charm and her easy approachability. She carried herself with such grace and easy confidence that she set a strong model of achievement and accomplishment for the young women passing through the halls of Macdonald Institute.

McCready's achievements and her service to Macdonald Institute were recognized when she was named a Fellow of the University of Guelph in 1972 and awarded an honorary degree by Guelph in 1984.

Educational Association, 1953, among roles with other organizations — made her an ideal selection for the position of director of Macdonald Institute as the institution turned its new-found status into substance.

There was no fundamental reshaping of Macdonald Institute's mission with these changes. The degree program and students gave Mac a renewed academic thrust that increasingly came to dominate the Guelph environment, but many of the old traditions remained. The outreach to rural Ontario continued. Farmers' daughters still received preferential treatment. The Women's Institute continued to regard Guelph and Macdonald Institute as its home base, and Girls' Conferences remained a feature of the post-war summer environment, still being used as a recruiting device for Mac. In winter 1944–45 the Women's Institute of Ontario petitioned the provincial government to establish a four-year degree program at Macdonald Institute, and when the program began, the Women's Institute immediately provided funds for four entrance scholarships.[226] And yet signs of change were present. There was talk of graduate work at Macdonald Institute, of extension work overseas in developing countries, of trying to attract men into the Mac programs.

CURRICULUM

The first main task faced by Mac administrators was to shape the curriculum of the new four-year degree program. The function of this program, as initially articulated, was stated thus: "While the training of homemakers is fundamental, the course will also qualify young women to act professionally in the field of dietetics; in extending home economics education in schools and colleges and in adult education programs."[227] This is suggestive of the limited vision that made this program a true product of its time. The fundamental aim of the program was to train young women who would be skilled and knowledgeable homemakers, rather than professional experts. This narrow-

Cooking classes in Mac after the war.

Left: *Cooking classes in Mac after the war.*

Right: *Misses Blochin, Bradt, McGuigan, and James in 1948.*

Left: *Sewing class work-room, circa 1950.*

Right: *Practising for the real world in the apartment in Macdonald Institute.*

Left: *Fourth-year Textile students in 1954.*

Right: *Textile students in their final year.*

ness was restated with a greater emphasis on professional training after McCready's arrival. The 1951 course calendar claimed that the objectives of the home economics program were to "qualify young women to act professionally in the field of foods and dietetics, clothing and textiles, and in extending home economics education in schools and colleges and in adult education programs."[228] Mac Institute continued to see itself as exclusively for young women who would eventually put their training to good use in their own homes; the program's professional ambitions remained limited. The rural emphasis of the program continued, as advertisements for the new degree program were placed in such journals as the *Farmers Magazine* and the *Ontario Milk Producer*.[229]

The four-year program itself was thoroughly academic. In the first year students took courses in bacteriology, chemistry, physics, physical education, and zoology, as well as English, art, clothing, textiles, and foods. This was followed in second year by botany, nutrition, household management, and physiology, as well as further courses in English, art, bacteriology, chemistry, clothing, and foods. The third year was taken up with courses in art, English, biochemistry, clothing, economics, foods, household management, sociology, and textiles. In fourth year students were expected to declare a specialization — either food administration or clothing and textiles — taking appropriate courses for the specialization as well as English and a few other courses. Students were required to obtain a passing grade of at least 50 percent in each course and an overall average of at least 60 percent; those failing a small number of courses could write supplemental exams the following September.

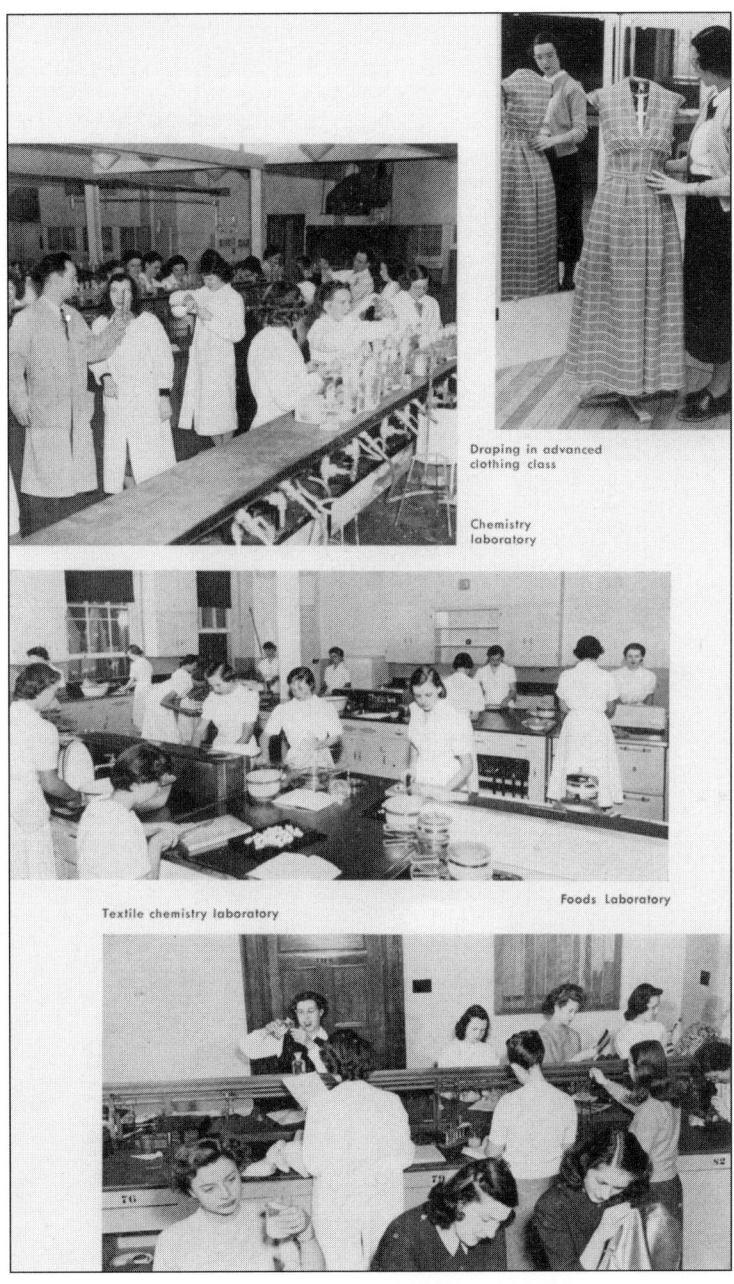

Various shots from classes during this era.

Draping in advanced clothing class

Chemistry laboratory

Textile chemistry laboratory

Foods Laboratory

Left: *In the new wing, here is the craft and leather workroom, 1955.*

Right: *Students woodworking in the early 1960s.*

Left: *First-year students in their "related art" class cutting lino.*

Right: *Students Shirley Ann McPhee, Mary Margaret Henderson, and Isabel Bierworth modelling their creations on the steps of Macdonald Institute, April 14, 1961.*

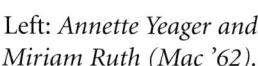

Left: *Annette Yeager and Miriam Ruth (Mac '62).*

Right: *Irene Collins and Diane Gingirick (Mac '64).*

 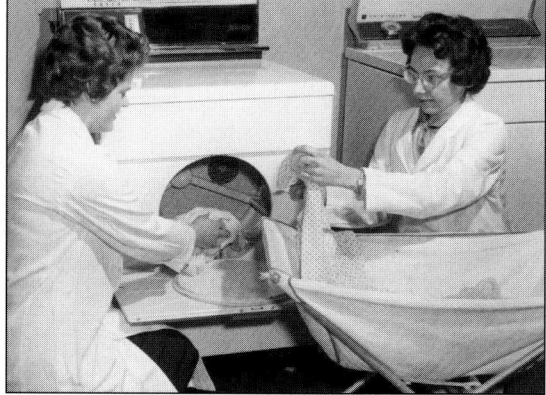

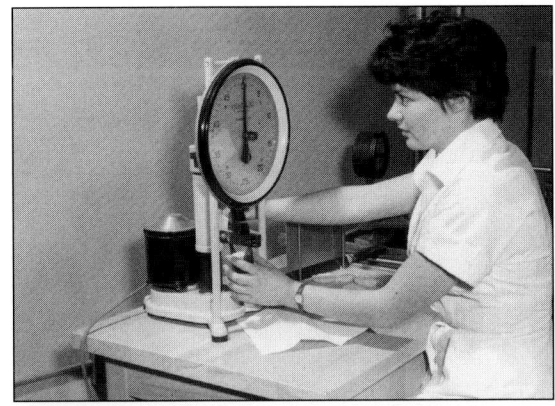

Left: *Gail Hunter (Mac '63).*

Right: *A. Bush and Rita Crow (Mac '63).*

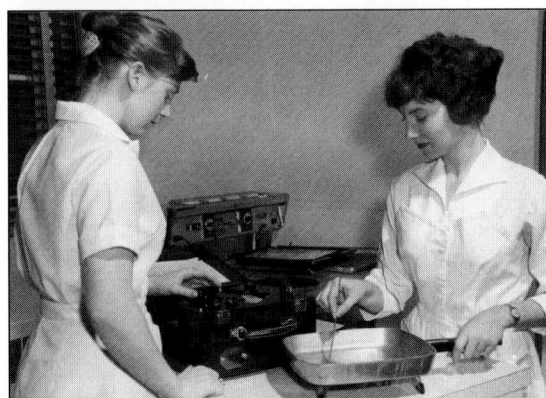

Left: *Wendy McCaul and Shirley Ann McPhee (Mac '62).*

Right: *Classes in food preparation and tasting.*

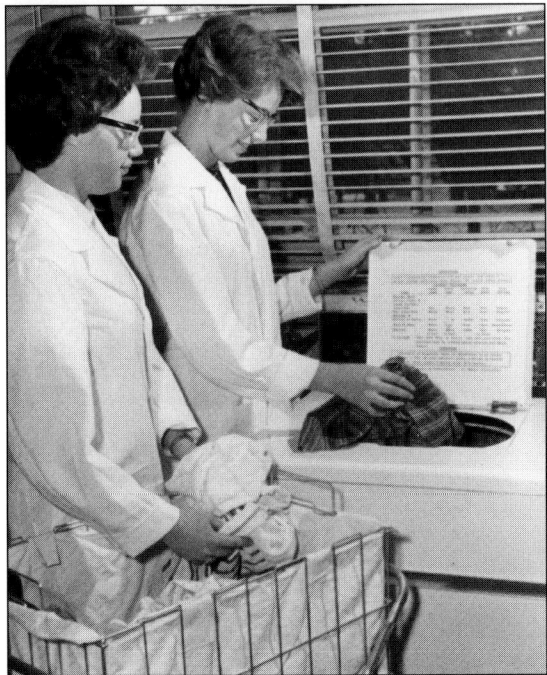

Left: *R. Archibald and A. Baak (Mac '64).*

Right: *Adele Shainline and Hazel Martin (Mac '63).*

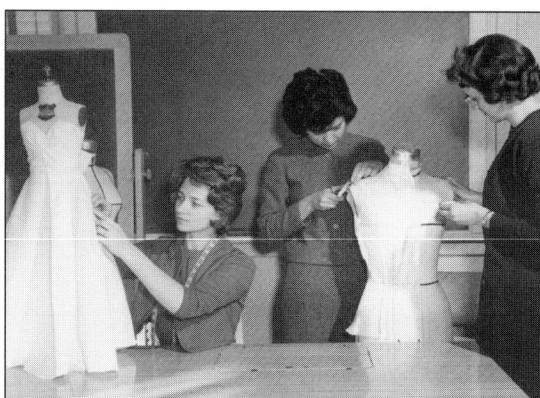

This curriculum changed somewhat over the years as courses were added or deleted, but its basic character remained. Students received a broad training in the scientific background to various foods and textile processes as well as a good general education in English, along with a slight exposure to some social sciences and humanities subjects. According to Dr. McCready, in 1955 the curriculum consisted of traditional science courses (43 percent of course time), social sciences and humanities (13 percent), and applied and professional courses (44 percent).[230] In 1958 a new fourth-year option, home management, was introduced, in which students would take courses in business management, advanced equipment, and other specialized subjects. There remained a strong emphasis on applied learning. Students interested in clothing and textiles could take such courses as tailoring and clothing reconstruction, and others could take such courses as interior decoration, in contrast to such electives as calculus, rural sociology, or statistics.

Macdonald Institute remained dependent on the University of Toronto for the viability of the four-year degree program. All program changes required approval of the Board of Household Science Studies at Toronto and of the university's senate; final exams needed to be submitted to the registrar of the University of Toronto.[231]

New scholarships underscored the academic thrust of the degree program. It has already been noted that the Women's Institute established entrance scholarships for degree students in 1948. In 1952 the Hoodless family endowed an award for a third-year student on the basis of general proficiency, with preference being given to girls from rural communities. W.M. Stewart of the Macdonald Company contributed funds for a new scholarship, and the Mac Alumnae established a bursary fund. Several food companies gave awards for top-performing students, and individual branches of the Women's Institutes established several prizes. By 1954 there were twenty-two different scholarships and awards handed out, and in 1960 the Mac Alumnae began a campaign to raise new scholarship funds. The alumnae loyalty to Macdonald Institute was remarkable; the 1960 Alumnae president stated: "The feeling of kinship found amongst Macdonald graduates is such that one might compare them with members of one large family. Just as each link in the chain determines the ultimate strength of that chain, so does each graduate determine the graduate strength of the school."[232]

The Macdonald curriculum was a reflection of home economics as an academic discipline at the time. An examination of the home economics programs in Canadian universities in 1952 confidently proclaimed that the "primary purpose of home economics education has been to promote better family living." This applied character of home economics to the practical issues of the home and family took second place to nothing within the discipline. "But in our time the family is assuming a new importance in which it is recognized that as go our homes so go our nations," announced the study. This sort of traditional rhetoric about the family/home was at the heart of home economics still. The fundamental task of home economics programs in universities was "to inspire homemakers for greater competence and enjoyment of their role." Only secondary was an interest in training young women for professional occupations that were related to family living. And yet there was the beginning of signs that perhaps the discipline was experiencing problems. It was difficult to judge the value of home economics training, admitted the author of the 1952 report, and both the American Home Economics Association and the Canadian Home Economics Association had initiated studies to evaluate the effectiveness of university-level programs in the discipline. Doubts began to surface about the effectiveness of trying to educate for home-making and professional work at the same time and in the same courses, and about the general quality of home economics programs in the universities.[233] But in the meantime Macdonald Institute's curriculum carried on with the traditional approaches to the discipline (as did the other home economics programs in Canadian universities).

The Macdonald curriculum also reflected contemporary society. As historian Terry Crowley has described it, "price controls spawned consumers' associations in which women assumed leadership to ensure compliance with the new regulations. A climate that believed the middle-class housewife should be the efficient manager of her husband's salary doubled the number of home economics students in the country between 1940 and 1960."[234] Authoritative expectations in society presumed that young women would marry and become full-time housewives, and in that role they would need all the expertise they could acquire to deal with the increasingly complex and demanding tasks assigned to "stay-at-home moms." Macdonald Institute would both teach young women to be better housewives and provide increasing numbers of home economics teachers who could pass on their expertise to a wider audience. Mac would also provide significant numbers of workers who could take their expertise into occupations such as dietetics, but contemporary social norms suggested that these women too would eventually find themselves as full-time housewives.[235]

What is striking about the curriculum is that for all the interest in the home environment and family setting manifested at Macdonald (and elsewhere), there was little or no study of the family itself. Rhetorical interest in the family was considerable. Pointing to the many social phenomena felt to be threatening the stability of the family, Margaret McCready complained in 1955 about the serious underfunding of research in the social sciences.[236] But Macdonald Institute's familial interests remained focused on particular elements of family life, rather than on the family itself. In the late 1950s there began a minor "packaging" of courses under the general rubric "child and family studies" but the offerings were slight — a general course in psychology, an elective course in child development offered in alternate years, and a course devoted to the most recent research developments in the field.[237] Given that limited interest and given the emphasis that would eventually be attached to this subject, it is important to note a new development in 1959.

One of the major innovations of this period was the Macdonald Institute Nursery School. Opened in September 1959, the nursery school accepted children of pre-school age (two to five years) who could be observed by Mac students as the children went about their daily activities. Planning for this began at least as early as 1955 with the deliberate intention of giving students an opportunity to study child development and to gain practical experience in dealing with young children. The immediate initiative came from Professor Doris Baskerville, who organized and planned the innovation. There was interest in building on the nursery school by developing a diploma course on nursery education. Although that did not occur, the nursery school offered a way of enriching the child studies portion of curriculum, and yet the founding of the school was announced as a way of providing a sound education *for* family life rather than *about* family life. Macdonald Institute still thought of its education as one fitting young women for better carrying out their homemaking tasks.

The initial nursery school opened from eight-thirty to noon each weekday morning and cost parents five dollars a week for each child. Lindsay Weld, who had been working on the research staff of the Institute of Child Study at the University of Toronto, was hired to supervise the nursery school. The nursery school had a capacity of twenty-five children and initially operated in the basement of Macdonald Institute, with a playground outside the west wing. Children were selected on the basis of age and sex and social background, with the aim of having as diverse a population as possible. By 1962 there was a waiting list for children to get into the school.[238]

As well, the diploma course continued to meet a demand among Ontario's young women. When the program started up again in 1946, its previous characteristics were maintained. The course did not offer training for any specialized occupations, but rather aimed to assist girls in meeting the varied demands of life, both at home and in their communities. The program's aim, declared the 1952 course calendar, was "to give practical instruction in the art and science of homemaking." Applicants were specifically warned that the program did not in itself lead to any specific jobs or provide any professional standing, although students who were thinking of non-university training in teaching or nursing or of entering the business world were encouraged to think of the diploma program as a valuable educational background. Applicants had to be at least seventeen years of age on entry and had to have completed at least two years of high school. Farmers' daughters and ex-service personnel were given admission preference; in the later 1950s preference was given to farmers' daughters and applicants from Ontario.

The diploma program changed in 1946 to a one-year program, signifying its more limited educational expectations. Most of the three-term program consisted of courses in foods, clothing, and textiles, paralleling the specializations that would be emphasized in the four-year program. In addition, diploma students took one-term courses in English, consumer economics, home nursing, family living, and physiology. The diploma program was quite popular immediately after the end of the war, with 105 students entering in 1946. By 1954 registration had fallen to thirty students and a maximum of forty was placed on the program to leave room for the degree students. The administration continued to encourage the diploma program, adding bunk beds to some of the residence rooms in the mid-1950s to facilitate a greater intake of students. In 1961 the entrance requirement changed to three years of high school, and students who did well in the diploma program might be considered for a second or third year of training in nursery school education. But this change was not a well-considered attempt to give new life to the diploma program, which increasingly did not reflect the academic aspirations of Macdonald Institute. In 1963, despite a large number of diploma applicants, the diploma program ended at Macdonald Institute — because it "unfortunately has not fulfilled its purpose as a supplement for rural girls" — and was transferred to Kemptville Agricultural College.[239]

There was some awareness that in the changing cultural environment of the late 1950s home economics was coming to be seen as "behind the times," no longer on the cutting edge of what the more progressive elements of society wanted for their young women. The emphasis on housewifely skills in particular received denigrating remarks. Where was the challenge to young women's minds in teaching them such applied skills as ironing or housecleaning, as the practice apartment did? Such remarks were aimed in part at the applied character of the education, but they also questioned whether many of the ideas and approaches of home economics as a discipline warranted a place in North American universities. The leading educators on the Guelph campus, both inside and outside Mac, were not yet ready to concede that some serious thinking was needed about the character of home economics education. Margaret McCready rallied to the defence of the education being provided by Macdonald Institute. In 1957, she wrote:

> Even now, can we remain complacent about the state of our families? Many are suffering breakdown due to divorce, desertion, juvenile delinquency, mental disturbances, and other ills. The logical attack on such problems is to educate and act to prevent them. Through study we should understand better the changing goals, values, and satisfactions in homemaking practices to-day.
>
> We believe that through our home economics studies we will produce leaders who have a creative attitude to homemaking, and who will be influential in promoting more constructive home and family life in which many disintegrating home influences will be avoided. ... At the same time as our grad-

uates are personally equipped to undertake good homemaking practices, they
are in demand in educational, business, and institutional fields of service.

On this defensive note McCready went on to talk about doing more of the same. In an
environment that had produced Betty Freidan's *The Feminine Mystique*, with its fundamental
questioning of the ways in which women were "trapped" in their isolated homes, McCready
talked not about rethinking the educational mission of home economics but rather of
expanding the existing educational thrust to include men and to involve greater research.[240] So
the Macdonald curriculum changed little and received no fundamental rethinking.

When faculty members at Macdonald Institute talked of preparing young women for the
world of work and when the staff talked about the rising number of married women in the
workplace, the work that the faculty members spoke of tended to be temporary — before
"settling down" to life at home as a housewife and mother — and tended to be secondary to
women's domestic work. Two faculty members, Evelyn Curran and Doris Baskerville,
addressed the issue of married women in the workforce in a 1956 article. Working outside
the home, they wrote, jeopardized the emotional and physical well-being of husbands and
children. And yet married women increasingly persisted in seeking paid employment
because they needed the additional income and because they needed an outside outlet for
their creative talents. They illustrated the "problem" by taking one example, that of Mrs.
Fromm of Waterloo County, whose husband owned and operated a turkey farm. Mrs.
Fromm, the writers delighted, had found an outlet for her talents without placing her family or home in jeopardy — she had developed a turkey pie business that could be run right
from the family farm.[241] No paid work could have been more traditional than a farm wife
developing secondary income from the basic farm enterprise. In highlighting — and roman-
ticizing — the family farm enterprise, Curran and Baskerville betrayed a fundamental inabil-
ity to come to grips with the growing phenomenon of the working mother. It was this reluc-
tance to move beyond the traditional approaches and understandings that flawed the home
economics enterprise in the post-war world.

At the same time, there were currents of change in Macdonald Institute that pointed the
way to the future. The development of the Macdonald Nursery School was one such change,
allowing students to study and analyze child behaviour. Another was the rising interest in
consumerism. Margaret McCready herself brought an active interest in studying consumer
behaviour, and she was joined by faculty members who saw in such new organizations as the
Canadian Association of Consumers a way of educating and protecting consumers, the great
bulk of whom were housewives. The new Home Management specialization, though it never

attracted large numbers of Macdonald students in fourth year, studied and analyzed marketing and consumerism, laying the groundwork for growth in this area.[242]

The alumnae described the programs in a way that emphasized the development of applied skills. For Food Administration majors, "practical application is the keynote, with quantity foods cookery experience in the Physical Education Building Cafeteria, and pantry and stock-room responsibilities at Macdonald Institute." Home Management students were registered in "a practical and necessary" program in which "emphasis is placed on efficiency in time and energy management, with many studies carried on in work simplification." Students in the Clothing and Textiles option took courses in weaving, clothing design, and fashion illustration, among others.[243] This emphasis on applied skills would soon be regarded as a problem.

The teaching of the Macdonald curriculum was facilitated by a major addition to the Macdonald Institute facilities in the early 1950s. A new west wing added to the Institute contained vital new facilities for the growing number of students. In the basement a craft centre had five areas equipped for work in ceramics, woodworking, metal, weaving, and leather; much of the use of these facilities was for extracurricular work, though there was some use by diploma and degree students in their courses. The first floor of the new west wing was turned over to the Textiles program. There were three large laboratory/classrooms, one for the diploma students and two for the degree program. The fourth-year laboratory had a fadeometer, a tensile-strength tester, a launderometer, two fume hoods, a hot-water bath, and drying ovens. Adjoining

West wing expansion, 1952.

Floor plan of the west wing expansion.

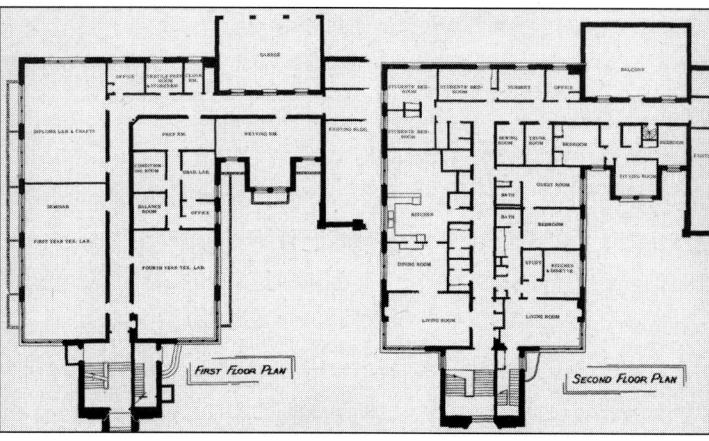

this lab were a balance room, a temperature-humidity control room with considerable testing equipment, and a small research laboratory. On the second floor was the Home Management apartment together with the supervisors' flat. The apartment consisted of a spacious living room and dining room, together with bedroom and bathroom facilities for six students. Considerable care was taken in furnishing the apartment to reflect what were considered to be the best of home decorating ideas, while taking into account cost and durability. The windows were framed by silkscreen print curtains depicting old and new Macdonald buildings. Canadian paintings hung on the walls; a stone fireplace graced one wall of the living room. The latest equipment brought the students' knowledge as up to date as possible, even if that raised their expectations about the level of equipment and furnishing in their own homes. The apartment, for example, was equipped with an automatic dishwasher at a time when such an appliance was quite rare in Canadian homes.[244]

Cooking lab, 1963.

Other renovations improved the facilities in the older parts of Macdonald Institute. New laboratories were added for the Home Management program, for home planning and arts, for advanced clothing, and for nutritional studies (including small animal experiments).[245] The result was up-to-date facilities in what had become the largest home economics program in the country. In 1962–63, Macdonald Institute registered 249 degree students and 41 diploma students. By that time the minimum cost per year was estimated to be up to $950, including tuition, room and board, books, and equipment. Education at Macdonald Institute was expensive, however, from the point of view of the Ontario government. The student-faculty ratio was a mere ten-to-one, making education at Mac a relatively expensive enterprise.[246] The "golden age" at Macdonald Institute was based on a level of expenditures not enjoyed by Ontario university students.

The new Home Management apartment opened in 1953–54. Six third-year students at a time made it their home for three weeks. This "dream apartment" was meant to contain the latest equipment and furniture and to represent the most recent trends and decorating ideas. The students in the apartment attended regular classes and looked after the chores associated with maintaining a household. The various "duties of the average housewife," in the words of one student, were handled in rotation by the six students. Every student had an assigned set of tasks and each student rotated through each set of assignments — marketing, budgeting, planning and preparing the meals, serving the meals, washing and ironing, cleaning, and other housework.[247]

The curriculum was rich with field trips. The students visited a wide variety of facilities — sites such as furniture factories in Stratford, textile mills in Toronto, prenatal well-baby clinics, child health centres in Kitchener, and numerous commercial kitchens in Toronto. There was an important continuing emphasis on applied knowledge.

The staff was relatively stable — Edyth Bray, Grace Frank, Jessie Lambden who carried on after being hired during the war, Louisa Brill, Mabel Sanderson, Eleanor Sandford, Mary Singer, Olive Wallace — and expanded in the late 1950s to include junior faculty members, such as Lila Engberg and Elizabeth Gullett, as well as a number of assistant instructors who remained on staff for only a short time. Staffing was difficult for Dr. McCready, who found that Mac salaries did not keep pace with good high school salaries. Some of the faculty members took leaves of absence to gain graduate degrees (usually doctorates) in various programs in the United States, resulting in an academically more qualified staff, one more in keeping with Mac's growing academic aspirations. Others spent their summers upgrading their qualifications at American universities.[248] Research programs expanded with such faculty members. Of particular note was the 1954 appointment of Gordon Couling, the first male to join the teaching faculty since the very first years of Macdonald Institute. Couling had been a part-time instructor at Mac for the past five years and now joined the full-time faculty; he taught art, art history, and home planning, adding an aesthetic dimension to the curriculum. By 1963 the twenty-eight faculty members had been reorganized into departments — Foods and Nutrition, headed by Mabel Sanderson; Home Management, led by Mary Singer; and Clothing and Textiles, headed by Edyth Bray. Most of the professorial rank had masters' degrees, and a few (McCready, Sanderson, and Singer) had their doctorates by the end of the period under discussion. By the late 1950s professorial ranks had been assigned and were being used to distinguish the Macdonald Institute faculty members as partners in a truly academic enterprise. Under the influential leadership of the president of the OAC, J.D. MacLachlan, the employment environment improved for faculty members. He widened salary categories and increased salary increments in order to distance remuneration more effectively from that of the civil service.[249]

The degree program, the large number of undergraduate students (relative to previous decades), the increasing number of graduate degrees among the faculty members (and the consequent interest in research), and talk of university status all led to greater academic aspirations by and expectations for Macdonald Institute. Such aspirations seemed more realistic when Mac grads began to return to campus as highly qualified academics in their own right. In 1961 Dr. Helen Abel joined the OAC's Extension Education Department. Abel was a graduate of the Mac diploma program in 1938, and had gone on to earn her PhD in rural sociology, to teach at Cornell University, and to publish extensively.[250] Throughout the 1950s there was sporadic public discussion of creating a university at Guelph, using the existing colleges as the basis for the new institution. Although there was no clear vision of what sort of university this might be, structural change did point the way to the new institution. In 1962 the three colleges at Guelph — the OAC, OVC, and Macdonald Institute — came together in a new academic structure, the Federated Colleges. Mac was now, at least structurally, on an equal footing with the other two colleges and was expected to "pull its weight" in academic terms.

 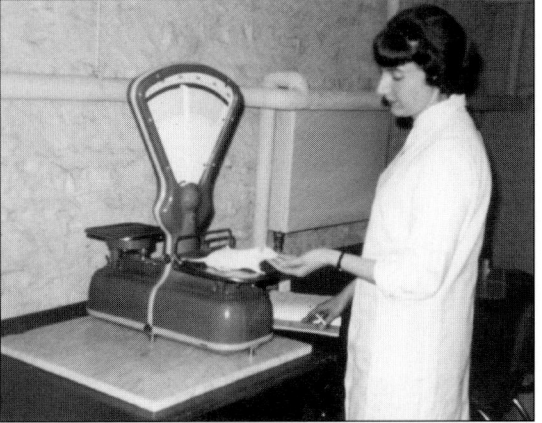

Left: *Students at work in a textiles lab.*

Right: *A Nutrition student working with a lab rat.*

One reflection of Mac's stronger academic aspirations was the renewed and increased interest in research among the faculty members and senior students. This was also a reflection of the enhanced qualifications and graduate degrees held by faculty members. With the expanded facilities opening in 1953 and 1954, some space could be devoted to research facilities. The nutrition experiments of Dr. Isabel Irwin, for example, allowed senior students to use guinea pigs and rats in experiments to test the effects of various diets on the metabolism of the animals. Students were exposed to scientific research methods and could observe the impact of various dietary supplements. Similarly, with the new machinery in the textiles labs students could carry out controlled experiments on various materials. This work, the facilities, and the fact that many more Mac grads were continuing on in graduate work encouraged discussion of graduate programs at Mac.[251]

The Macdonald Alumnae showed signs of increased activity. In the fall of 1961 they became well enough organized and enthusiastic enough to start a regular newsletter distributed to all Mac alumnae. Regular branches met in five cities in southern Ontario and by 1962 there were more than eleven hundred paid-up members. The Alumnae began to put concentrated effort into raising scholarship funds for Mac students.[252]

STUDENT LIFE

Life began again at Macdonald Institute in September 1946 when the first students returned. The *Librani* yearbook suggested that the return of the Mac Hall girls to the campus "has caused everyone to radiate friendliness." The *OAC Review* commented:

> The first and most salient change has been the return of the Mac Hall students to the campus. The long awaited girls are back and to say that the Aggies are happy about the whole thing is a pathetic understatement. ... We look forward eagerly to the resumption of tea-time hops, college proms, and the girls' participation in the activities of the major societies.[253]

All of the traditional extra-curricular clubs were soon active with Mac participation: the Student Christian Movement, the Union Literary Society, and the philharmonic society, all with Mac representatives on the executive. Other OAC clubs soon incorporated what seemed to be token Mac representation.[254] In 1950 a home economics club began. In 1946 the Mac students were all drawn from Ontario, but within a few years there was somewhat greater diversity; Macdonald Institute would never return, however, to the cross-Canada and international representation that it had witnessed in its early decades of existence. There were a number of girls' athletics teams — archery, basketball, rifle, volleyball, badminton, hockey, skiing, and swimming. In 1950 and 1951 and again in 1959 the girls' archery team won national intercollegiate championships.

Left: *Inter-collegiate archery champs, 1959.*

Right: *Practice makes perfect. Our champion team in 1959.*

Initiation welcomed the new students but the actual initiation rituals were tame events. Mock courts were common and the new students were forced to wear some form of distinctive attire. The 1949 frosh, for example, were required to wear white hats and name placards around their necks; aprons signified the character of the education they were about to commence. There were also shared events with the OVC and OAC students, such as a wiener roast at the Dairy Bush.[255] Initiation began to be downplayed in 1957, being replaced with orientation — a way of creating group spirit and social contacts without the often immature antics of the past. "There was a noticeable lack of ridiculous costume among the Mac freshettes," commented the dean of women, "and didn't they look ever so much prettier?"[256]

The changing diploma and degree programs meant that life at Macdonald Hall was noticeably different. For the diploma students the Macdonald experience was now only one year in duration and consequently more transient than in the past. For the degree students, however, there were four years to "put down

Frosh initiation in 1949.

roots" and make the campus "their own." There was a Macdonald Hall House Committee, a Watson Hall House Committee, a Macdonald Institute Students' Council, and each degree year had its own "year executive." The girls earned plaudits for the efforts and success with which they contributed to student government. "They have taken over a great share of the government at [Mac Hall] and they have been doing an admirable job of it," reported the *OAC Review*. By 1959 student government was opened to greater student participation by involving the whole Mac student body (rather than just the fourth-year students) in the elections for student government.[257] It had not taken long for the degree-program students to have an impact. The degree students had more opportunity to get involved in campus extra-curricular activities and to form social attachments, both among themselves and with boys from OAC and OVC. This did not prevent the diploma girls from continuing the reputation of the diploma program as the "diamond ring" course.

Residence life remained a central element in the social dynamic of the campus. Girls developed close friendships, cliques formed, and networks of acquaintances shared many experiences. The common pleasure of anticipating and preparing for the dances, the creation of an often co-operative residential atmosphere, the shared displeasure at the constricting residence rules, and the sharing of time and ideas together all helped to create an environment of common experiences. These were often lived out in informal residence parties with food and conversation — "hen parties" to use a contemporary descriptor. The camaraderie created was manifested in the development of Mac pins and blazers for the girls to wear.[258] But it was not only the shared residence life that created this bonding. The Mac girls tended to share a large number of courses and to have the same course assignments; they wore the same lab uniforms and tended to dress in a more formal manner than their female counterparts on other campuses. In contrast to later students, the young women of Mac in the 1950s shared a great deal in common with each other, and this resulted in a strong sense of fellowship and camaraderie.

The regulatory environment continued to be strong. College authorities felt it necessary to articulate a dress code in the early 1950s: slacks and bedroom slippers were inappropriate dress for classes or for wearing to the Creelman dining hall. An exception was made for girls taking chemistry labs, where blue jeans might be permissible. When girls were permitted to wear slacks to Creelman on Saturdays in 1963, it was headline news in the *Ontarion*.[259] Authorities were intent on maintaining a code of conduct that represented the girls as "young ladies." The girls, on the other hand, were intent on finding ways to make the regulations as unrestrictive as possible and often were able to find ways around the more onerous rules.[260]

Many of the girls chafed at the restrictive environment. They complained about the "mothering approach" taken by Macdonald Institute and the faculty members. The staff was unwilling to allow the girls to take responsibility for their education. Instead, attendance was taken at lectures and monthly reports were made on each student. Mac students often felt that they were coddled in their courses and that courses were not as demanding as they might be so that most students could pass. "This come-under-my-wing attitude," commented the *Ontarion*, "was consistent with a small college and it was thought that when Macdonald Institute was enlarged in later years it would tend to move away from this."[261]

In the late 1940s and early 1950s there was adequate room in the two residences, Macdonald and Watson, to accommodate all out-of-town students. By the late 1950s the situation had changed. The Mac program formally promised residence accommodation to all first-year students wishing it; the trade-off was that many second-year and third-year students were forced out of residence to find accommodation in town. Students did return to residence for their final year, however, cementing the social relationships and group sentiment that had developed over the preceding years.[262]

The social swirl of pre-war years retained its pulse. Major dances were at the heart of campus social life, becoming almost monthly highlights of the social calendar — the Hallowe'en dance, the Sadie Hawkins dance, the Mac Hall formal or semi-formal, Conversat, the College Royal Ball, and the graduation dance. As highlights of the campus social environment, these dances celebrated heterosexuality in an indiscriminate manner. The Sadie Hawkins dance was a popular chance for the Mac girls to take the initiative and to "dress down." The *OAC Review* reported that the 1950 Sadie Hawkins "was a huge success. Hard times' dances really are fun when the girls can wear slacks and the boys forget jackets and ties. There were some rather unusual corsages the boys had but quite in keeping with the evening." Corsages included such ingredients as celery, marshmallows, and peanuts.[263] Much planning and effort went into the events, on the part of both the hardworking organizers and those attending. For the first time, third-year Mac students joined third-year OAC and OVC students in organizing Conversat in 1951.

The height of the social "season" remained Conversat. Planning for the great event took several months and the anticipation of the night lasted for many weeks. "The social highlight of the year," commented one observer. "You see more expensive decorations, ravishing gowns, pretty girls, and handsome men than at any other function on this campus. It is the dance you must attend at least once in your college career. For this great occasion the girls are booked months ahead of the event."[264] When the new Physical Education Building opened in 1959, it became the new site of Conversat.

Soon after the Mac girls returned, regular Saturday dances were being organized by rotating groups of girls — twenty-five cents for girls, fifteen cents for boys, to cover the cost of food and drink. These dances were not the success they had been in the pre-war years and appear to have been discontinued in 1948. At other times the girls would organize co-ed sleigh rides, using the OAC horse teams.[265] The dances did not consciously exclude those who were not heterosexual; the dances were simply part of what one historian has called the construction of "normalcy" — the articulation and acting out of an environment in which there was only one form of behaviour that could be recognized and approved.[266] Indeed heterosexual alliances dominated much of the social life of Mac. In the fall of 1951, the third-year girls of Mac '53 commented that Mac '52 "has outdone itself in getting married and engaged" and Mac '53 responded with a marriage and two engagements of its own. Marriage and engagement notices appeared in a steady trickle.[267] The growing acceptability of student marriages reflected a North American trend. But marriage was not intended to interfere with completion of the young women's program; those marrying before graduation tended to remain in school until the completion of their program.[268]

Miss Margaret McKinlay, the first College Royal Queen, 1951.

College Royal combined social activity with academic expertise. Mac students took pride in displaying their achievements to the public and in demonstrating some of the latest innovations in their field. The prizes awarded are suggestive of the kinds of home economics work that was underscored by College Royal — an award for the highest number of points in the crafts section; a championship award for the clothing section; an award for the student obtaining the highest number of points in the cooking section; the grand champion trophy for the student obtaining the highest number of points throughout the home economics division; the reserve grand champion trophy for the student with the second highest number of points in the home economics division; a trophy for the diploma student receiving the highest number of points in the home economics division. Mac girls, especially those with a rural or 4H background, were also active in showing animals and in judging. Students were encouraged to participate and to display their best work in cooking, clothing, and the fashion show. Beyond that there were the activities aimed at facilitating fun and enjoyment — the boys' cake-baking contest and the square-dancing competition, for example. College Royal was about having fun but also a way of emphasizing the skills and expertise being developed by the academic programs on the Guelph campus.

And yet there were problems with what went on at College Royal, as with such teaching practices as the apartment. These events presented a side of home economics whose place in a modern university environment was coming to be doubted. There was talent in baking a good pie or in sewing a neat seam, but was this really what home economics was about?

Should universities be teaching students how to operate as efficient homemakers or was such applied work better learned elsewhere? The six students in the practice apartment for three weeks rotated through six jobs — manager, cook, assistant cook, laundress, housekeeper, and waitress. College Royal awarded prizes for cooking and baking, for sewing and needlework. These were the faces that a Macdonald Institute education displayed to the public and they did a disservice to the genuinely analytical work that these young women carried out as part of learning in foods and nutrition, textiles, or home management by downplaying the public face of such study. The prominence of the practical skills elements of the educational experience at Mac led to fundamental questioning of home economics programs.

By September 1948 the diploma students were joined by the first twenty-five degree students. The number of degree students rose quickly as the four years of students accumulated, but the annual intake increased only gradually. By 1950, the new cohort of degree students was forty-one in number. The combined number of degree students now outnumbered the diploma students, but the diploma program continued to meet a demand from among young women; the average intake in the early 1950s was over seventy students annually.[269]

The girls in Macdonald Hall continued to be subjected to a set of rather stringent regulations. There was a curfew of eleven o'clock, and the residence doors of Mac were kept locked in the early 1950s, at least, so that boys calling for their dates were required to wait on the steps. In the post-war environment these regu-

Were we or weren't we taking ourselves seriously? The diploma '61 logo, from Libranni, *1961.*

lations chafed somewhat more than in the past. The rules at Mac Hall and Watson Hall "are pretty stiff," according to the *OAC Review*. One frustrated aggie student commented that the rules requiring early return and banning men from the girls' rooms were enough to inhibit him from dating a Mac girl: "Perhaps there are others too who have found Mac Hall girls much to their liking, but who cannot adjust themselves to the kids' rules we must face when we take them out." The rules were "ridiculous for girls of college age," complained the *Review*. Another writer suggested that the "oppressed" girls were relieved of any personal decision-making or responsibility. Mac "girls" were treated like children and placed in an environment where they could avoid adult responsibility for four years.[270] The regulations, however, did not prohibit the

Left: *First-year sleigh ride and dance, 1947.*

Right: *The Class of '56 in April 1956.*

Left: *The Class of '58 during an etiquette class.*

Right: *The shooting club in the late 1950s.*

Left: *The 1959 badminton team.*

Right: *Swimming pageant stars in the late 1940s.*

Left: *Macdonald Institute Majorettes in 1961.*

Right: *Alumni Weekend, June 13, 1963.*

development of a environment conducive to amorous liaisons; the Mac Hall reception rooms gained a well-deserved reputation as a place for "necking."[271]

Others, presumably a small minority, objected to the effect that the women's presence had on the moral standards of the campus. The students, complained one letter writer, were showing signs of moral degeneration. For example, some women were smoking on campus, and alcohol and "necking" were too prevalent at campus dances.[272]

For the most part the criticism of the girls and their protective rules took the form of good-natured mockery. As had occurred in the pre-war years, there were occasional hockey contests between the girls and some group of campus boys, with the boys adopting some form of overt "handicap." Others suggested that the Mac girls should form a football team — so that they could play in a "powder puff bowl" to a packed audience.[273]

Macdonald Hall remained the focus of male pranks on campus. The pranks themselves varied from year to year, and their timing was only partially predictable — Hallowe'en, for example. In the fall of 1948, the aggies attempted to move a carriage into the Mac Hall foyer, but could not get it past the second set of front doors. Another time, rooms were filled with feathers. In the spring of 1954 there were at least three "invasions" of Macdonald Hall, as the authorities called them; girls were dumped out of their beds and the lighting system went off. The following year the pranks became more frequent, culminating in a more serious one: a steer was left to roam the ground floor of Mac Hall, causing considerable damage to the library. So-called "panty raids" were not uncommon.[274]

For the first time, in this post-war environment, the administration began to take notice that Macdonald's all-female character might not be the best idea. In 1955 Margaret McCready talked publicly about the desirability of attracting young men to the study of the family.[275] But for the most part, Mac seemed comfortable in its all-female character. Indeed gender was celebrated increasingly on campus. College Royal, which was coming to be the leading public event on campus, was more overtly constructed by gender. The president of College Royal was always a leading male from the OAC, and for the first time in 1951 students selected a College Royal queen — a young woman celebrated for her skills, popularity, and attractiveness. College Royal featured contests in cooking, baking, and crafts as well as a fashion show (first begun in 1950), all dominated by Mac girls, but the Mac girls joined in other elements of College Royal, particularly the showing of animals for judging. Female cheerleaders were a new addition to the OAC athletics landscape at this time.

In the mid-1950s the academic and social life at Mac was enriched by annual trips to New York City, arranged by Gordon Couling. Intended to expose the girls to the richness of Manhattan architecture and museums, the trips were at least as important for their social

side. Girls attended a Broadway play and did considerable sightseeing; some managed to get into local night clubs. The exposure to the cosmopolitan life of a huge city was an eye-opening experience for most of the participants.[276]

The culmination of life at Mac was graduation. Once a year, usually in May or June, the graduating classes would gather to celebrate their academic achievements and to receive their degrees or diplomas. The Mac degree students shared graduation ceremonies with the OAC year with which they had shared so much during their four years on campus together. The girls receiving their degrees would wear white or light-coloured dresses, which they had made as one of their clothing projects, topped with black academic gowns. They made a particularly attractive picture as they paraded to the ceremony. The diploma students had separate graduation ceremonies. The day was crowned by a graduation party arranged at some nearby spot where dancing and socializing could continue late into the night.

By 1964 Macdonald Institute had made great strides. A four-year degree program had been successfully established and it had become the largest home economics program in the country. Mac students were competing successfully for jobs in the open market, particularly as teachers of home economics and as dietitians. Mac had developed new and headier aspirations as an academic enterprise, aspirations that befitted an institution that was about to become part of a new university, independent of the University of Toronto. And yet at the same time there were new, public doubts about the efficacy and appropriateness of home economics as a discipline. These doubts affected Mac and its staff to such an extent that some staff could envision a time when home economics would disappear from universities.[277] The fate of Macdonald Institute, as it passed its sixtieth anniversary, depended on its response to these pressures and opportunities.

V

MACDONALD TRANSFORMED, 1964–1970

Macdonald Institute entered the fall of 1964 as part of a newly incorporated body. The University of Guelph had come into existence, using the three long-time colleges — the OAC, the OVC, and Macdonald Institute — as the founding base of the university. As the discussions of plans for the new university proceeded, "Macdonald Institute and its principal had a difficult time making their voices heard in Toronto and Margaret McCready was given very little opportunity to influence the direction of the change the colleges were about to experience."[278] New programs in arts, social sciences, and sciences were added to provide the basis for a comprehensive university. The new university now granted its own degrees and was no longer

The first BHSc grad from the University of Guelph, May 21, 1965.

dependent upon the University of Toronto. Academic and student life became more complex as the number of courses and programs mushroomed and as Guelph acquired the trappings of a modern university.

At first these changes seemed to affect Macdonald Institute relatively little. Dr. Margaret McCready continued on as dean, guiding the fate of Mac and its students with her usual charm and energy. The young women of Mac stood out on campus for their conservative

Left: *Typical classroom activities from this era.*

Right: *Fashion shows of clothing created in class were very popular.*

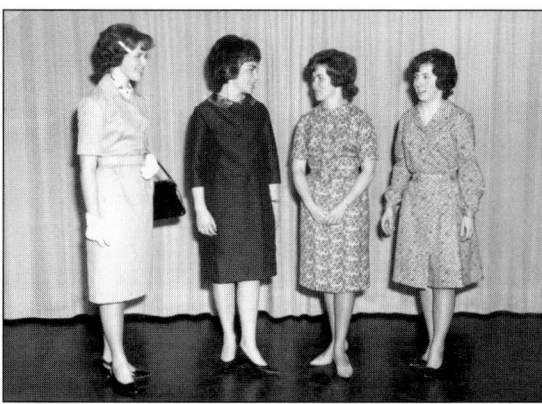

Left: *Mac '65 tailoring class.*

Middle Right: *Miss Bray's sewing class.*

Bottom Right: *Students created many designs from scratch.*

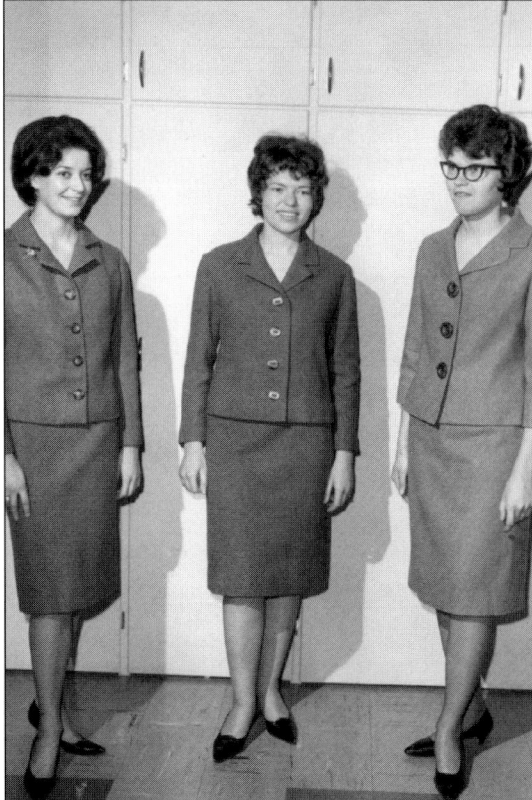

style of dress. Macdonald Hall remained a female centre of the campus, though now there was a greater variety of women students living there. The Macdonald Alumnae remained a source of considerable strength to Macdonald Institute, providing scholarships and a sense of continuity with the past. The Women's Institutes of Ontario continued to voice their support for Mac and for its expansion in the face of growing student and societal demand.[279]

One of the consequences of the creation of the University of Guelph was the severing of Macdonald Institute's ties with the Ontario Department of Agriculture. With the breaking of this link, it followed that Mac no longer had a special mission or responsibility to rural concerns or the young women of rural society. Mac was now free to find its own market among the various elements of Canadian society. In truth the mission to rural women had been diminishing for some time as more and more Mac students came from urban and suburban areas.

THE PROCESS OF CHANGE

Underlying the switch to university status were currents of disquietude and change. The 1960s was a decade of turmoil, challenge, and change, affecting no groups more than youth and women. It was thus not surprising that Macdonald Institute became a focus for some of this challenge and change. The source of that challenge came from several directions.

First, it came from the leadership of the university. The president of the university, J.D. MacLachlan, articulated some basic qualms about the philosophy and content of the Macdonald Institute curriculum. Did a home economics program belong at a university, he wondered? Did such a program involve the sort of research and analysis typical of a university program, or was it better suited to a community college? An OAC alumnus and local educator voiced some of MacLachlan's concerns in other words:

> You see the [existing] Colleges, in my view, lacked a vision or notions of what a more complete education was all about. In many respects, I think OAC and Macdonald Institute in particular and, in part, OVC were more technological institutions than colleges of a university and it seemed to me that for the very vitality of learning, a more broadly based program was necessary.[280]

At least as fundamental a challenge came from the home economics discipline itself. Self-doubts and concerns were not new to the discipline across North America, as discussed in the 1950s. There were worries that home economics was not keeping up with the times, not evolving to reflect the changing character of society and the changing position held by women and the home in that society. The traditional rhetoric about the centrality of the home and family and of women's place there rang increasingly hollow in the 1960s.

In 1958 Doris Baskerville, the dean of women at Macdonald Institute, responded to the idea that applied training such as home economics had no place in the modern university. Society had undergone vast changes since the turn of the century, she argued, and home economics had not kept pace with the changes.

> Never in the history of mankind have so many changes taken place in the manner of life and work. … Look at the home. Technical advances have made it within the realm of possibility that most women will have homes of their own. … Social changes have made it possible, and now we might almost say necessary, for every girl to become gainfully employed and thereby becoming completely independent.

It was questionable, Baskerville wrote, whether home economics graduates could answer fundamental questions about the contemporary family. Home economics implies within its name the understanding and dissemination of information that will be useful in making effective homes and families, she continued. But the discipline had failed to meet that challenge. It had failed to give its graduates the necessary information and knowledge to be of use to the bewildered homemakers of the post-war world. Home economics need-ed more research and greater academic respectability, Baskerville argued.[281]

Baskerville's thoughts were not effectively articulated, but she had made a basic leap in her expectations of home economics. No longer was the discipline to be judged by its abili-ty to train good homemakers. Instead it should be seeking to train professionals — dietitians, teachers, demonstrators, research workers. These "embryo professionals" needed an educa-tion that would be primarily about "giving them ideas and skills which will make them more effective people." The article was more important for the disquietude that it revealed than for its solution to the problems addressed.[282] Nevertheless, it is clear that at least some of the fac-ulty at Macdonald Institute shared the growing concerns that home economics was becom-ing outmoded and was failing to keep pace with the times and with the changing university environment. In fact, the Macdonald program had been training professionals for years already, but the rhetoric and philosophy of the program still pointed to a traditional home economics discipline that sought, as a primary function, to prepare young women for their life as homemakers. That was what needed to change.

The third challenge came from broader societal changes. Much had changed socially since the founding of Macdonald Institute. Canada was now an urban society. By 1966 almost three-quarters of the population lived in urban areas. The greatest growth rate occurred in suburban areas of metropolitan centres; by 1961, 45 percent of all city dwellers lived in the suburbs. The birth rate, having climbed during the famed baby boom of the 1950s, was settling back to earlier levels. The marriage rate began to decline as young people postponed marriage. The continuing impact of the baby boom produced many new jobs in the teaching profession. The continuing growth of service industries and clerical sectors gave rise to increasing employment opportunities for women. Rising wages attracted more women, particularly married women, into the workforce. For increasing numbers of women, being a full-time housewife was a temporary experience or an experience not known at all, as women with children joined the surge of women into the labour force.[283] The education provided by Macdonald Institute needed to reflect this changing reality.

This challenge was reflected in the broader women's movement of the 1960s — the so-called second-wave feminism — and in the reform of home economics across North America. Second-wave feminism brought with it new expectations of freedom and equality. Women, it was argued, had a right to education free of the restrictive gendered boundaries of the past. Home economics was no longer the post-secondary education of choice for many young women; women wanted and demanded unrestricted access to all sectors of the post-secondary educational environment. Schools were challenged to move away from earlier sex-role stereotyping and to treat young women and men in new, more egalitarian ways. Indeed the time had quickly come when the label "home economics" was considered a retrograde one and a disadvantage to those to whom it was applied. When Margaret McCready asked at one American campus how closely the Hotel Management program was associated with the local Home Economics program, the response made clear the negative connotations now linked to home economics: "the name Home Economics hurts a [hotel] program such as ours … we minimize all references to the college and emphasize the name of the department."[284] To cope with the problem, home economics programs across the continent were beginning to change their names and to restructure. This new attitude about the traditional term "home economics" was reflected as well in a decision by the National Research Council (NRC) of Canada in the late 1960s that henceforth the NRC would not accept scholarship applications from home economics students; instead, the students would have to claim a developed specialization in an area such as foods, nutrition, or textiles, for example.[285]

The most immediate impact of these challenges came from the new president of the university, J.D. MacLachlan, who was in a position to make his concerns heard. He took full advantage of that position to push for reform of Macdonald Institute. He pushed McCready to reconsider the type of education being offered through Mac. He asked, for example, how clothing and textiles would be taught in twenty-five years. In May 1965 MacLachlan attended a faculty meeting in Mac "to tell us what he envisages as our program of development and expansion at Macdonald Institute." MacLachlan began by denying rumours that plans for Macdonald Institute had been shelved in favour of other departments. He acknowledged the need for increased facilities but suggested that more fundamental planning and consideration of the type of education being offered were necessary before proceeding with expansion. The first stage, he challenged the faculty, was to articulate an educational philosophy — where was Mac going in each program area and how each program area related to broader developments and programs on campus. Once this rethinking had been completed, then expansion and building programs would be considered.

MacLachlan was expansive in his approach to the future, speaking of the erection of another building to meet Mac's physical needs. But first and foremost he called for a recasting of Mac's educational philosophy: "Our first task is to establish the primary educational concepts for Household Science education at this university, projected to future requirements and educational philosophy."[286] In expressing such concerns MacLachlan was echoing the sorts of anxieties that were plaguing almost every home economics program in North America at this time. His vice-president academic, Burt Matthews, made the same point to Dean McCready in 1966 when he asked, "Is our current program in Home Economics the one which is most suitable for the 1970s?" In asking such a question, he was laying down the fundamental challenge to Macdonald Institute. Matthews went further, suggesting the kind of detailed concerns that the senior administration harboured. Of the proposed program changes in 1966, he wrote:

1. Does the content provide opportunities for the student to do critical thinking?
2.   Has the content been examined carefully for evidence of proliferation?
3. Has the time spent for manipulative skills requiring little or no intellectual content been reduced to a minimum?[287]

Home economics' reputation as a discipline, deserved or not, was shaping the kind of reforms being promoted.

Margaret McCready, now dean of Macdonald Institute, had her own concerns looking toward reform. Most interestingly, McCready talked of new ways in which men students might be attracted into Mac programs. The emphasis here was on bringing in young men rather than on reform, but reform was implicit in this strategy. Implicit too in this strategy was an end to any emphasis on training young women to be effective housewives, but McCready did not articulate this. Instead she came up with specific tactics that facilitated the overall strategy. She was particularly interested, for example, in the development of a food management program which, she felt sure, was the sort of program in which men would be interested.[288] McCready also discussed the possibility of changing the name of the home economics degree so that more men would consider joining the program.[289] She was not afraid of change, proposing new programs in food management and in interior design and important changes in the child and family studies curriculum in December 1964. She also brought forward proposals to revamp the curriculum of all of the major streams of study in Macdonald Institute to prepare students more effectively to teach the revised Ontario high school curriculum.[290] The dean was also concerned about expanding the facilities at Macdonald Institute to take in the increasing numbers of students that

Dr. M.S. McCready, dean of Macdonald Institute.

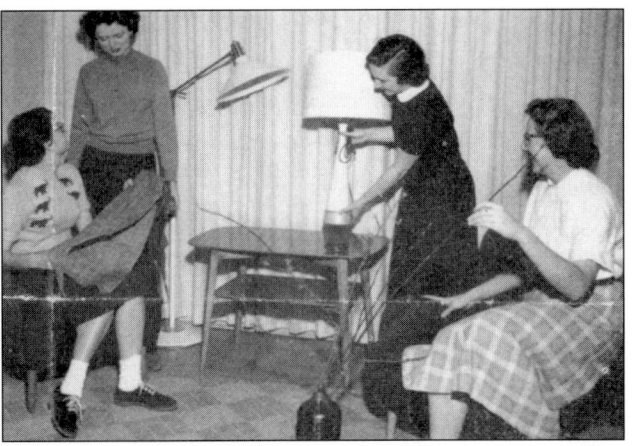

Home planning labs.

she expected to arrive after 1964. But her concerns tended to be less fundamental and more tactical. She proposed, for example, that the number of Home Management apartments be expanded, perhaps by building two or three houses for this purpose, so that all of the young women then passing through the program could receive the sort of housewife and management training received by whole cohorts in the past.[291] McCready seemed bent on considering more immediate responses to the new situation in which Macdonald Institute found itself. It is unclear whether she was resistant to more fundamental rethinking of the program or simply caught up in Mac's more immediate problems. Whatever the reason, there was a tendency for McCready not to see change in broad, fundamental terms.

McCready struck a planning committee, consisting of herself and the department heads, to consider the problems and to map out new directions for Macdonald Institute. A draft of the committee's extensive report was submitted to President MacLachlan in June 1966. The committee proposed that there would be four departments in the new Macdonald Institute, all modelled very much on past experience: Foods and Nutrition; Home Management; Clothing and Design; and Textiles. This proposal to revamp and expand Mac's administrative structure is surprising, given that the president had already rejected the idea in senate executive committee in 1965.[292] The 1966 proposals called for nineteen regular faculty members, supplemented by thirteen part-time instructors, a calculated ratio of 15.5 students per faculty member. The programs would grow with an undergraduate intake of 140 students each year, including 40 students in the spring semester who were expected to be "above-average students" entering before completion of Ontario Grade XIII. Macdonald courses would begin to include elective students from the BA and BSc programs. Graduate programs, which started at Mac in 1965, would become an increasingly important part of the teaching.

A small number of new programs was envisioned as instructors became available and as student demand warranted. A four-year program in Food Administration or Food Management would build on existing strengths at Mac and would, hopefully, attract male students. The most significant innovation was the inclusion of a minor concentration of courses in Child and Family Studies within the Home Management major and within the BA program. A minor program in Textile Science would be offered in the BSc program. A new major would be developed in Design — housing and interior decoration. Finally the report looked to the establishment of a general program in home economics without specialization. McCready thought of these proposals as radically changing the home economics program, so much so that she proposed that a new degree be awarded, signifying a basic break with the past.[293]

More important than the details was the 1966 report's discussion of the underlying philosophy of Macdonald Institute's education. The Macdonald programs, explained the report, involved students for half their time in courses in the arts and sciences and half in professional courses. This "broad and liberal education" ably prepared students for the many occupations in which Mac graduates found employment — teaching, social welfare and public health, consumerism, extension services, and public relations. The demand for workers in these fields would continue for the foreseeable future, thus ensuring that an education at Macdonald Institute would continue to fulfill a needed role in society. At the university, household science played a valuable role by spanning the gap between the social sciences and the life sciences, and Macdonald Institute should thus be expected to grow at the same pace as the other groups of disciplines.[294]

The report met with a critical response from President MacLachlan. Lacking in the report, he argued, was "any reference to design or philosophy of BHSc education in the light of other new developments. Where, he commented, was the consideration of the program's relation to the education offered at Ryerson Institute or the new community colleges? What distinguished the BHSc program from the education offered at these colleges and what advanced the BHSc "over and beyond their objectives"? The BHSc program demanded a "depth of understanding of the principles and scientific basis of the subjects taught" if it were to continue. "Nothing in the brief," he continued, "suggests that these objectives have been developed in the design of the educational program to meet them. Brief suggests no change contemplated in undergraduate pattern at present. This is a highly important issue before design of added physical resources is contemplated." With these disparaging remarks, the president rejected the administrative expansion entailed in making textiles a separate department and sent the planners back to the drawing board.[295]

McCready and her senior faculty members seemed incapable of reconceptualizing the Macdonald Institute program. Rather than recasting the Mac program in dramatic new ways, McCready and her collaborators had focused on minor changes within the existing program. They suggested the same basic shape and content for the program and talked largely about expansion of the existing departments. While some aspects of the existing Macdonald Institute would almost inevitably be a part of any restructured program, McCready and her supporters seemed unable to escape the bonds of "the way things had always been done." The broader forces at work were pushing Macdonald Institute towards much more fundamental change.

President MacLachlan's more considered response to the 1966 proposal was more substantial and just as fundamental. He was quite dissatisfied with the review undertaken by Dean McCready. Knowing that Margaret McCready would be stepping down as dean in 1968 MacLachlan initiated the search for her successor immediately. The successor would be named associate dean for a one-year overlap and would undertake a new review and assessment of the Mac programs. This plan was continued by President William Winegard when he succeeded MacLachlan in 1967. Dr. Janet Wardlaw, who had joined the Foods and Nutrition Department in 1966,

Dr. McCready and Dr. Wardlaw planning the future of Macdonald Institute.

Dr. Janet Wardlaw

Born and raised in Toronto, Janet Wardlaw received her BA from the University of Toronto and undertook her dietetic internship at Royal Victoria Hospital in Montreal. In 1950 she earned her MSc in community nutrition from the University of Tennessee. In 1963 she graduated from Pennsylvania State University with a PhD in foods and nutrition. Wardlaw also had an active career in the public sector. In 1947–49 as a dietitian she participated in a school meal study for the Canadian Red Cross. Following that, she was employed as a nutritionist with the Michigan Department of Health and subsequently with the Toronto Health Department. In 1956 she joined the Faculty of Food Sciences at the University of Toronto where she remained until 1966, taking a two-and-a-half-year leave of absence to obtain her PhD.

In 1966 Janet Wardlaw joined Macdonald Institute at the University of Guelph, and in 1968 was named dean-designate to succeed Dr. Margaret McCready. As dean-designate, Wardlaw played a major role in the substantial restructuring of Mac that resulted in the creation of the College of Family and Consumer Studies. In 1969 she became dean of FACS and remained in that post until 1983. In the fall of 1983 Wardlaw served as acting vice-president academic of the University of Guelph; following a period of administrative leave she was appointed in July 1984 as associate vice-president academic and remained in that post until her retirement in 1987. In 1989 she was named Fellow of the University of Guelph. From 1985 to 1992 Wardlaw served as chairman of the board of governors of the International Development Research Centre.

was named associate dean and dean-designate in December 1967. Wardlaw's assignment was, in her own words, to "work with faculty, alumni and students in reviewing the Bachelor of Household Science program and developing a plan for a program which would justify the expansion of Macdonald Institute in terms of enrolment and related physical facilities."[296]

Dean Janet Wardlaw, 1969.

Wardlaw immediately set to work appointing a small faculty committee charged with the task of preparing a report on the present status of home economics in Canadian education at all levels and on Macdonald Institute's place in that educational system. The report was to focus on future plans for home economics at the University of Guelph, building on a base at Macdonald Institute; the future plans were to include both undergraduate and graduate education, as well as research and continuing education. Wardlaw wisely adopted a highly consultative process for the preparation of this report. Regular lunch-time meetings were held to discuss various sections of the preliminary report; since faculty brought their lunches to the meetings, the report came to be known as the "lunch bag brief." Questionnaires were mailed to alumnae of Macdonald Institute, soliciting information about their professional activities and their reflections on how their Mac education had met their professional needs. A 74 percent response rate indicated the strong level of interest and concern among alumnae.[297] This process of consultation must have been enhanced by the important addition of new faculty members in these years. Foremost among these additions was Dr. Janet Wardlaw herself, who joined the Foods and Nutrition Department in 1966. Of particular note, Dr. Jean Sabry joined the Foods and Nutrition Department in 1967 from the University of Toronto, where a reorganization of the Household Science program was creating considerable discontent; Dr. Elizabeth Miles came to the Foods and Nutrition Department after receiving her PhD from Pennsylvania State University; Dr. H.R. Richards joined Macdonald Institute in 1964. In 1968, Dr. Kathleen Brown, a specialist in family economics, returned to Mac after several years away while earning her PhD in the United States. These additions to the faculty added new and experienced voices to the debates over reform of Macdonald Institute.

Within months the brief was prepared and presented to the board of governors. The university senate approved detailed plans on the basis of the brief in November 1968.

Macdonald Institute was reorganized into two departments, Family Studies and Consumer Studies, to take effect the following July, ending the old departments, and a new school, Hotel and Food Administration (HAFA), was established. New degrees were initiated — a Bachelor of Applied Science (BASc) for Family and Consumer Studies and a Bachelor of Commerce (BCom) for Hotel and Food Administration — as a way of signalling a fundamental break with the past program. During the Christmas break that year faculty members gathered for a work session at a conference centre in the Bolton area to flesh out the details of the new undergraduate programs, drawing up course descriptions.

Wardlaw's Academic Brief made a convincing case for the retention of home economics in a new form. Implicit in the document was the fundamental belief that home economics was no longer about giving young women the skills they needed to create and maintain an effective home and family environment. Instead the program should be about taking social scientific approaches to the study of humans as social beings, particularly within the family group, and integrating these approaches with some of the more applied analyses of the family and the home. Reform of some of the major home economics programs in the United States along these lines was already well underway and the results looked promising. Married Mac grads already exceeded the national average for labour force participation — 53 percent of married Mac grads were presently employed, compared with 36 percent of married university graduates nationally — so the trend was already well-established. This new educational approach would be aimed at producing professionals who could benefit from an "integrated approach in applying knowledge to the improvement of the well-being of individuals and families."[298] Indeed there was a strong pool of students for such a program, argued the brief. Macdonald Institute offered far and away the largest program of its type in the province of Ontario, with almost three times the number of undergraduates as its next largest competitor. There were close to three times as many applicants for the Mac program as there were actual student admissions. Here was a program for which high demand existed and which could readily be changed to reflect current academic trends.

What was more, Mac had already instituted some of these changes. Its graduate programs had started in 1965 and were already the largest in home economics in the province. Plans for future growth were laid out. There would be forty graduate students in Family Studies by 1980, it was predicted, and fifty-two in Consumer Studies. Paralleling the growth in graduate work was the developing research profile of Macdonald faculty members. Existing research agendas in foods and home management had been augmented with new research in applied human nutrition and in textiles. In short, Macdonald was already taking advantage of the new university environment to strengthen its academic character. Macdonald Institute was already changing, leaving the older traditions of home economics behind and making the best of new opportunities. It was time to formalize these changes and to promote them.

The home economics program of Macdonald Institute had served a vitally important role in giving the young women of Ontario, particularly rural Ontario, a post-secondary institution of their own where they could learn and mature largely apart from the "chilly climate" of gender bias that dominated Canadian campuses. Macdonald Institute had offered young women a place to grow, and over the years thousands had taken advantage of the opportunity. They had acquired fundamental information and skills to be used in the homes they built; the graduates had often placed themselves in positions where they could employ their knowledge and skills in the workplace as dietitians, institutional managers, social workers, and teachers; as teachers in particular, a career on which Macdonald Institute had always focused, the graduates had been in a position to pass on their knowledge to future generations of young women. But the time for change had come. The idea of home economics, as it had been understood, represented an older and increasingly dated view of both womanhood and the function of post-secondary education, and Macdonald Institute would have to change if it were to survive.

 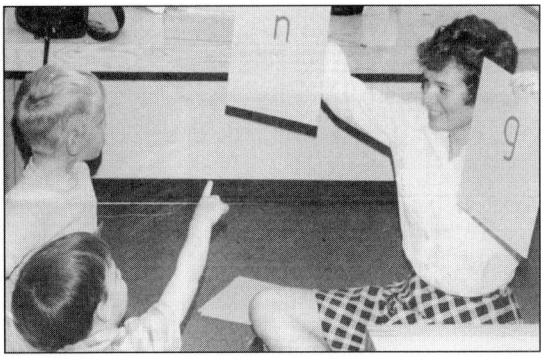

Left: *Mac's lab school, where hands-on experience made the difference.*

Right: *Another picture from the lab school.*

The best of the older traditions had been retained, however, as in the continuing extension work with outside agencies. In addition to the extension work with groups with non-professional interests, such as the Women's Institutes, Macdonald now offered short courses to professional groups, such as the Nursery Education Association of Ontario, the Ontario Hospital Association, and the Ontario Institutional Laundry Managers Association. To each of these groups some of the Macdonald faculty members had offered short courses in the late 1960s, providing professional training to association members. Assistance to Women's Institutes and to programs for provincial girls planned by the Department of Agriculture's Home Economics Branch remained an accepted part of Macdonald's outreach, but the professional programs put a new light on the developing expertise at Mac.

To reflect this existing change in Mac's educational pratice and to promote further change, the Academic Brief recommended a major reorganization of Macdonald Institute. First, the term "home economics" would be dropped. The term was out of fashion and denoted an older understanding of the subject that was no longer desirable to convey. The brief recommended that the new academic enterprise should be called "Macdonald Institute of Family and Consumer Studies." There would be two major departments in the new Institute — one focusing on "a study of the family as a social unit" and the other on "family members as consumers of goods and services." The brief continued:

> Recent interviews with employers of home economics graduates in the province revealed a common concern regarding the need for professionally educated individuals with an understanding of the sociological factors affecting families; with skill in communicating with families at all levels of society; and with knowledge of the physical and biological needs of family members in their various home settings, whether these be actual family homes or substitute homes of an institutional type. The graduate of a traditional home economics program was considered to fill these needs in part but to lack an adequate understanding of the sociological factors affecting the family and their relationship to physical needs. In addition the employers saw the desirability of increased emphasis on theories and skills in communication as they related to implementation of knowledge by home economists.[299]

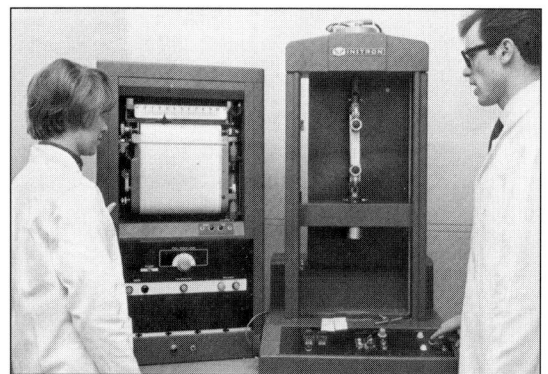

Open house at Mac in 1967.

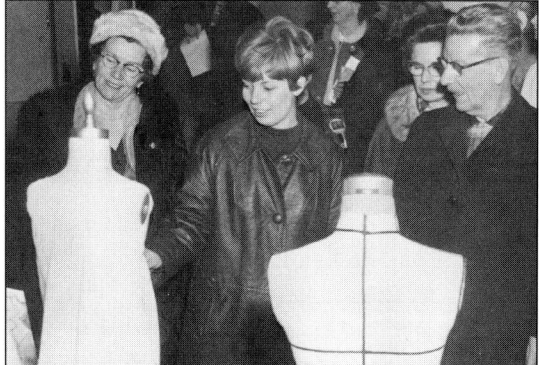

Left: *Another shot from the Mac open house in 1967.*

Right: *Proof that cookies are a major food group. Open house, 1968.*

Similarly, there was a demand in the marketplace for graduates who could appreciate not simply family needs, but also business and marketing operations, consumer behaviour, and the mediating processes between the consumer and the producers of goods and services. Education with new emphases and with a downplaying of the ties to an older form of home economics would characterize the new educational philosophy.

The two new departments would focus and present their expertise in new ways. The Department of Family Studies would emphasize the study of the family as a social system. The focus here would be on human development in terms of biological, sociological, and physiological aspects and on family relationships, family economics, and family management. The Department of Consumer Studies would emphasize the interrelationships between consumers and the producers and distributors of goods and services utilized by families. The subject matter would go beyond consumer economics and consumer behaviour to study consumption processes from the point of view of the consumer. The existing elements of Macdonald Institute would be distributed between these two departments. Family Studies, Applied Human Nutrition, and Early Childhood Education would all be housed within the Family Studies Department. Consumer Studies and Textiles would be housed within the Consumer Studies Department.

The emphasis within these new programs would be entirely on training for professional opportunities. Family Studies students, for example, would not only take courses in family relations and family economics, but also develop strength in the behavioural sciences and in communications. This would prepare graduates not simply for the traditional jobs in secondary school teaching or in home economics extension services, but also for work in community service agencies. Students in Applied Human Nutrition would have a choice of a minor emphasis in administrative dietetics, therapeutic nutrition, or community nutrition, in keeping with the recently revised academic requirements for entry into the Canadian Dietetic Association. The Administrative Dietetics program would be strengthened by a new link to the Hotel and Food Administration program. The program in Early Childhood Education would meet the growing demands of a changing society. The rising labour force participation of married women, and in particular of married women with young children, indicated an increasing need for child care facilities. This, combined with the growing awareness of the needs of disadvantaged preschool children, suggested a high demand for university-trained specialists in early childhood education, and the new Mac program would be ready to meet this demand.

The Academic Brief's case for Consumer Studies was somewhat less clear or persuasive. The emphasis on the study of consumerism was straightforward. Graduates of this program would be able to provide liaisons between the consumer and the producers/merchandisers of goods. Graduates could find jobs in business and industry and in government agencies concerned with consumer education and consumer protection. Students would take an emphasis on consumer economics or on foods, the latter preparing for entry into the food industry as a consumer consultant. Also available would be an emphasis on textiles and clothing or on housing. These various program concentrations made a less coherent package than did the Family Studies focus. The place of textiles and housing was unclear and the rationale for their inclusion was weak, leaving the impression that they were included simply because the older Macdonald program contained these elements and a place for them had to be found. There was also some confusion between studying consumer behaviour in order to produce professionals who could best exploit consumer tendencies for industry, and analyzing consumerism on behalf of agencies attempting to protect consumers in the marketplace.

Throughout the Academic Brief the emphasis was on professionalism. These new programs would prepare graduates for important jobs in the world of business, teaching, and government and service agencies. They would be characterized by their intention to meet the continuing and changing needs of society in the workplace. Gone was any discussion of training young women for their place in the home. The new Macdonald Institute would emphasize professionalism and the job market. A Macdonald Institute with strong academic credentials proclaimed its newfound strength in graduate programs and in research by faculty members and graduate students. This was a Macdonald Institute which, while retaining many of its existing strengths, left behind the attitudes and terminology of home economics. Macdonald Institute claimed its place in the academic environment of a university.

The Academic Brief was not merely defensive, though it certainly was that in part. It also articulated a new agenda that aimed to place Macdonald Institute at the forefront of education in its field in Canada. Taking advantage of the contemporary concern for intellectual dependence on the United States, the brief pointed out that most academics with a doctorate had received their advanced training at an American campus. If Mac were allowed to grow and develop as it envisioned, that dependence on the United States would be ended by the rise of Canadian graduate programs and the production of qualified Canadian PhDs in the field.

The university senior administrators now had the kind of progressive vision for Macdonald Institute for which they had been hoping. The changes proposed by Wardlaw's 1968 Academic Brief were largely adopted. Nevertheless, it was up to the new College of Family and Consumer Studies to prove itself. A December 1968 memorandum of the Senate Committee on Academic Administrative Organization pointed to the "continued uneasiness expressed by some members of the Committee on the proposals for the academic administration of the program presently within Macdonald Institute." The committee nevertheless approved the creation of a new and separate college housing Family and Consumer Studies as well as HAFA. The entire process had one further result: a new leader had been found in the person of Janet Wardlaw.

SCHOOL OF HOTEL AND FOOD ADMINISTRATION

One of the few truly innovative elements of Dean McCready's original 1963 proposals was the idea that a new program should be developed in food management. This proposal rested on several foundations. McCready was convinced that it was in Mac's best interests to cease its existence as a bastion of female difference. Macdonald Institute needed to present itself in the new university environment as open to both sexes. If Mac was going to retain any political influence on campus, it would have to grow significantly, and the easiest way to do this was to bring in men as well as women. McCready wasted no time in forwarding a proposal for a new program in food management in December 1964.[300]

At the same time the hotel and restaurant industry regarded the 1964 university expansion at Guelph as an opportunity to meet what was regarded as a major need on the part of the industry. The lack of any university programs providing qualified food managers and administrators left a serious lack of qualified personnel across the country. The new plans at Guelph offered "our big chance to win full university-level education," commented a leading magazine in the industry. The magazine article pointed to the knowledge in food science at the OAC and to Macdonald Institute's long experience in training food and nutrition specialists.[301] The industry emphasized its interest in a Guelph program by holding a large conference of the Canadian Restaurant Association at the University of Guelph in April 1966. The influence of the industry took on a greater prominence when it became clear that significant funds would be raised within the industry to support the start-up costs of the program.

Although the idea of HAFA began as a modest food management program, the intention to expand into restaurant and hotel administration had always been present. The industry thought in terms of a full-scale university program in hotel, restaurant, and institutional management from the early discussions in 1963, and the 1964 Macdonald Institute report to senate echoed this. McCready was cautious, making hotel and restaurant administration a long-term goal for the food management program. However, when an outside consultant, brought in by the food study committee, pushed hard for a hotel management program (including plans for an on-campus hotel students could use for workplace learning), the plans expanded. Influential too were a number of leading examples of such programs at American campuses that were much admired in Guelph, such as Cornell University.[302]

In the meantime Macdonald Institute was fighting off an attempt by the OAC to co-opt the proposed food management program and incorporate it within a broader program in food science. The university senate established a food study committee in 1965 that soon began talking of a broad-based initiative focusing on a science degree program that would include a wide range of studies of food — food science, food technology, and food management. McCready readily saw the threat to Macdonald Institute's plans in such an initiative and warned Mac colleagues that they needed immediately to begin to think how "our college can best be integrated with the Food Management course, or, if we must insist on further development of facilities which would enable the Food Management to extend beyond Restaurant Management to Hotel, Motel and other Institution Management studies."[303] There is a hint here that by including the hotel features of HAFA, the program could be made less attractive to the OAC. When the committee's 1966 report proposed a program in food science and management, Dean McCready and Dr. Mabel Sanderson issued a minority report. They rejected the idea that food science and food management belonged together in a single department, pointing to the different sorts of students attracted by the two areas and the different program requirements. These objections were seconded by other influential voices from the OAC and the result was that two distinct programs were soon being discussed. Macdonald Institute's potential role in the food management program had been preserved.[304] McCready and leading Macdonald faculty members envisioned food management as a way of reshaping the character of education at Macdonald in the quiet struggle to retain a significant profile on the Guelph campus. They also pointed to Mac's long-standing interest in applied food science.

As a business program, Food Management — and later the Hotel and Food Administration program — had no natural home on the Guelph campus. This was the first commerce degree being offered at Guelph. The OAC did, however, have a large number of departments that focused on some aspects of food science, and the Department of Agricultural Economics dealt with many aspects of the business side of the food industry. McCready had an ongoing struggle to retain the possibility of HAFA being housed at Macdonald Institute. The matter was not resolved until the fall of 1967, when the executive committee of the university senate recommended that the program should be closely associated with household science. In the long run, the decision to house HAFA within Mac may well have rested on their shared interest in applied study and research. Certainly it was central to the plans for HAFA that the new unit have a good deal of autonomy, leading to its establishment as a school, rather than just another department.

The business and applied character of the HAFA program was finally and formally set-tled by the debate over the degree that HAFA undergraduates would earn. For some time it was assumed that the degree would be a BSc, but when the matter was finally decided in the fall of 1969 — after students had already started in the program — the university senate decided that the degree would be a bachelor of commerce (BCom).

Hotel and Food Administration did not play a major role in Wardlaw's 1968 Academic Brief on behalf of Macdonald Institute. HAFA's role and its academic program were still not well developed at that point, awaiting the appointment of a director of the new school. HAFA had not been part of Dr. Wardlaw's mandate when drawing up the Academic Brief. Only at the end of the process was a very short Part II regarding HAFA added to the Academic Brief, on the request of the vice-president academic.

STUDENT LIFE

The regulatory environment of Mac relaxed noticeably with the onset of university status, the environment of the late 1960s youth revolution, and the broader spectrum of students on campus and in residence. Macdonald Hall and Watson Hall lost their special status as a home for Mac girls and were opened to young women from all sectors of the campus. While the students of Macdonald Institute were thus exposed to a greater variety of students, there was a concomitant loss of cohesion among Mac girls as they no longer shared a common residence life for most of their time at university. By 1969 the students were spread among fourteen residences that accommodated twenty-seven hundred occupants.[305] In 1965 attendance cards became voluntary for instructors in individual courses and were no longer submitted to the dean's office. A few years later regulations were changed so that attendance at lectures or labs was no longer compulsory. In 1967 residence curfew regulations were dropped, so that all girls were able to stay out as late as they wished on any night of the week.[306] In general the university relied on an internalization of the rules of proper conduct, using an overt regulatory environment much less. The course calendar commented, "In general the University expects that students will conduct themselves in a civilized manner which respects the rights of others at all times. More so than other institutions in society, the University Community must be a self-disciplined community dedicated to and upholding the values of learning, rational inquiry and mutual respect."[307] One of the striking changes of the new university environment was the intro-duction of a spring semester, with an intake of freshmen students in May as well as in

Left: *Registration lineups, the start of frosh week in 1969.*

Top right: *Frosh week initiation in 1967.*

Middle Right: *Conversat, 1970.*

Bottom Right: *Float titled "Mac girls always get their man" at homecoming, 1969.*

Left: *Mac Hall Formal, December 2, 1966.*

Right: *Another picture from the Mac Formal in 1966.*

Complex B, as South Residence was known in 1969.

September. There were thus two different intakes of first-year students and slightly less cohesion among the incoming cohort than there had been in the 1950s.

The costs of education increased across the 1960s, particularly the non-tuition costs. By 1968 students were paying $237.50 each semester and residence fees had risen to $460 per semester.[308] There was now a broad range of scholarships and awards available to Mac students. A number of county groups and Women's Institutes had established awards valued at $100 or more to assist young women to attend Macdonald Institute, and the assistance thus given was important in establishing a network of student support that would be the envy of other colleges at the university. The number of students also increased — forty new students each spring semester and a further one hundred in the fall.[309]

Top Left: *College Royal Queen Miss Joanne Glover, 1965.*

Top Right: *College Royal, 1969.*

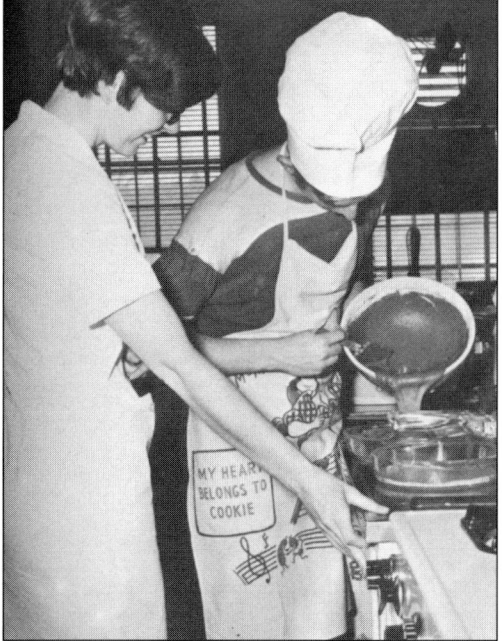

Bottom Left: *College Royal 1968 chocolate cake baking contest. This famous contest featured Mac girls talking their partners through the steps of making a scratch cake.*

Bottom Right: *Another famous College Royal contest — the patch sewing contest. Here Doug Hedley, OAC '65, sews a patch onto Vikey West, Mac '68. Judges were Edith Bray and Padre Young.*

There was a strong sense of community among the faculty. In the early years an annual faculty dinner was held, and staff and faculty joined in sponsoring a child through the Save the Children Fund. Such a sense of community was important in facing the difficult debates regarding curriculum reform and administrative restructuring.

The students too shared a well-developed sense of community. There were still many shared activities that drew the students together. The January winter carnival, for example, featured ice sculptures, skating, and entertainment, and College Royal continued to draw students into various events. The Macdonald open house at College Royal focused on the many skills that the students were developing, and the fashion show gave many of the young women an opportunity to display the clothes they had designed and made. Elsewhere at College Royal students participated in showing animals or in the square-dance competition and attended one of the several Curtain Call shows in War Mem Hall. For a while a Macdonald Institute formal replaced the traditional Mac Hall formal before it too disappeared. Student clubs, reflecting the various majors, played an increasingly important role in fostering a sense of community among the students, particularly after the creation of FACS in 1970. Clubs in child studies and in applied human nutrition were matched with later clubs as new majors emerged. The students of HAFA, because of the large number of courses common to the program, developed an especially noticeable sense of community and belonging.

The student body at Macdonald Institute remained female in the 1960s, but the faculty membership was beginning to change. Gordon Couling was no longer the sole male; Dr. H.R. Richards joined the Department of Textiles, Clothing and Design in 1964, and George Fuller and Keith Slater joined soon after. As well, the all-female leadership altered when Richards became head of his department in 1965. This prepared the way for the more extensive changes of the 1970s and 1980s throughout FACS.

Nineteen sixty-eight was a challenging year for the Macdonald faculty and alumnae. "They faced up to major changes," Wardlaw points out, "the phasing out of the program

Left: *Alumni tea, 1965.*

Right: *Alumni tea in 1967. One of the many celebrations to mark Canada's centennial. Here J.D. McLaughlin and his wife host the alumni in their home.*

Alumni Seminar Series in 1970. Dr. Wardlaw, Annette Yeager, and guest speaker Jeanne Lynch.

Left: *Alumni Weekend, 1970. Children of alumni on the cannon.*

Right: *The alumni hold a reception for Dr. McCready on her retirement ...*

... and another one for Dr. Wardlaw on her new appointment.

which they had known and the acceptance of a new undergraduate program and a new departmental organization."[310] In addition, the much beloved Margaret McCready had retired. In 1970 these changes were completed with the formal alteration of the name of the college. Henceforth Macdonald Institute would be known as the College of Family and Consumer Studies (FACS). Similarly the graduates of this new college would receive new degrees — Bachelor of Applied Science (BASc) or Bachelor of Commerce (BCom). These were intended to be reflective of the new departure in the education offered through Macdonald Institute.

The changes were central to the new FACS, but it is important to realize just how much the Academic Brief had built on the old Macdonald Institute and just how many changes were already underway at Mac prior to 1968. The founding of the nursery school in 1959 had pointed to the new emphasis on early childhood education. The new graduate programs established in 1965 were the basis of important new initiatives in research and training. The plans for HAFA were well underway and were largely independent of the Academic Brief. McCready's leadership had been of central importance in laying the groundwork for change. The next step was to translate the strong Mac foundation into the new vision of FACS.

The new FACS was not perfect. It was the product of compromise, and realistically sought to accomplish what was possible in the existing circumstances. It was necessary, for example, to retrain the existing faculty, some of the older of whose training now placed them on the margins of the educational enterprise. Some of the changes would take time — the replacement of faculty, for example — and were constrained by the finite resources available. But Macdonald Institute was now on a new path, one that had great promise.

VI

THE FACS YEARS,
1970–1998

During the 1960s Macdonald Institute had undergone a great deal of turmoil and debate. By 1970 most of the debate had ended and the basis of a new beginning on older foundations had been created. The traditional tasks of Mac had been reshaped and expressed through a new academic structure, the departments of Family Studies and Consumer Studies. A new school had been added, the School of Hotel and Food Administration, and these three units now made up the College of Family and Consumer Studies (FACS). New degrees were in place for the students in these programs. But this fresh start was a demanding one. It still remained to make these changes meaningful, to give substance to the new forms of education now expressed in all of the reforms that Macdonald Institute had witnessed. The task was not an easy one for FACS.

The new college had the advantage of building on the solid foundations of Macdonald Institute, which had a reputation for successful education over almost seventy years and had an established market among the young women of Ontario. FACS had proven leadership in the person of its dean, Dr. Janet Wardlaw, who had instigated and now oversaw the fundamental changes. There were a number of experienced and increasingly well-qualified instructors. But FACS also had some disadvantages. Of necessity the new college contained elements of the old

Left: *The FACS years.*

Right: *The graduating class of FACS '72 presenting Dean Wardlaw with the brass building plate.*

Left: *An aerial view of the FACS buildings.*

Right: *The new name plate.*

Macdonald Institute that reflected the older "home economics" traditions in an environment that was trying to break away from many of those traditions. The two departments were hybrids in which various disciplinary elements had deliberately combined to form interdisciplinary units. The School of Hotel and Food Administration (HAFA) was starting afresh with a small and inexperienced faculty. The task ahead would be to mould the departments and the school into effective, intellectually challenging units individually and collectively.

NEW BEGINNINGS

Planning for the HAFA curriculum had been deferred until the first director was appointed, in the expectation that the director would do much of this work. In December 1968 Donald Greenway was named the first director of the school. Greenway had impressive credentials in both industry and the education field. Until recently he had been executive vice-president of the National Restaurant Association. Before that he had been at the centre of the reorganization of the hotel management curriculum at Washington State University and then director of the School of Hotel, Restaurant and Institution Management at Michigan State University.[311]

Greenway remained in Guelph for only a very short time, leading to some unfortunate delay and confusion in preparations for the start of HAFA. Greenway did, however, help to find a successor. George Bedell was appointed director in June 1969, just a few short months before the first HAFA students were to arrive. Bedell too had good credentials, particularly in industry, where he had been director of management training programs and of the business and technical advisory service of the National Restaurant Association in the United States. He lacked the academic experience of Greenway and had the distinct disadvantage of a late start. Nevertheless, Bedell pressed ahead with his task. He proved to be very good at establishing an effective learning environment and was highly regarded by students for his caring attitude and behaviour.

George Bedell.

HAFA's program was established first and foremost as a business degree. The arrangement with the hospitality industry was that the industry would provide the funds for erecting the HAFA building and the university would provide the operating funds. The program had just the one major and this gave the program and its students a good deal of cohesion and sense of unity, much like Mac in its earlier days. In the early years of FACS, HAFA was the only academic unit awarding the BCom at Guelph.

Family Studies and Consumer Studies began the 1970s seeking new department chairs, making for even more discontinuity as well as a greater opportunity for new beginnings. Dr. Kathryn Kopf became the new chair of Family Studies in the spring of 1970. Dr. Kopf had joined the department less

HAFA students continue to be united in spirit and purpose.

Richard Vosburgh in 1974.

than two years earlier and focused her teaching and research on education for family living. During her leadership some highly qualified appointments were made to the department, helping to set the academic tone for years to come. Kopf also enhanced relationships with outside agencies and teachers' groups. In Consumer Studies an outsider was brought in to give fresh leadership to the somewhat disparate elements of the department. Dr. Richard Vosburgh came from the University of Toronto's Faculty of Management Studies and his research centred on marketing and consumer behaviour. He would be a stabilizing

Left: Beth Parks, FACS '79 Consumer Studies student, conducting consumer research.

Right: G.R. Osbaldeston, deputy minister of Consumer Affairs, with Drs. Wardlaw, Vosburgh, and Upton.

Sensory and Consumer Preference testing labs in Mac in the late 1970s.

force in Consumer Studies as chair over the next decade. Under the leadership of Dean Janet Wardlaw, there was strong encouragement of cross-disciplinary research among the faculty in HAFA, Family Studies, and Consumer Studies, keeping alive some of the strengths of the old Mac alliance. In time, however, this faded, particularly after the departure of Wardlaw, and the various disciplines retreated more into their own areas.

The students kept entering. HAFA took in a first student cohort of thirty young men and women, realizing Margaret McCready's dream of expanding the Mac student body to include men. The two departments accepted 180 entering students (40 in the spring semester and 140 in the fall), and increased admission to 250 by 1972. This growth continued throughout the decade, so that total enrolment in the three units doubled in the 1970s.[312] The first BASc degrees were awarded in the spring of 1972 and the first BCom degrees the following year. Dean Wardlaw was kept busy with many public and professional appearances explaining the curriculum reforms and administrative reorganizations that lay behind the new degrees.

New space was also acquired for the work of FACS. Across the road from Macdonald Institute stood an old "temporary" clapboard building left over from the Second World War occupation of the campus. This had long been the Textiles Building, modestly refurbished, and it continued in this role. In the early 1970s Macdonald Hall, which many alumnae still

Originally built to be the "temporary" home of the Wireless School in the 1940s, the Textile Building continues to be used.

regarded as their home on campus, received some much-needed renovations. The wooden staircase was removed, replaced by a safer, fire resistant stairway. The reception room to the right of the front door, where dancing had occurred for the Mac Hall formal, was replaced by more residential rooms. Everywhere bright colours were introduced, ceilings were lowered, and the appearance was one of "crisp, clean lines." In Macdonald Institute a student-faculty lounge complex was completed from renovated space.

The most important new space was the Macdonald Stewart Hall, which would house the HAFA program. Late in 1973 construction began on the new west wing of Macdonald Institute, which was planned to house the faculty and students of HAFA. At that point there were only 163 students and 5 faculty members, but the additional space would facilitate much-needed expansion — the projected enrolment was 370 students with 15 faculty members. The new Macdonald Stewart Hall had the most up-to-date teaching facilities in FACS and they were made use of by all of FACS over the years

Macdonald Stewart Hall opens on October 25, 1975.

Left and right: The HAFA building.

to come, but the building was designed specifically to meet the needs of HAFA students. Laboratories with modern kitchen equipment, computing facilities, seminar and lecture rooms, and office space were all included.[313] The facade was designed to complement Macdonald Institute, using red brick to blend the old with the new. The building opened in 1975, thanks to the generous support of the hospitality industry through the Hospitality Industry Founders' Fund, whose contributions made it possible to construct the new building entirely without government funding.

New space was also added when a house on University Avenue, immediately north of the existing Macdonald Institute building, was renovated in 1975. This building was used for

Right: The Lab School's playground in the 1970s.

office space and for an expansion of the nursery school. The existing nursery school and laboratory had focused on children aged three and four; now the school expanded to include younger toddlers. Space for offices and classrooms was always in demand. On three separate occasions in the 1960s and 1970s the faculty of Mac/FACS developed detailed plans for construction of

Left: The children registered in the Lab School's Nursery School program plant trees behind Macdonald Institute. This area will be made into the Adelaide Hoodless Garden for Macdonald's centenary in 2003.

Right: A group shot of the tree-planting ceremony.

a new building, but on each occasion financial constraints forced the abandonment of the plans. Instead, FACS made do with renovated space largely in Macdonald Institute as older laboratories, the Home Management apartment, and the dean's suite were all converted to office space over the years. As well, new space was added in several converted houses on University Avenue East.[314]

There were six programs from which FACS students could choose: Hotel and Food Administration; in the Family Studies Department, Family Studies, Child Studies, and Applied Human Nutrition; in the Consumer Studies Department, Textiles and Consumer Studies. The potential for specialization increased in the 1970s as students could declare their major at an earlier point in their university career. Students already entered HAFA directly, and in 1972–73 students in the other departments could choose to enter their major in their first semester and to begin specialization beyond the introductory core courses in their third semester. At the third semester, the programs of specialization began to diverge considerably from one another. About half the entering students in 1972 declared a major upon entry. This stood in marked contrast to the old BHSc program, where students took most of the same courses for their first three years and did not declare their specialization until their final year. As well, in 1972 the university adopted a pass-by-course system, giving the students increased flexibility in course scheduling.[315] In 1974–5 the first male to graduate from Family and Consumer Studies, outside HAFA, earned his degree, but Family Studies in particular remained almost exclusively a female bastion.[316]

Kenneth Devine, FACS '75 Child Studies, was the first male graduate of Macdonald Institute. Ken was a Grade 4 teacher from Toronto.

While women students overwhelmingly predominated, Family Studies acquired an important complement of male instructors during the 1970s, breaking the long-standing dominance of women professors. In 1970 Dr. Ed Herold joined the department, followed by Dr. George Kawash in 1972; Dr. Bruce Ryan in 1975; Dr. Richard Barham in 1976, as chair; and Dr. Andor Tari in 1977. The staff now had an influential complement of men for the first time. Ryan, an educational psychologist, brought his expertise to the preschool/daycare field, traditionally an area of female competence. Tari, also an educational psychologist, focused his research on the effects of fathering on achievement motivation in children, adding an

important additional dimension to the studies of childhood and parenting. By 1979 there were just eighteen men students enrolled in the entire FACS program outside HAFA, although this number was increasing noticeably.[317]

There were new research programs to take advantage of the scholarly environment. Some of these took advantage of the links now available to other social science departments in the new university environment. In 1968 the university founded the Centre for Educational Disabilities and named Dr. Dennis Stott as chair. Stott was a member of the Psychology Department but his research and activity overlapped the interests of many in

Dr. Dennis Stott of the Centre for Educational Disabilities.

Family Studies. The centre focused on studying and correcting the various learning disabilities experienced by young children and thus meshed nicely with Family Studies' teaching and research interests in child development, although the amount of interaction with Family Studies was limited. The centre soon grew into a five-room remedial school where five staff members and a number of volunteers met bi-weekly with the children participating in the centre's programs. In 1974 Dr. Griffith Morgan joined the Family Studies Department and assumed leadership of the centre. Under his leadership the centre was active in providing psychological assessments of school-age children; the children and their parents could use the psychological reports to understand better their children's educational needs. The centre assessed between one hundred and two hundred clients a year. At the end of the 1970s the centre was closed after an academic review concluded that while it was performing a useful public service, it was doing little to serve the students or the university and insufficient research or teaching functions were being performed.[318]

Family Studies faculty members brought a wide range of research interests to bear in their teaching. In 1971 Dr. Kathleen Brown began to publish *The Consumer Interest*. Brown edited the newsletter with the assistance of a grant from the Canadian Consumer Council. The publication contained information regarding legislation, meetings, publications, and conferences of interest to people in the consumer field. In her teaching, Brown pushed her students earlier than many other faculty members to go to the primary literature and emphasized skills in learning and critical thinking.

Dr. Kathleen Brown.

In 1970, Professor Anne Callagan joined the Department of Family Studies. She was unusual in that she did not have a doctorate but began a research program nevertheless. Professor Callagan's research compared families at all income levels in their adjustments to a physical or emotional disability in the mother. The project utilized interviews with family members, observation, and follow-up contacts over a three-year period, and aimed at uncovering the extent to which family roles were redefined and workloads rearranged in the face of the mother's disability. Not surprisingly, the study revealed that stress was a major element of the family environment, particularly financial stress.[319]

Other long-term faculty joined the Family Studies Department and added their research and teaching to a growing pool of well-qualified instructors. In 1972, for example, Dr. George Kawash brought his interests in developmental psychology to the department and began to teach courses in parent-child relationships, child development, and mental health

Professor Joe Hornick teaching a family studies class in Mac Institute in the 1970s.

principles. Kawash played an important role in helping to create an interdisciplinary department and in bringing a social science approach to applied human nutrition, in which he collaborated with several faculty members.[320]

In 1970 Dr. Ed Herold joined the Department of Family Studies, bringing a new dimension of family behaviour within the analysis and study carried on in FACS. Herold was a specialist in sexuality and in the early years brought that interest to bear on issues of sex education. "Healthy sexual functioning," he argued, "is seen as essential to the mental health of individuals and marital relationships." The study and understanding of sexuality thus lay at the heart of any program aiming at the study of the family. Effective sex education, Herold suggested, complemented the informal sex education that occurs constantly in modern western society with the exposure to sex in the media.[321] Herold's courses attracted considerable student attention and support and were important in the maturing process of the Family Studies program. He also began a very popular outreach program by organizing an annual conference on human sexuality that drew specialists in the field from a wide geographical and workplace background, helping to draw attention to the FACS program and its scholarly approach to important topics. A further outreach development was Herold's production of *It Couldn't Happen to Me* (1974), a film about adolescent pregnancy.

Dr. Jean Sabry.

Dr. Jean Sabry led an effective group of faculty members in applied human nutrition. She had been trained as a classic experimental nutritionist, carrying out laboratory bench work looking at human nutritional requirements. But on her arrival at Guelph she soon embraced the interdisciplinary environment in Family Studies, moving to examine the behavioural side of nutritional research. Increasingly she turned her research to the psychological and social factors that influenced nutritional behaviour. Sabry's first doctoral student, for example, was Donna Woolcott in the late 1970s, who herself later became a mainstay of Family Studies. Woolcott's doctoral research examined the personality and social-psychological factors that influenced the nutritional health of men in the insurance industry. With such research Sabry led the applied human nutritionists in new directions.

Faculty elsewhere in the college exposed students to new research interests and approaches. In HAFA Dr. Elizabeth Upton, a specialist in institutional foods services management, began to introduce her students to the marvels of the computer. She developed a computer-based program that simulated the dietary department of a large, modern hospital. Patient needs and meal requests were fed into the computer and the computer in turn produced: a food item file detailing all the foodstuffs being used in the food preparation, serving as an inventory check; a nutrient file listing the nutrients of the foods being served; and a recipe file listing the quantities of ingredients needed for cooking. Upton herself was on the leading edge of computer-assisted dietary management and brought

Dr. Elizabeth Upton.

this new technology to the students at FACS. Through such research and teaching Upton made students aware of the advantages and limitations of computer-assisted work and exposed the students to some computer technology as it was beginning to impact the worlds of work and learning.[322]

In Consumer Studies, new faculty brought their research and intellectual interests to bear on the education of FACS students. From its Macdonald antecedents, Consumer Studies had inherited an expertise in food, housing, and textiles. By the early 1970s two new majors were in place in the Department of Consumer Studies — in Consumer Studies and in Textile Science. The Consumer Studies major had several streams of emphasis, including food (focusing on the product side), housing, clothing, and consumer behaviour, with the

last two having the highest student enrolment. Textile Science had low enrolments, and this, combined with the departure of faculty members specializing in this area, led to the gradual decline of Textile Science by the mid-1980s. The food emphasis too declined over the years, as faculty members such as Dr. Elizabeth Gullett left.

Valerie Allen and Jean Hume in the food labs, 1989.

New emphases appeared. The new chair, Dr. Richard Vosburgh, began to recruit some long-term members of the department whose influence would be considerable. In the early 1970s, for example, Dr. John Liefeld, Professor Trevor Watts, and Dr. Marjorie Wall joined the department. Liefeld's early research involved a study of consumer behaviour and informative labelling of textiles and other products. Through such studies he sought an understanding of the nature of the

Left: *Dr. John Liefeld,*
1972.

Centre: *Trevor Watts.*

Right: *Dr. Marjorie Wall.*

marketplace, the behaviours of consumers and sellers, and the interactions among consumers, products, and sellers. Some of this research was funded by the federal government's Department of Consumer and Corporate Affairs. Liefeld's research informed his teaching in such courses as Communication and Behaviour, Communication in the Market Place, and Consumer Decision Processes.[323] His research interests meshed well with the traditional attention paid to textiles by FACS. Louise Heslop brought her expertise to bear in the area of consumer behaviour and was important in enhancing that emphasis in the department before leaving in the early 1980s.

Left: *Louise (Bazinette)*
Heslop.

Right: *Heslop from her*
1967 yearbook.

Similarly, housing had long been a topic of interest in Macdonald Institute. Consumer Studies took on responsibility for this subject, hiring Joan Simon in 1971 to teach and conduct research in the area. Simon was interested in interior housing design regarding areas of aesthetics and efficiency, but she also brought a new ecological perspective to the department, articulating in her courses some of the growing environmental concerns regarding unplanned, extensive growth of our cities and housing. Simon's knowledge in the field of architecture added an important dimension to the housing expertise in the department, and when she was killed in an accident it was a considerable loss to the department.[324] In time, Consumer Studies moved away from the product development side of the discipline to the consumer behaviour side.

Research had assumed a new and prominent position in the FACS profile. Reflective of this was the fact that in the period 1974–1979, research funds received by faculty in the college increased by 150 percent.[325] Such statistics helped to change the profile of the college in the university and among the wider public.

Joan Simon.

FACS continued Macdonald Institute's traditions of educational outreach. Like Mac in the 1960s, much of this outreach took the form of continuing education conferences and workshops for professionals in the field. There were workshops in family economics and in human relations in family life education, for example. FACS co-operated with the Early Childhood Education Association of Ontario to conduct workshops on the creative use of children's literature and on infant development for persons working in programs for infants and pre-school children. A number of Ontario dietitians attended a workshop focusing on Elizabeth Upton's research into food and nutrition management with computer assistance; this was run with the co-operation of the Ontario Hospital Association and the Ontario Dietetic Association.[326] A less formal form of outreach was the annual alumnae seminars, which began in 1968 and continued on through the 1970s. These were designed to maintain alumnae ties with FACS while giving faculty and alumnae an opportunity for intellectual exchange.

A different form of outreach occurred with the Ghana project. During the 1960s there had been modest interest at Mac in sharing some of the educational benefits of a home economics program with underdeveloped countries, especially in Africa. Graduates had occasionally gone off to developing countries for several years and their exploits had been reported to alumnae. In 1970, as part of a broader Canadian International Development Agency project in the areas of agricultural science and home science, FACS developed a close relationship with the Department of Home Science at the University of Ghana. Dr. Margaret

Left: *Margaret McCready in Ghana.*

Right: *Judith Lean and Cathy Armstrong showing Ghanaian souveniers to Joan Jenkinson, 1972.*

McCready, after her retirement, accepted a short-term position as chair of the Ghana department for two years; this began prior to Guelph's active involvement. In 1972 McCready was replaced by Dr. Lila Engberg, who had taught occasionally at Mac over the previous fifteen years and had extensive experience working in Africa. With the support of several other Canadians, often with FACS ties, these women carried out an ambitious educational project in Ghana over the next several years. The flow of benefits from this University of Guelph program was very much two-way, as FACS opened its doors to Ghanaian exchange students, while FACS students, administrators, and faculty members travelled to Ghana.[327] The 1970–78 program was followed by a later project, 1987–90, under Richard Barham's direction, between FACS and the University of Ghana's Department of Home Science, which was designed to provide further graduate training for Ghanaians so that a master's program could be introduced in Home Science. There was considerable enriching of the perspectives of all involved, to the benefit of the FACS program overall.

FACS was also enriched in these early years by increasing external support. Particularly noteworthy was the H.H. Harshman Foundation, which provided generous endowed funds for several scholarships at both the undergraduate and graduate levels. The Harshman Foundation also sponsored academic conferences, the first being in November 1972, entitled "Food in a Changing Society." This conference capitalized on the broad range of faculty expertise and drew on faculty members from all three units. The academic conferences were important in maintaining interdisciplinary initiatives within FACS.

Yet through all the changes and developments of the 1970s, FACS struggled to reinvent itself. On the eve of Macdonald Institute's seventy-fifth anniversary in 1978, Dean Janet Wardlaw commented on the continuing sly remarks that the education at FACS was "really home economics, isn't it?"[328] By the end of the 1970s the FACS programs had taken substance, consisting of extensive training in applied and social sciences; the old emphasis on skills training had disappeared. A new applied program, HAFA, was gaining strength and had added a new degree to the offerings from FACS. The old Macdonald Institute, in the form of FACS, continued to change as the 1980s approached, building on some of the changes of the 1970s to deal with research problems and teaching in fresh ways. FACS took advantage of the hiring opportunities offered in the 1970s to make some very important appointments in all sectors of the college that helped to set a new tone and approach to teaching and research. The reinvention of Macdonald Institute was well underway.

Student life had taken on a new character as well. Gone were the days when "Mac girls" congregated in Macdonald Hall and Watson Hall, sharing a highly developed community life and spirit. FACS was now part of a growing university and FACS students were spread across

Left: *Making the symbolic first hole on the seventy-fifth anniversary Restoration Project are Nancy (West) Sawyer, Mac '62, and Marilyn (Inglis) Robinson, Mac '55.*

Right: *The new student lounge under construction.*

Left: *Macdonald Institute as it looked in 1978 for its seventy-fifth anniversary.*

Right: *FACS, room 102 after being refurbished for the seventy-fifth anniversary. This room will be the site of the Alumni Heritage Room in 2003.*

Left: *The grand opening on Alumni Weekend, June 1978.*

Right: *Conclusion of the speeches.*

The new lounge completed.

Left: *Club life was very important. Here Child Studies '76 leave their mark on the cannon.*

Right: *Class of FACS '76 in the old basement lounge.*

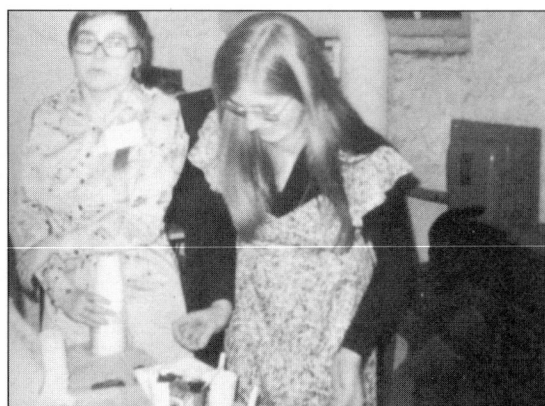

Left: *The class of FACS '79 enjoying treats from the Mac-FACS Alumni Association during the annual dessert party in the class's final semester.*

Right: *Dr. Vosburgh and students in the 1970s.*

Left: *FACS '75 at the dessert party.*

Right: *Nutrition club (FACS '79) with Dean Wardlaw.*

The Keg, a home away from home for many students.

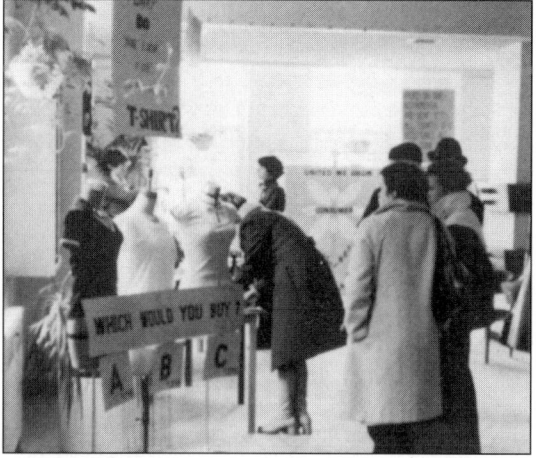

Left: *FACS '79 fundraiser. Bringing nutrition to the masses in the UC.*

Right: *College Royal textile display, 1976.*

Left: *The winning entry from FACS '79 at College Royal 1978.*

Right: *The Consumer Foods display from 1979.*

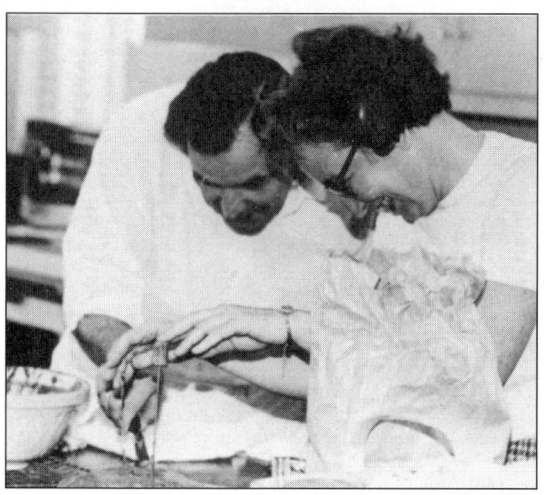

Bottom Left: *Dean Wardlaw and President Winegard in the 1973 cake baking contest. They tried for many years before …*

Right: *… they finally won in 1975, proving practice does make perfect.*

Left: *Liz O'Neil and friend were the grand champions in the chocolate cake baking contest in 1973.*

Right: *Rosemary Clark, Mac '59, talking to the FACS '75 grads about the services the Alumni Association offers.*

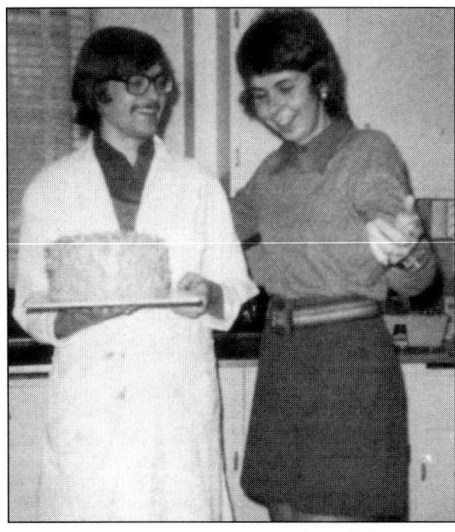

The program from the ring ceremony in 1978.

Pledge to Accompany Presentations of the
Professional Home Economics
Graduation Ring

"In accepting this ring as a symbol of our profession, I pledge:

— to demonstrate my competence in the body of knowledge unique to my facet of Home Economics

— to further the development of human resources through working in conjunction with other disciplines

— to help families and individuals realize a more satisfying life

— and to live creatively in a changing world."

Presented By
Ms. Bonnie Lacroix
Ontario Director, Canadian Home Economics Assoc.

Valedictory to Accompany Presentations of the
College of Family and Consumer Studies
Graduation Ring

"To commemorate our graduation from the program in Family and Consumer Studies, we have chosen to accept this graduation ring. Within this ring the unity of the five majors — Child Studies, Consumer Studies, Family Studies, Applied Human Nutrition and Textiles is symbolized. The students in each of the five majors, although unique in their particular emphasis, have shared experiences and friendships which have brought us together in fellowship. We hope that in the future this ring will serve to remind each of us of our years as a part of the College of Family and Consumer Studies at the University of Guelph".

Presented By
Dean Janet Wardlaw
College of Family and Consumer Studies

8:00 p.m.
Thursday, March 30, 1978
Faculty Club Lounge, University Centre
Wine & Cheese to Follow

the campus, taking courses, living in various residences, and generally mixing with the student population. The social and political dominance of the OAC students had ended, to be replaced by a student environment in which leaders came from a wide variety of programs, many of which were considerably larger in student numbers than FACS. While the sense of community within FACS was noticeably diminished, there were still strong associations with the various majors, enhanced by active student clubs — the child studies club and the applied human nutrition club, for example. As well, many of the majors had only a limited number of elective courses, so that the students within each major took many courses together and developed a somewhat weaker version of the older Mac sense of community; this was particularly noticeable within HAFA.

THE 1980S

The achievement of a decade of experience with the FACS curriculum provided an appropriate opportunity for a review of FACS and its teaching experience. The Child Studies major added further closely monitored practicum experience with children. Some form of the practicum had been part of the Child Studies and the Applied Human Nutrition programs from their beginnings; the Family Studies major had a regular course that included practicum experience in a local community agency. The practicum was an important part of the applied character of the degree program and occupied a central place in the philosophy of the Family Studies programs.

Claude Guldner.

In 1980 the Marriage and Family Therapy Centre, later renamed the Couple and Family Therapy Centre, was established under the direction of Professor Claude Guldner. Guldner came to Guelph with a well-established reputation in therapy and counselling, helping to give the new counselling centre instant credibility. This added an important new dimension to the graduate program at FACS. Students were soon earning master's degrees in Family Therapy, and the FACS program was undergoing accreditation reviews by the American association that certified graduates. Attention to couples and family therapy strengthened the attention given to broader facets of the family beyond child studies, adding a real enrichment to the Family Studies offerings. Accreditation by the American Association of Marriage and Family Therapy enhanced the program's credentials and gave it a broader profile. The centre operated a clinic where students could get hands-on experience in counselling.

In the late 1970s a conscious decision was made to add a further dimension to the Family Studies program — in gerontology. The study of aging and the elderly would address a developing social issue and would present a Family Studies program that now addressed the entire life course. Dr. Anne Martin Matthews was the first to be hired, followed in 1981 by Dr. Joan Norris and Dr. Joseph Tindale. Led by Martin Matthews this team established the Gerontology Research Centre in 1983, funded for six years by a strategic grant from the Social Sciences and Humanities Research Council. At the end of the period the Gerontology Research Centre became a partner in CARNET, the Canadian Aging Research Network, which, in collaboration with the University of Toronto and the University of Manitoba, was funded by the National Centres of Excellence program. The Gerontology Research Centre, along with CARNET, played an important role in establishing productive research links with other sectors of the University of Guelph, particularly among the social science departments. Important connections were made with researchers in geography, psychology, sociology, and rural planning and development, foreshadowing the more formal administrative links established after 1998.

This new emphasis on gerontology translated into substantial changes for students and faculty. A Gerontology major was introduced for undergraduates in 1985, and at the same time Gerontology students were accepted into the graduate program. The Gerontology Research Centre provided a forum for both graduate students and faculty where they could discuss their common research interests. The centre developed a useful infrastructure in support of research and the preparation of grants proposals.

Institutions such as the Couple and Family Therapy Centre, the Gerontology Research Centre, and the Child Study Laboratory School helped to give Family Studies and its programs an important profile on the Guelph campus and to emphasize the special areas of research interest. But they drew resources away from the department and its teaching responsibilities. There was tension between the teaching and research responsibilities when it came to distributing somewhat scarce resources. When Richard Barham became dean in 1983, leadership in Family Studies fell to Dr. Bruce Ryan.

Faculty research continued to give Family Studies national prominence. In the mid-1980s, for example, Dr. Donna Lero participated in a national research network examining family needs for child care, current child care use patterns, as well as affordability and availability of child care facilities across Canada. The survey centred on case studies of 336 families chosen

Dr. Richard Barham

Born in New Zealand, where he took his first degrees, Richard Barham graduated with his PhD in educational psychology from the University of Alberta in 1971. He began his teaching career in the Department of Educational Psychology at Alberta before returning to New Zealand, where he taught in the education department of the University of Otago. In 1976 he was recruited to become chair of Family Studies at Guelph and remained in that position until 1983. In 1983 he succeeded Janet Wardlaw as dean of the College of Family and Consumer Studies. As dean, he provided significant leadership to the college in a difficult period of financial restraint and scarce resources. In 1994 Barham stepped down as dean, returning to active membership in the Department of Family Studies.

to reflect the diversity of the Canadian population and to include sufficient numbers of child care user groups. One purpose of the study, conducted for the federal government, was to provide the state and interested community groups with reliable information on provision and use of child care facilities and to assess some of the options for future provisions.[329]

In Consumer Studies the emphasis on consumer behaviour translated easily into a marketing emphasis and gave the program a fresh new perspective. The department had the new leadership of its chair, Professor Monty Sommers, who, like his predecessor Richard Vosburgh, had come from the Marketing Faculty at the University of Toronto. Sommers developed a number of important initiatives. He opened the curriculum up to new approaches, as for example when he hired Dr. Grant McCracken, bringing a cultural anthropologist to Consumer Studies; when McCracken left after a few years the initiative was abandoned. More successful was the idea of shifting to an emphasis on marketing and of abandoning specializations, such as food and textiles, that no longer attracted many students. Sommers began the process by which the Consumer Studies program focused on marketing; the process was completed in the late 1980s by Sommers's successor as chair, Dr. John Pratschke.

George Bedell left HAFA in 1979 after serving two terms as director. As Canada was not yet producing senior academics in the field, his successor was an American, Tom Powers. Powers came to Guelph from Pennsylvania State University, where he had been professor-in-charge of the associate degree in Hotel and Food Service. Powers's great contribution to the HAFA program was a greater concern with scholarship. He created an environment in which

Tom Powers.

faculty members wanted to acquire PhDs and he used money from the Hospitality Founders' Fund to support young faculty members going to American doctoral programs, there being no similar Canadian programs at the time. This paralleled programs in the OAC in the 1950s, when faculty there felt academic pressure to upgrade their qualifications and found it necessary to travel to the United States for their PhDs. In this way HAFA gained important young faculty who were well trained in the new ideas current in the field and who could operate on level terms with faculty members in other disciplines. Faculty members such as Julia Christiansen Hughes, Iain Murray, Cathy Ralston, and Joe Barth all benefited from this scheme. Powers also entrenched links with the hospitality industry by going out and asking what industry leaders wanted from the Guelph program. What was more, he made every attempt to satisfy industry needs. Most prominently Powers established executive development programs, designed to provide training for managers and executives already in the industry. The Advanced Management Program for the Hospitality Industry (AMPHI) offered short courses designed to prepare senior executives in the hospitality industry. The Hospitality Developers course did the same for middle management. Powers also introduced the case study approach to classes, using his contacts with industry to gain access to company records for the creation of the case studies. By the time Powers's term as director was finished the school had grown to four hundred students.

In 1987 Powers was replaced by Professor Michael Nightingale, from England, who had had extensive teaching experience and had worked on a management level for the hotel and catering industry. Nightingale built on the strengths of HAFA and added new dimensions to the program. HAFA introduced graduate programs at the instigation of Dean Barham. A master's degree in Management Studies (MMS) commenced to turn out graduate students in the field. This degree began with a considerable research focus that was lost when the degree was renamed and reshaped into a business administration (MBA) degree. Dr. Robert Lewis was brought to Guelph from the University of Massachusetts to

Michael Nightingale.

head the graduate program, and Lewis's reputation as a leader in scholarship and hospitality education helped to establish the new programs on a sure footing and to enhance HAFA's scholarly reputation. HAFA also expanded its undergraduate numbers, which approached six hundred before declining somewhat, and added more faculty members to cope with the rising numbers of graduate and undergraduate students.

Nightingale was disturbed by the lack of experiential courses in the HAFA program. It was at this time that the co-op program was introduced in HAFA, soon becoming the largest co-op program in the university. Up to 25 percent of the undergraduate student body enjoyed the benefits of hands-on learning experience in industry, leaving their courses at Guelph temporarily for two, eight-month periods (later changed to a single period of one year). Other programs were introduced to add broader cultural experience to the HAFA program. Courses in French did not last very long because of low student enrolment, but a program offering a semester abroad in France proved to be more popular.

THE 1990S

The 1990s were a difficult period for most university campuses in Ontario. In the face of the government's social contract and cuts to university funding most programs faced important contractions. FACS was no exception. To cope with the reduction in government funding the University of Guelph introduced an early retirement program that affected a number of departments disproportionately, cutting back on regular teaching faculty at a time when student enrolment in the university as a whole continued to rise. Family Studies, for example, lost faculty members to retirement, early retirement, and resignation, and fewer than half of these were replaced. Fortunately for Family Studies, it could control the damage somewhat by restricting the number of entering students. There were also reductions in elective course offerings as departments focused on their own program's students.

Nevertheless, despite these difficulties, new developments were possible. A PhD program began, for example, in Family Relations and Human Development. A new relationship also began with the long-time nursery school program.

In 1990 fresh new facilities were opened for the university's Child Care and Learning Centre, the successor to the original Macdonald Institute Nursery School that had begun in the late 1950s. The original school had long made do with facilities in the basement of Macdonald Institute, supplemented by an outdoor playground and additional facilities for toddlers in a converted house on University Avenue East. Now the Child Care and Learning Centre acquired up-to-date facilities in keeping with its mandate both to act as a child care centre for children of the university and Guelph community and to facilitate learning for students in the Child Studies program.

The centre itself had extensive facilities. Rooms were set aside for the separate care of infants, toddlers, pre-school children, and kindergarten-age children. One-way observation booths looked onto each of these rooms, equipped with microphones so that the children could be both heard and watched. The observation booths facilitated extended use of the facilities by students, particularly those in Child Studies. The rooms themselves were stocked with above-standard equipment. Outdoors, an extensive playground provided space for organized and free play among the children. In the mid-1990s the centre's facilities were expanded to include classroom space for teaching Child Studies students who were in the centre working on their practicum. The Child Care and Learning Centre played a vital role, under the leadership of Barb Stuart, in providing vital learning facilities for the Child Studies students. As well as conducting detailed observations of the young children, the third-year students gained useful experience in working directly with the children as part of the students' field placement experience.

As well, funding was found for an expansion to the Macdonald Stewart Building. Opened in 1995, the extension provided much-needed space for HAFA and for Family Studies. This helped to ease some of the long-standing tensions and resentment about the unfulfilled

Left: *The ceremonial first shovel in the HAFA expansion, June 22, 1994.*

Right: *The trees come down for the new facilities.*

Left: *The footings go in.*

Right: *It finally starts looking like a building …*

Left: *… and it is almost complete.*

promises of building extensions and new space. The new addition contained office space, seminar rooms, and classrooms with U-shaped seating arrangements suitable for greater interaction among the students.

In Consumer Studies the evolution towards a marketing program was completed in the early 1990s. This was best symbolized when the BASc degree was ended for the program and the BCom was adopted. The Consumer Studies program now had two majors: one very successful program in Marketing Management, which had high student enrolments; and another in Housing and Real Estate (developed by John Pratschke and John Auld), which struggled over the following years to obtain satisfactory student support. To further enrich both majors a co-op program was added in the mid-1990s, allowing students on a regular basis (alternating with time at school) to spend time in the paid workplace, putting into practice some of the knowledge and skills they were learning at school. This program of change was completed by the new chair in the early 1990s, Dr. Marjorie Wall. About one-quarter of the students took up the co-op option, for which a minimum 70 percent average was required.

When Michael Nightingale became the new dean of FACS in 1994, he was eventually replaced by Dr. John Walsh as director of HAFA. Walsh brought a fresh enthusiasm to the position. He was the first Canadian-trained director of HAFA, a sign of a growing maturity in the academic side of the industry. Under Walsh's leadership the long-standing interest in tourism received greater emphasis. Courses that had long taught tourism to HAFA students were now used as the basis for a second undergraduate program, Tourism Management.

FACS continued to draw generous support from alumni, particularly the long-term alumnae from the early decades of Macdonald Institute. In 1992 the estate of Dorothy Britton, a diploma graduate of 1932, turned over $1,320,000 to scholarships at FACS. In the late 1990s the estate of the late Audrey Yeandle, a diploma graduate of 1925, donated $475,000 for bursaries to students in Family Studies and Consumer Studies. At approximately the same time the estate of Katherine Beck, a diploma graduate of 1922, donated $480,000 for scholarships. The donations added significantly to the bursary and scholarship funds available to students, and spoke well of the education received in the 1920s and 1930s and of the attachments and loyalty created during the time spent at Mac.[330]

The CSAHS Merger

One form of the 1990s retraction at the university shifted the administrative framework within which FACS operated. The financial exigencies of the mid-1990s placed pressure on all sectors of Ontario universities. One of the ways in which the University of Guelph responded was to consider administrative restructuring as a way of rationalizing the use of resources. The Strategic Planning Document, known locally as the Bunce report, discussed a number of ways in which administrative restructuring might occur at Guelph, including the

FACS Scrapbook

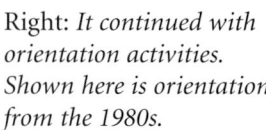

Left: *University life in the FACS years started with registration at the Athletic Centre.*

Right: *It continued with orientation activities. Shown here is orientation from the 1980s.*

Left: *There was lunch at the president's house …*

Right: *… and friends to make.*

Right: *And always Mac Institute was part of student life …*

Left: *… leading to that day when the degree is finally granted. Convocation 1979.*

Right: *FACS and HAFA students in the late 1980s.*

Left: *Here Dr. Vosburgh and Mike Taylor check out a diagram of a cow before attempting to milk it, 1974. He wasn't as successful as Dean Wardlaw!*

Right: *After the milking competition during Aggie Week '75, Dean Switzer, President Forster, and Dean Wardlaw check out her results. Our own honourary Aggie wins by one millimetre!*

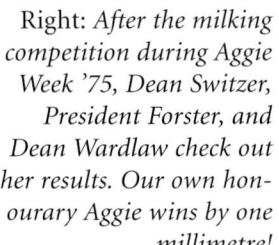

Left: *As always our college is well represented during College Royal. Here the crew from the famous HAFA restaurant take a break after another successful year.*

Right: *Preparing for the restaurant in the early 1990s.*

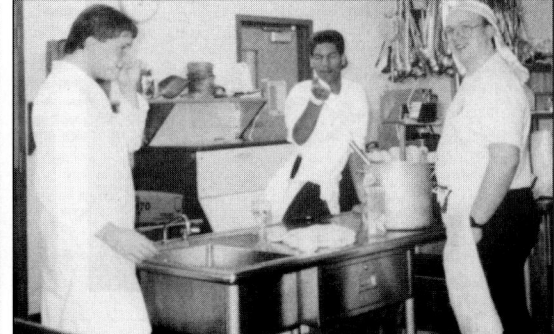

possibility of merging the College of Family and Consumer Studies and the College of Social Science. FACS was the smallest of the seven colleges on the Guelph campus and some felt that it suffered politically because of that. There was also a question of economies of scale — the hope that less money would be used for administrative purposes and more for teaching if the administrative apparatus of the university could be reduced. Finally, there was the hope that there would be intellectual and instructional synergy created among the various components of the two colleges if a merger occurred.

The idea of merger initially met with resistance in various sectors of the two colleges, but pressure was exerted by the senior administration of the university to give the idea serious consideration as a means of rationalizing resource allocation and creating a structural environment in which some fruitful cross-disciplinary work might occur. From 1995 to 1998 extensive discussions were held, particularly within the dean's councils of the two colleges, where, as the saying goes, a "full and frank" exchange of views occurred. As well, the two colleges had separate consultation processes. In FACS, for example, Dean Michael Nightingale set up a committee of faculty members, students, and alumni to ensure that all sectors of the college were consulted; open forums were occasionally held to discuss aspects of the merger idea.

Finally a consensus emerged that merger of the two colleges was an acceptable idea with the potential for fruitful synergy among the component units. The joint dean's councils drew up a merger document that was adopted by all of the departments involved. The new college was to be called the College of Social and Applied Human Science and began its life in 1998 with Michael Nightingale as its first dean. The new college built on pre-existing collaboration between the two colleges. The BCom program of HAFA and Consumer Studies had developed important links with the Department of Economics; Family Studies, particularly through its Gerontology and Child Studies programs, had useful links with Psychology, Sociology, and Geography. These links had developed without a merged college structure and without merger may have continued to flourish, but the expectation was that a unified college would facilitate co-operation, both at the teaching and research levels. There was also a political advantage in that CSAHS became the biggest college on the Guelph campus. FACS went from being the smallest college on campus to a member of the largest college, and now had the potential of greater political influence within the university. Thus in 1998, a new expanded college emerged, the College of Social and Applied Human Sciences, containing all of the components of the previous FACS.

Professor Michael Nightingale

Born in the United Kingdom, Michael Nightingale received extensive training and education in the hotel and foods industry. After receiving his diploma in hotel operations from the Westminster Technical College, he passed the membership examinations of the Hotel and Catering Institute. Studying part time at Manchester College of Commerce, he added to his credentials the Technical Teachers Certificate of the City & Guilds of London Institute and the Higher National Certificate in Business Studies. At the same time Nightingale began to teach in the field. In the early 1960s he lectured in hotel and catering subjects at Hollings College before becoming Education Officer of the Hotel and Catering Institute in London. For the next nine years he acted as chief executive to the Hotel, Catering & Institutional Management Association and its predecessor the Hotel and Catering Institute. Here he gained extensive experience with the industry in England and with managing a large organization that represented over twenty thousand members.

After leaving the Hotel, Catering & Institutional Management Association in 1976, Professor Nightingale moved into consultancy work within the industry, in which work he remained until he accepted the post of director of HAFA at the University of Guelph. He became dean of FACS in 1994 and then dean of the newly merged college, CSAHS, 1997–2000. In 2000, he moved into senior levels of administration of the University of Guelph as a whole, becoming vice-provost academic and chief academic officer for the University of Guelph–Humber.

EPILOGUE

The year 1998 saw the College of Family and Consumer Studies subsumed within a new organizational structure, the College of Social and Applied Human Sciences. But the antecedents in Macdonald Institute were still apparent and played a vital role in the new college. The dean and the central administrative offices were located in the long-standing Macdonald Institute building. The new college created a research centre to emphasize some of the research strengths across the various departments; called the Centre for Families, Work and Well-Being, it was headed initially by two faculty members from Family Studies (now newly named Family Relations and Applied Nutrition), Drs. Kerry Daly and Donna Lero. Michael Nightingale, the first dean of CSAHS, was replaced in 2000 by Dr. Alun Joseph.

Under the new college structure, some new initiatives were taken that affected the older FACS units. In 2002 the university senate approved a name change for

Dean Alun Joseph.

*Macdonald Institute
then …*

… and now.

HAFA. Henceforth the School of Hotel and Food Administration would be known as the School of Hospitality and Tourism Management, to reflect more accurately the type of education it offered. In that same year approval was given for a change in the majors offered by Family Relations and Applied Nutrition. The major in Applied Human Nutrition remained; what changed was combining the three previous majors in the family studies area into two — Gerontology remained a separate field, and Child, Youth and Family became a new major. Change will continue in the future.

Dr. Alun Joseph

Born in Wales, Alun Joseph received his PhD in geography from McMaster University. After teaching briefly elsewhere, he joined the Geography Department at Guelph in 1978 and began a long career of teaching, research, and administration. He had been department chair of Geography for eight years, 1992–2000, when he became the second dean of CSAHS.

Joseph had developed important ties with FACS through his interest in gerontology. His long-standing research interest in rural population dynamics and health care provision brought important strengths to the Canadian Aging Research Network. Through the Gerontology Research Centre and CARNET he collaborated with Dr. Anne Martin-Matthews in several research projects and publications investigating the problems faced by the rural elderly and health care issues for working people with aging family members in need of care. This collaboration was an important manifestation of the kind of ties being created by the expanding research activity in FACS.

But throughout this evolution, many elements of the traditions and experience of Macdonald Institute remained. The study of the family continued to be an area of special emphasis and expertise. But now no echoes were heard of the moralistic rhetoric of Adelaide Hoodless; rather, the faculty and students now examined a wide body of literature on the life course and some of its characteristic and non-characteristic elements. Faculty and student research pursued questions and data exposing the intricacies of individual and collective behaviour of persons at various or comparative stages of the life course. The new School of Hospitality and Tourism Management and the long-standing Department of Consumer Studies were natural outgrowths of Macdonald Institute's interests in food, food management, consumption, and consumer behaviour. The research and teaching continued to reflect a predominant emphasis on the applied, in the teaching, as reflected in practicum courses and the popularity of co-op programs, and in the research of graduate students and faculty. Macdonald Institute, which had begun its life as a haven for the education of young women, had evolved into a college that accepted women and men on an equal footing, and yet in practice women continued to dominate the classes of Family Relations and Applied Nutrition; informally, the college still played a special role in the education of women.

And yet women's education had changed dramatically since 1903. It had changed structurally in that women were no longer seen to need a segregated place of education. Instead, women were now fully incorporated into the halls of learning. In the case of home economics the systemic barriers to gender equality had disappeared. A segregated place of learning — of women, for women, by women — was no longer considered appropriate or desirable.

At the same time, in the 1960s, the special rural mission of Macdonald Institute came to an end. Rural society in general and rural women in particular no longer received the special and focused treatment represented by the Ontario Department of Agriculture's historic commitment to Macdonald Institute in the early twentieth century.

And yet Macdonald Institute had survived this double blow to its fundamental mission and character. Mac had reinvented itself, building naturally on its past characteristics to produce a new place of learning designed to meet the social and educational needs of a new era. Some of the old traditions of home economics — the training in housewifery and in manipulative skills — had quickly disappeared once change began, but many of the strengths remained. The very fact that Macdonald Institute successfully reinvented itself in the 1960s and has continued to build on that success suggests the strength of the institution itself and of its leadership.

Through the years a succession of remarkably able women found in Macdonald Institute a vehicle for their own achievement and personal success. Here was a post-secondary institution of learning where women's leadership was assured, in contrast to most colleges throughout the

twentieth century. Mary Urie Watson, Olive Cruikshank, Dorothy Lindsley, Margaret McCready, and Janet Wardlaw all received opportunities to demonstrate their administrative abilities and their leadership potential in what was otherwise a male-dominated academic world. Often these women found that those opportunities were restricted by the broader administrative world of the Ontario Agricultural College and the Ontario Department of Agriculture — all dominated by male administrators. The challenge to these women was considerable, but so was the opportunity. Women made Macdonald Institute the success that it was, despite considerable obstacles. Macdonald Institute was used as a vehicle to success by its leaders, its faculty members, and its students. After 1968, FACS opened its offices to increasing numbers of male faculty and male administrators, and yet the FACS departments and programs continued to offer opportunity to women, albeit no longer in an exclusive environment.

Reading the accounts of the cohorts of women who passed through the halls of Macdonald Institute and Macdonald Hall over the decades, one is struck by the variety of women who used Macdonald Institute to meet individual needs. Young women used Mac to gain some independence from home and family; some sought simply the sort of skills they would need in running their own homes and families. Not a few wanted the skills to compete in the workplace, even if only for a few years until the young women had gained some experience and were ready "to settle down." Some simply sought education, wanting "to better" themselves; in its early years Mac offered a particularly accessible education to those who for whatever reason had not completed their high school education. Middle-aged women too sought out an education at Macdonald Institute, particularly in the early decades, hoping to give themselves enhanced employment opportunities. A few women found themselves with the opportunity to teach at Macdonald Institute, often accepting lower salaries for the pleasure and status of teaching at the post-secondary level. The success that Macdonald Institute enjoyed was created by these women, with their varying motivations.

"My hope is constant in thee" — the motto from the stained glass windows in the stairwell at Mac Institute. As Macdonald Institute enters her second century we know she will endure and continue to be an important part of life at the University of Guelph.

MAC AT 100
by Scott N. Schau

A day at Macdonald Institute,
February 2003

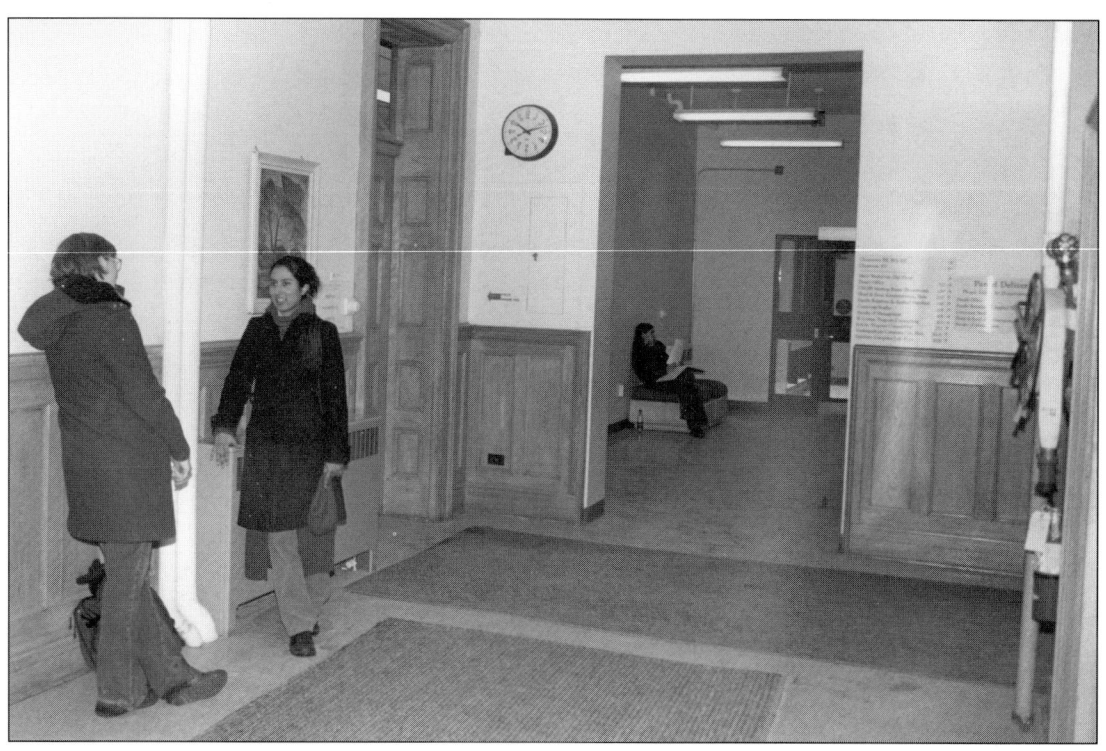

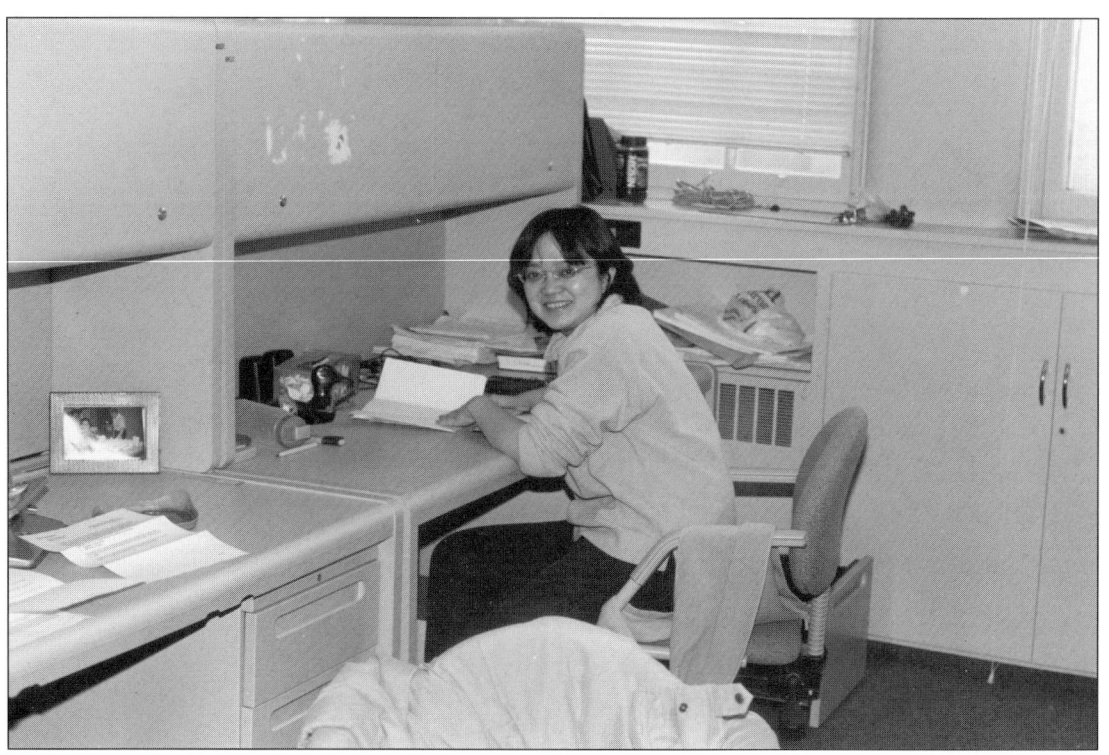

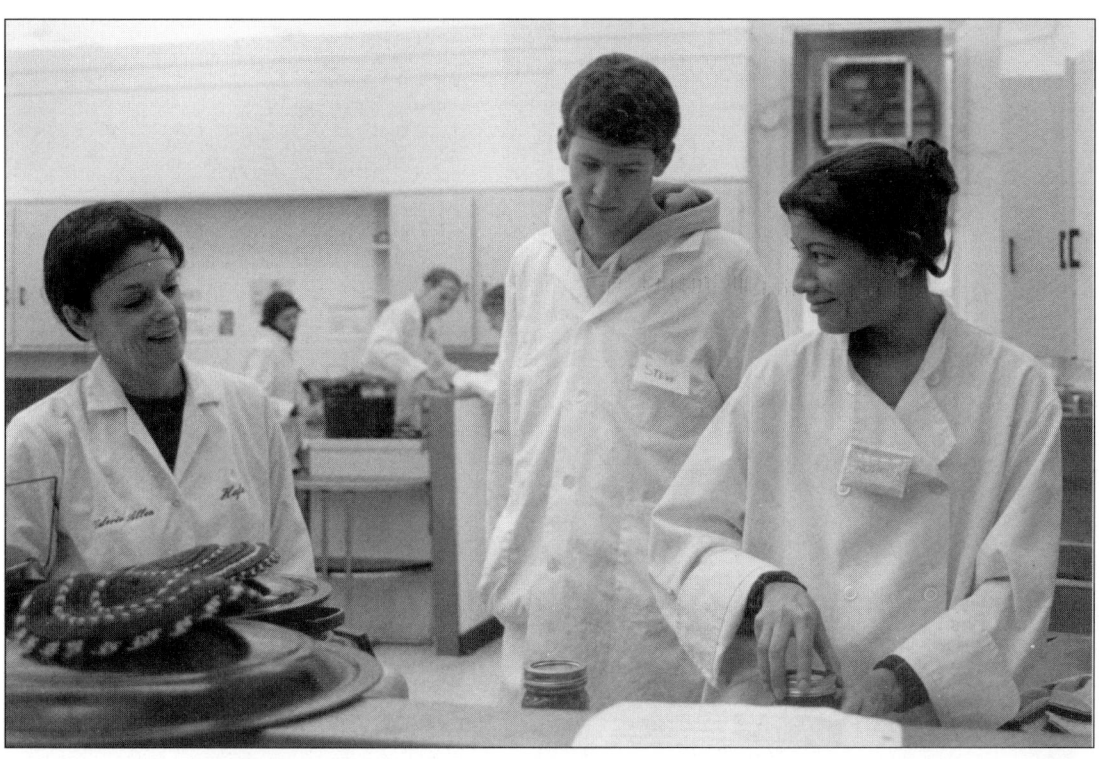

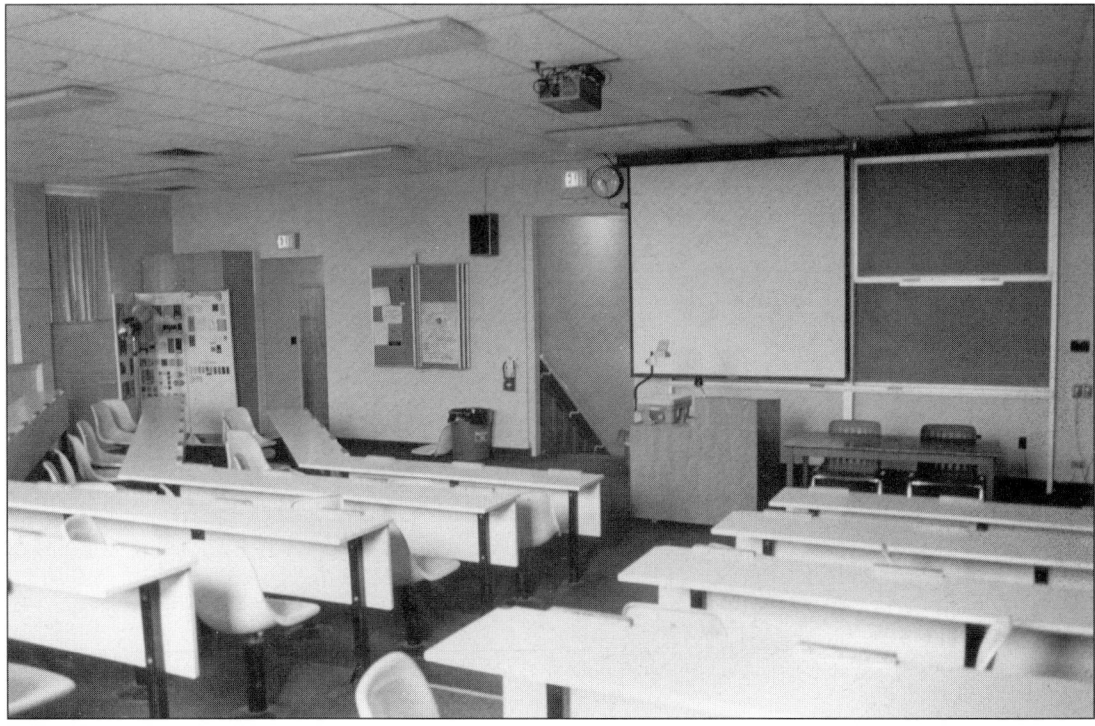

NOTES

1   J.M. Taylor, *Fashioning Farmers: Ideology, Agricultural Knowledge and the Manitoba Farm Movement, 1890–1925* (Regina: Canada Plains Research Centre, 1995).

2   A. Adams, *Architecture in the Family Way: Doctors, Houses, and Women, 1870–1900* (Montreal: McGill-Queen's University Press, 1996).

3   A.B. McKillop, *Matters of the Mind: The University in Ontario, 1791-1951* (Toronto: University of Toronto Press, 1994), 141.

4   See, for example, L. Rose, "The Womanly Sphere of Women," in Ontario, *Sessional Papers*, #24 (1906), Report of the Women's Institutes of Ontario, 30-34.

5   *Proceedings of the Sixth Annual Lake Placid Conference on Home Economics*, cited in I. Bevier and S. Usher, *The Home Economics Movement* (Boston: Whitcomb and Barrows, 1906), p. 21.

6   C. Manthorpe, "Science or domestic science? The struggle to define an appropriate science education for girls in early twentieth-century England," *History of Education*, 15 (1986), 195-213; D.E. St.John, "Educate or Domesticate?: Early twentieth century pressures on older girls in elementary schools," *Women's History Review*, 3 (1994), 191-218; R. Bayliss, "Flexner, Smithells and Home Economics," *Journal of Educational*

Administration and History, 8 (1976), 9-18; Bayliss, "Home Economics and the Special Reports," *ibid.*, 7 (1975), 18-27; J. Matthews, "Education for Femininity: Domestic Arts Education in South Australia," *Labour History*, 45 (1983), 30-53; McKillop, *Matters of the Mind*, 177.

7   R.S. Harris, *A History of Higher Education in Canada, 1663-1960* (Toronto: University of Toronto Press, 1976), 284-285.

8   L. Ambrose, *For Home and Country: the Centennial History of the Women's Institutes of Ontario* (Erin, Ont.: Boston Mills Press, 1996), 40.

9   The most comprehensive biography of Hoodless is Cheryl MacDonald, *Adelaide Hoodless: Domestic Crusader* (Toronto: Dundurn Press, 1986); more analytic and insightful are: T. Crowley, "Madonnas before Magdalenes: Adelaide Hoodless and the Making of the Canadian Gibson Girl," *Canadian Historical Review*, 67 (December 1986), 520-547; and Crowley, "Adelaide Sophia Hunter (Hoodless)," *Dictionary of Canadian Biography*, XIII, *1901–1910* (Toronto: University of Toronto Press, 1994), 488-493.

10   I. Bevier and S. Usher, *The Home Economics Movement* (Boston: Whitcomb and Barrows, 1906), 34-36.

11   H.H. Dean, "Dairy Instruction at the Agricultural College," Ontario, *Sessional Papers*, #22 (1904), 162.

12   UGA, Hoodless Family Papers, box 1, correspondence file, J. Mills to A. Hoodless, Guelph, 9 March 1900: "I am glad to know that you are favourable to the establishment of such a Department in connection with the College; and I shall be glad of any assistance which you may render in this direction." OAC faculty members occasionally lectured in bacteriology and chemistry at Hoodless's Hamilton school; see R.M. Stamp, "Adelaide Hoodless, Champion of Women's Rights," in R.S. Patterson, et al., eds., *Profiles of Canadian Educators* (Toronto: D.C. Health, 1974), 213.

13   *Ibid.*, J. Mills to J.W. Robertson, Guelph, 31 October 1901; *ibid*, A. Hoodless to [Sir W. Macdonald, n.p., 8 November 1901].

14   S.B. Frost and R.H. Michel, "Sir William Christopher Macdonald," *Dictionary of Canadian Biography*, XIV, *1911 to 1920* (Toronto: University of Toronto Press, 1998), 689-694.

15   *Ibid.*, G.W. Ross to J.W. Robertson, Toronto, 18 February 1902; *ibid.*, J. Mills to Robertson, Guelph, 17 February 1902; *ibid.*, Robertson to Mills, Ottawa, 15 February 1902; *ibid.*, Sir W. Macdonald to Robertson, Montreal, 13 February 1902; *ibid*, Order-in-Council, 7 March 1902.

16   *Ibid.*, J. Mills to A. Hoodless, Guelph, 10 May 1902; *ibid.*, R. Harcourt to Hoodless, Toronto, 2 January 1902; *ibid*, A. Hoodless to [Sir W. Macdonald, n.p., 8 November 1901].

17   *Ibid.*, box 3, clippings file 1904; *ibid.*, clippings file 1903, Toronto *Globe*, 3 October 1903; E.M. Ferguson, "Early Days at Macdonald," *The OAC Review*, Oct. 1908, 54-56; *ibid*, Fall 1955, 28-29.

18   *Ibid.*, box 1, correspondence file, J. Mills to A. Hoodless, Guelph, 5 October 1903; *ibid.*, Mills to J.W. Robertson, Guelph, 5 January 1904; *ibid.*, "Things to be aimed at"; *ibid.*, "Things to be aimed at."

19   *Ibid.*, J. Mills to J.W. Robertson, Guelph, 1 April 1903.

20   *Toronto Star*, 15 September 1950; *Guelph Mercury*, 15 September 1950; *Globe & Mail*, 15 September 1950; RE1 MAC A0014, box 2, file 1915–20, M.U. Watson to Miss Mills, Ayr, Ont., 26 August 1915.

21   *Ibid.*, [A. Hoodless] to G. Creelman, Hamilton, 18 August 1904; Macdonald, *Hoodless*, 141-144. In October 1912 the WI of Ontario presented Macdonald Institute with a portrait of Adelaide Hoodless, "President of Macdonald Hall"; the reading room in Macdonald Hall was redecorated and refurnished in keeping with its lofty status as home to the portrait. That portrait now hangs in Macdonald Institute. (See *The OAC Review*, Dec. 1912, 166, June 1913, 509-510.)

22   UGA, Watson correspondence, RE1 Mac A0014, box 2, file 1915–17.

23   Ontario, *Sessional Papers*, 1904, 37, part IV, the OAC Report #14, 147; City of Guelph Inventory of Heritage Structures, #1047; City of Guelph Building Inventory, #91.

24   *The OAC Review*, Dec. 1914, 182-185; City of Guelph Building Inventory, #90; RE1 MAC A0014, box 1, file 1918–19, M.U. Watson to A.E. Knight, [Guelph], 22 January 1918.

25   James Mills, *Provisional Announcement of the Macdonald Institute Ontario Agricultural College for 1903–1904* (Guelph, August 1903), 6.

26   The Manual Training program moved out of Macdonald Institute in 1907 though it continued to offer elective courses to Mac students in such subjects as plain carpentry, woodcarving, art metal work, basketry, and colour work, aiming at giving students an understanding of principles of construction and an appreciation of aesthetics. See *The OAC Review*, June 1907, 465-469.

27   Small numbers of women began to attend OAC after the dairy school opened a short-course in 1893, but women were not admitted to the degree program in OAC until 1918. A.M. Ross and T. Crowley, *The College on the Hill: A New History of the Ontario Agricultural College, 1874–1999* (Toronto: Dundurn Press, 1999), 51, 63.

28   M.L. Friedland, *The University of Toronto: A History* (Toronto: University of Toronto Press, 2002), 184.

29   Watson's standard explanation for this was that the Macdonald and Toronto programs simply did not mesh easily; to what extent this is accurate is unclear. It is, of course, possible that friction was developing between the two programs, exacerbated by the Ministry of Education transferring its accreditation of the teacher training program in 1915 and/or that the academic quality of the Macdonald courses was judged inadequate by authorities at the University of Toronto. (See, for example, UGA, Watson Correspondence, RE1 MAC A0014, box 1, file 1920, M. Watson to V. Donaldson, [Guelph], 26 May 1920.)

30   UGA, Watson Correspondence, RE1 MAC A0014, box 1, file 1916–17, M. Watson to L. McMechan, [Guelph], 23 Feb. 1916.

31   G. Greenwood, "A Country School Equipment," *The OAC Review*, Feb. 1908, 285-288. Grace Greenwood was a graduate of Columbia University's Teachers' College and a Mac instructor in teaching methods.

32   *OAC Calendar 1912–1913*, 84-86; UGA, Watson Correspondence, RE1 MAC A0013, box 1, file 1920, M. Watson to B. Summers, [Guelph], 4 February 1920; J.E.T., "Home Economics as Related to Institutional Housekeeping," *The OAC Review*, June 1911, 521-522.

33   UGA, Watson Correspondence, RE1 MAC A0014, box 1, file 1916–17, M. Watson to E. Zavitz, [Guelph], 27 July 1916; *ibid.*, Watson to H. Pirie, [Guelph], 19 April 1917.

34   *The OAC Review*, April 1914, 361.

35   *OAC Calendar 1912–1913*, 83.

36   On the place of domestic art in this curriculum, see *The OAC Review*, May 1906, 397-399. On the sewing curriculum, see *The OAC Review*, Jan. 1908, 250-252. *OAC Calendar 1912–1913*, 71.

37   *OAC Calendar 1910–1911*, 82; UGA, Watson correspondence, RE1 Mac A0014, box 1, file 1913–16.

38   This parallels the growing tendency to provide professional expertise on child-rearing and to decline to rely on the transmission of knowledge and skills from parents and female networks. See: C. Comacchio, *'Nations Are Built of Babies': Saving Ontario's Mothers and Children, 1900–1940* (Montreal: McGill-Queen's University Press, 1993); K. Arnup, *Education for Motherhood: Advice for Mothers in Twentieth-Century Canada* (Toronto: University of Toronto Press, 1994).

39   For one view of the short-course program, see E.M. and A.D., "Macdonald as Seen by

Short Course Students," *The OAC Review*, Feb. 1912, 277-278.

40   UGA, Watson correspondence, RE1 Mac A0014, box 1, file 1913–16. This became such a standard explanation for rejecting urban applicants that it was drawn up as a form letter.

41   In the United States there was a similar tendency towards a more rigorous curriculum without totally counteracting the stigma; see Bevier and Usher, *Movement*, 41.

42   Ironically, the WI conventions moved to Convocation Hall at the University of Toronto (as well as to Massey Hall in Toronto), paralleling the 1915 loss of the teacher training accreditation to the same university.

43   Ambrose, *For Home and Country*, 38-39.

44   A.M. Ross and Terry Crowley, *The College on the Hill: A New History of the Ontario Agricultural College, 1874–1999* (Toronto: Dundurn Press, 1999), 65, 72-73.

45   Bringing middle-class values and behaviour to rural Canada was not quite so easy as the founders of the OAC and Macdonald Institute believed and as the administrators and faculty of those two institutions found out; see Prof. W. Lochhead, "The Agricultural College and Rural Life," *The OAC Review*, Feb. 1907, 258-260.

46   UGA, Watson correspondence, RE1 Mac A0014, M. Watson to J.B. Spencer, [Guelph], 12 December 1916 and attached memo "Macdonald Institute Loan Collection"; *ibid.*, box 2, file 1915–20, G.C. Creelman to M. Watson, Guelph, 29 October 1917.

47   Ambrose, *Home and Country*, 50-51.

48   UGA, Watson correspondence, RE1 Mac A0014, box 1, file 1914–15, M. Watson to C.N. South, [Guelph], 26 Oct. 1915; *ibid.*, Watson to B. Hamilton, [Guelph], 29 January 1920; McKillop, *Matters of the Mind*, 198-202.

49   Watson appears to have done the hiring of staff and faculty members, the OAC president simply retaining control over the number of hirings; see UGA, Watson correspondence, RE1 Mac A0014, box 2, file 1905–1919, M. Watson to G.C. Creelman, [Guelph], 18 May 1905. Watson's own networks within domestic science tended to be American and, given her own educational background, she tended to turn to the U.S. in recruiting instructors; see: *ibid.*; *ibid.*, Watson to L.I. Pratt, [Guelph], 22 June 1916.

50   The OAC faculty members and Adelaide Hoodless were not included in these calculations. McKillop, *Matters of the Mind*, 277 points out the infrequency of female academic appointments on other campuses; in this regard, domestic science faculties stood out in contrast to their contemporaries.

51   A. Hoodless and M.U. Watson, *Public School Household Science* (Toronto: Copp Clark, 1905); UGA, Watson correspondence, RE1 Mac A0014, box 4, file extension 1909–15,

B.R. Andrews to M. Watson, New York City, 6 January 1909; *ibid.*, M. Van Rensselaer to Watson, Ithaca, N.Y., 28 January 1915.

52   *The OAC Review*, April 1907, 349.

53   E.M. and D.W., "Summer Vacation of a Homemaker," *The OAC Review*, Oct. 1911, 46-47, tells of two students returning home for the summer and being called "homebreaker" rather than "homemaker" because of their challenges to their mothers' home regimen.

54   UGA, Watson correspondence, RE1 Mac A0014, box 1, file 1914–15, M. Watson to C.N. South, [Guelph], 26 Oct. 1915.

55   The positive student perspective is suggested both by the large number who kept in touch with Mac after graduation and by Hazel Staebler's account, "Benefits and Advantages of Macdonald Institute Courses," *The OAC Review*, Jan. 1910, 228-231. C.M. Crowe, a graduate of 1913, commented: "I have yet to meet the Macdonald graduate who regrets the time she spent within those halls of learning." (*Ibid.*, Nov. 1913, 92-93.)

56   *The OAC Review*, December 1904, 182-186, Nov. 1912, 83; Ross and Crowley, *College on the Hill*, 95-96.

57   For descriptions of initiation see: *The OAC Review*, Oct. 1907, 42, Nov. 1908, 111-112, Oct. 1909, 43-44, May 1910, 455, Nov. 1910, 96-97, Nov. 1911, 102, Nov. 1912, 84, May 1913, 442-443, Dec. 1913, 179, Oct. 1914, 58-59, Feb. 1915, 226, June 1915, 435, Oct. 1915, 67.

58   *The OAC Review*, Jan. 1910, 230, June 1910, 490, Jan. 1914, 205, Oct. 1914, 56-57, Oct. 1915, 68.

59   One manifestation of this sense of community was a Mac publication, *Public Opinion*, published apparently by the students and exhibiting the camaraderie and joking common among those with a shared sense of community. (See RE1 MAC A0152.)

60   UGA, RE1 OAC A0145, H.B. Mullein to M. Watson, 4 December 1905; *ibid.*, Watson to Mullein, [Guelph], 8 December 1905.

61   Elections were held and, judging from notes in *The OAC Review* (July 1915, 466, Nov. 1915, 104), there were some two dozen officers chosen for different posts.

62   E.M. Ferguson, "Early Days at Macdonald," *The OAC Review*, Oct. 1908, 55-56.

63   In this self-contained character, Macdonald Hall resembles the University of Toronto's use of the Lillian Massey Home Economics building, where a wide range of facilities were provided for women, allegedly matching the men's exclusive facilities in Hart House. The self-contained character had an element of isolation. When Creelman Hall dining room opened in 1914 right across the road from Mac Hall, the girls nevertheless remained in their own dining room. Girls were "allowed" to "go into town"

in the late afternoon but otherwise they were required to stay on campus, except on weekends and with notice. There was only one telephone in Macdonald Hall for contact with "the outside world"; see *The OAC Review*, June 1913, 574.

64 UGA, Watson correspondence, RE1 Mac A0014, box 1, file 1916–17, M. Watson to D. Weir, [Guelph], 10 February 1916.

65 See, for example: *The OAC Review*, Jan. 1907, 205, Nov. 1907, 108-109, Dec. 1907, 173-174, March 1912, 328.

66 For purposes of discussion here, until 1964 I will be treating the student body of both the OAC and OVC as male, ignoring the small number of young women in these two programs.

67 This echoes the courtship styles of the time; see B. Bailey, *From Front Porch to Back Seat: Courtship in Twentieth-century America* (Baltimore: Johns Hopkins University Press, 1988), where courtship in the girl's family home gave her considerable ability to control the character and pace of courtship.

68 There is a good description of the 1905 Hallowe'en Ball in *The OAC Review*, Dec. 1905, 149-151.

69 Carnival was first mentioned in *The OAC Review*, Feb. 1915, 219.

70 For a contemporary description of Conversazione, see *The OAC Review*, March 1911, 318-320. See also, Ross and Crowley, *College on the Hill*, 101-102.

71 *The OAC Review*, Feb. 1914, 258.

72 *The OAC Review*, Jan. 1912, 224, Feb. 1912, 273, Oct. 1912, 34, March 1913, 320; McKillop, *Matters of the Mind*, 251; *Macdonald Institute Alumnae News*, February 1962, 6. At least on some occasions, the campus YW/YMCA organized games and music for those couples who did not wish to dance; see *The OAC Review.*, Jan. 1914, 206.

73 "Much Ado About Nothing," *The OAC Review*, Dec. 1908, 199. See also, for example, *ibid.*, April 1910, 385-386, April 1911, 383-384, June 1911, 524, March 1915, xviii.

74 See, for example: *The OAC Review*, Jan. 1908, 230-232, April 1912, 396-397, Feb. 1913, 272-273, April 1913, 354-355, 383, Nov. 1913, 93.

75 *The OAC Review*, July 1911, 570-572; Ross and Crowley, *College on the Hill*, 96.

76 M.U. Watson in 1911, in Ontario, *Sessional Papers*, #14 (1913), Report of the Women's Institutes of Ontario, 1912, 41.

77 Notification of the withdrawal arrived so late in Guelph that the 1915-16 Calendars had already been printed; see UGA, Watson correspondence, RE1 Mac A0014, box 1, file 1914–15, Secretary to P. Stanley, [Guelph], 6 July 1915. Two years earlier the ministry had withdrawn its accreditation for the University of Toronto's one-year pro-

gram, making the abrupt reversal of that earlier decision that much more surprising.

78   UGA, Watson correspondence, RE1 Mac A0014, box 1, file 1913–16, M. Watson to M. Dawson, [Guelph], 14 June 1914; *ibid.*, *passim*.

79   J.A. Allen, "The Practical Value of Technical Training in Domestic Science in the Home," *The OAC Review*, March 1911, 328. See also, UGA, Watson correspondence, RE1 Mac A0014, box 5, file letters personal 1915-20, M. Hutton to M. Watson, Druid, Sask., 26 June 1920.

80   RE1 MAC A0014, box 5, file on World War One, *passim*; *ibid.*, W.J. Hanna to M.U. Watson, Ottawa, 22 December 1917; *ibid.*, J. Muldrew to Watson, 20 December 1917; *ibid.*, Watson to W.A. Wilson, 23 February 1918; *The OAC Review*, Dec. 1914, 142, Feb. 1915, 227, Nov. 1915, 103, Dec. 1915, 175, April 1916, 341, June 1916, 422, Feb 1917, 264, Dec. 1917, 179, April 1918, 360.

81   *The OAC Review*, Nov. 1914, 58.

82   *The OAC Review*, May 1918, 404-406, 440-43, Dec. 1918, 195, 198-199.

83   RE1 MAC A0014, box 1, file 1918-19, M.U. Watson to A. Keegan, [Guelph], 26 November 1918; *ibid.*, E. Jamieson to Watson, Oshweken, Ont., 24 December 1918; *ibid.*, Watson to Jamieson, [Guelph], 28 December 1918; *ibid.*, Watson to V.L. Harmer, 2 January 1919; *ibid.*, box 2, file 1918-20, Watson to J.M. Taylor, 14 November 1918. See also, for example, *ibid.*, W.H. Garland to Watson, Toronto, 8 October 1918; *ibid.*, R.J. Hopper to Watson, Brantford, Ont., 1 November 1918; *The OAC Review*, Nov. 1918, 134-135.

84   RE1 MAC A0014, box 2, file 1918-20, M.U. Watson to J. Clark, [Guelph], 28 January 1920; *ibid.*, Watson to P. McLeay, 30 January 1920; *ibid.*, J.C. Grant to Watson, Vancouver, 29 January 1920 and *passim*; *ibid.*, box 1, file 1920, Watson to A.D. Watson, [Guelph], 9 March 1920; *The OAC Review*, March 1920, 363.

85   RE1 MAC A0014, box 2, 1918–20, M.U. Watson to W. Frank, [Guelph], 27 March 1920; *ibid.*, A. Hill to Watson, Sarnia, Ont., 30 December 1918.

86   RE1 MAC A0014, box 2, file 1905–19, M.U. Watson to Miss Pott, [Guelph] 15 July 1919, and attachment; *ibid.*, G.F. Plant to Watson, London, Eng., 11 October 1919; *ibid.*, F.C. Blair to G.C. Creelman, Ottawa, 15 November 1919.

87   RE1 MAC A0014, box 1, file 1920, M.U. Watson to D. Marsten, [Guelph], 1 June 1920; *ibid.*, box 2, file 1920, Watson to Miss Vernon, 13 February 1920; *ibid.*, Watson to C.M. Wadge, 15 April 1920.

88   RE1 MAC A0014, box 1, file 1918–19, L. Chilton to M.U. Watson, Ottawa, 6 May 1919; *ibid.*, Watson to Chilton, [Guelph], 10 May 1919; *ibid.*, "Training Courses for Soldiers'

Wives and Daughters." See also, file 1919-20, Lt. O.B. Binkley to the OAC, Harrogate, Eng., 28 July 1919; *ibid.*, box 5, file on World War One, Watson to Secretary, Great War Veterans Association, [Guelph], 24 February 1919; *ibid.*, file extension 1919–20, M. Williams to Watson, Toronto, 28 April 1920.

89   RE1 MAC A0014, box 1, file 1916–17, G.A. Locking to M.U. Watson, Emo, Ont., 10 May 1917; *ibid.*, box 3, file supplies 1918–20, Watson to Moffat Stove Co., [Guelph], 19 August 1915; Annual Report of the OAC and Experimental Farm, 1915 in Ontario, *Sessional Papers*, #30, 1916, 38-40; Annual Report of the Women's Institutes, in *ibid.*, #41, 1916, 176-177; *Calendar*, 1916–1917, 98-99.

90   RE1 MAC A0014, box 4, file extension 1916, "Macdonald Institute Loan Collection," [1916].

91   RE1 MAC A0017, box 14, file 1920–22 and *passim.*

92   RE1 MAC A0014, box 1, file 1914-15, M.U. Watson to B. Sharpe, [Guelph], 2 July 1915; *ibid.*, file 1920, Watson to G.V. Jamieson, 12 April 1920.

93   RE1 MAC A0014, box 1, file 1914–15, M.U. Watson to L. Cook, [Guelph], 2 July 1915.

94   Annual Report of the Minister of Agriculture, in Ontario, *Sessional Papers*, 1927, #21, 34.

95   Ross and Crowley, *College on the Hill*, 104, 113.

96   RE1 MAC A0017, box 1 file 1920–24, R.H. Clemens to O. Cruikshank, Arthur, Ont., 31 July 1922; M.B. Cruden, to Cruikshank, Fergus, Ont., 17 June [1922]; *ibid.*, box 8, file 1926-28, [O. Cruikshank] to W. Schenck et al., [Guelph], 1 February 1926; *ibid.*, box 14, file 1927–28, J. Carroll to Cruikshank, Toronto, 10 January 1927.

97   RE1 MAC A0014, box 2, file 1905–19, M.U. Watson to L.I. Pratt, [Guelph], 22 June 1916.

98   RE1 MAC A0017, box 6, file 1920–29, OAC staff meeting, October 1929. Cruikshank regretted when J.B. Reynolds stepped down as president of the OAC. "I shall miss him greatly, I can hardly bear the thought of working under any other President, but I expect to give it a trial anyway." (See RE1 MAC A0017, box 2 file 1928, [Cruikshank] to A. Laird, [Guelph], 18 July 1928.)

99   Report of the OAC for 1928, in Ontario, *Sessional Papers*, 1929, #30, 6. While a student at Mac in 1914, Bradley had been chosen Athletic President; she was lauded as "a born organizer … [and] one of the very nicest and best all-round girls and good sports that ever entered Macdonald Hall." (*The OAC Review*, Oct. 1914, 56.) A scholarship was established in Bradley's memory to be awarded to the graduating student with high marks in foods and cooking who "is considered to be the most faithful in her work, and most thoughtful of others." (See, *ibid.*, 51.)

100   Compare RE1 MAC A0063 (Nellie Harcourt) with RE1 MAC A0045 (Clara Maxwell).

101   RE1 MAC A0017, box 4, file 1923–25, [O, Cruikshank] to G.M. Sneyd, Montreal, 13 July 1924; *ibid.*, box 9, file appointments, [Cruikshank] to W.B. Roadhouse, [Guelph], 8 June 1928.

102   RE1 MAC A0017, box 8, file 1926–28, J. Bradley to O. Cruikshank, Guelph, 16 February 1928 (italics in original).

103   Faculty members received a salary ranging between $1400 and $2800, but paid for their own room and board. See RE1 Mac A0017, box 9, file 1920–30, [O. Cruikshank] to D.A. Cowan, [Guelph], 22 September 1922.

104   RE1 MAC A0017, box 6, file 1920–29, O. Cruikshank, Guelph, [April 1924].

105   Report of the Minister of Agriculture, in Ontario, *Sessional Papers*, 1922, #29, 10.

106   RE1 MAC A0017, box 3, file 1929–30, [O. Cruikshank] to M. Seaborn, [Guelph], 14 December 1929; *Libranni*, 1948.

107   RE1 MAC A0017, box 1, file 1920–24, [O. Cruikshank] to V. Smith, [Guelph], 21 April 1921; McKillop, *Matters of the Mind*, 291; R.C. Brown and R. Cook, *Canada, 1896–1921: A Nation Transformed* (Toronto: McClelland and Stewart, 1974), chapter 15.

108   RE1 MAC A0014, box 1, file 1920, M.U. Watson to V. Donaldson, [Guelph], 26 May 1920.

109   University of Toronto Archives, Falconer Papers, A75-0008-001, Minutes, 23 February 1923; *ibid.*, 5 May 1924; *Calendar*, 1921–1922, 68; RE1 MAC A0017, box 6, file 1920-29, [O. Cruikshank] to J.B. Reynolds, [Guelph], 28 April 1922; *ibid.*, Reynolds to Cruikshank, 22 April 1922.

110   RE1 MAC A0017, box 6, file 1920–39, [O. Cruikshank] to W.B. Roadhouse, [Guelph], 26 January 1928; *ibid.*, box 4, file 1928–29, [Cruikshank] to A. Laird, 19 November 1928.

111   *Calendar*, 1917–1918, 92; *ibid.*, 1921–1922.

112   *Calendar*, 1922–1923, 73; *ibid.*, 1925–1926, 67; *Year Book*, 1926, 53; RE1 MAC A0017, box 3, file 1920–39, [O. Cruikshank] to W.B. Roadhouse, [Guelph], 26 January 1928.

113   *Year Book*, 1926, 72; *ibid.*, 1927, 74.

114   RE1 MAC A0014, box 1, file 1918–19, M.U. Watson to D.E. Smith, [Guelph], 1 May 1918; *ibid.*, Watson to C. Evans, 8 May 1919.

115   RE1 MAC A0014, box 1, file 1919–20, A.R. Coffin to M.U. Watson, Truro, N.S., 3 March 1919; *ibid.*, Watson to Coffin, [Guelph], 10 March 1919; *ibid.*, file 1917–18, Watson to M. Hutchings, 27 March 1918; *ibid.*, file 1919–20, Watson to J. Cameron, 30 October 1919.

116   *Calendar*, 1923–1924, 73; RE1 MAC A0017, box 2, file 1920–22, [?] to J. McCallum, [Guelph], 2 August 1922; *ibid.*, box 4, file 1920–22, [O. Cruikshank] to A.H.U.

Colquhoun, [Guelph], 18 July 1922; *ibid.*, box 9, file 1920–30, 24 January 1924; *ibid.*, Colquhoun to Cruikshank, Toronto, 8 February 1924.

117 RE1 MAC A0017, box 6, file 1920–29, O. Cruikshank to J.B. Reynolds, [Guelph], 16 April 1924, attachment.

118 RE1 MAC A0017, box 6, file 1920–39, [O. Cruikshank] to W.B. Roadhouse, [Guelph], 24 January 1928.

119 RE1 MAC A0017, box 1, file 1920–24, [O. Cruikshank] to M. Campbell, [Guelph], 15 March 1922; *ibid.*, [Cruikshank] to E.P. Bailey, 19 April 1922; *ibid.*, box 6, file 1920–29, [Cruikshank] to J.B. Reynolds, 3 January 1922; *ibid.*, box 5, file 1938-39, [Cruikshank] to C. Marshall, 4 March 1939; *The OAC Review*, January 1931, 265-266. In the fall of 1929 a committee was struck to investigate the possibility of acquiring a practice house on campus, to replace the apartment; see RE1 MAC A0017, box 8, file 1929–31; *ibid.*, box 7, file 1932–34, [O. Cruikshank] to G.I. Christie, [Guelph], 6 July 1932.

120 RE1 MAC A0017, box 2, file 1926–27, [O. Cruikshank] to I. Payne, [Guelph], 22 August 1927.

121 RE1 MAC A0017, box 8, file 1920–25, newspaper clipping of July 1925.

122 RE1 MAC A0017, box 4, file 1928–29, E.C.S. to Mrs. Gurnett, [Guelph], 22 January 1929; *ibid.*, E.C.S. to Judge M. Patterson; *ibid.*, E.C.S. to J.L. Rutledge; *ibid.*, box 6, file 1920–30. Other students studied marketing at such sites as the Canadian Rail and Harbour Terminals Cold Storage Warehouse, White & Company Food and Vegetable Warehouse, and the Royal Winter Fair.

123 RE1 MAC A0017, box 6, file 3, [O. Cruikshank] to Mrs Hamilton, [Guelph], 23 January 1924; *ibid.*, box 6, file 1920–29, [Cruikshank] to G.I. Christie, 13 May 1929.

124 RE1 MAC A0014, box 1, file 1919–20, G.P. Allen to M.U. Watson, Mt. Forrest, Ont., 1 August 1919.

125 RE1 MAC A0014, box 1, file 1920, B. Hamilton to M.U Watson, Galt, Ont., 23 January 1920; *ibid.*, A0017, box 2, file 1923–25, H.M. Ogilvie to Secretary, Port Hope, Ont., 3 September 1924.

126 RE1 MAC A0014, box 2, file 1905–17, M.U. Watson to H.W.T., [Guelph], 14 March 1916, 27 March 1916.

127 RE1 MAC A0014, box 1, file 1917–18, M.U. Watson to L.C. MacNutt, [Guelph], 6 September 1918.

128 RE1 MAC A0014, box 1, file 1917–18, E. Lumsden to M.U. Watson, Galt, Ont., 22 December 1918.

129 McKillop, *Matters of the Mind*, 322-361.

130   On the 1920s students from South Africa, see *The OAC Review*, January 1934, 250-251; April-May 1934, 441.

131   RE1 MAC A0017, box 6, file 1920–29, [O. Cruikshank] to J.B. Reynolds, [Guelph], 6 December 1926. See also: *ibid.*, box 8, file 1926–28, 25 April, 1928; *ibid.*, box 3, file 1920–29, Cruikshank to W.B. Roadhouse, 12 January 1928.

132   RE1 MAC A0017, box 3, file 1920–39, [O. Cruikshank] to W.B. Roadhouse, [Guelph], 26 January 1928, attachments; *ibid.*, 3 September 1926.

133   RE1 MAC A0017, box 3, file 1920–39, W.B. Roadhouse to J.B. Reynolds, Toronto, 11 October 1921; *ibid.*, [O. Cruikshank] to W.J. Bell, [Guelph], 22 October 1921; *ibid.*, box 3, file 1929–30, 20 September 1930; *ibid.*, Bell to Cruikshank, Kemptville, Ont., 25 September 1930.

134   RE1 MAC A0017, box 3, file 1920–39, *passim*; *ibid.*, [O. Cruikshank] to J.S. Martin, [Guelph], 2 September 1925; *ibid.*, Cruikshank to W.B. Roadhouse, 3 September 1926.

135   A good example of the sort of letter recommending several graduates can be found at RE1 MAC A0017, box 11, file 1923–24, [O. Cruikshank] to Dr. W.J. Robinson, Wingham, Ont., 28 December 1923. A list of Mac placements for 1924 can be found at *ibid.*, [Cruikshank] to Miss Elthorpe, 22 August 1924, enclosure.

136   RE1 MAC A0014, box 5, file extension 1917, M.U. Watson to B. Roadhouse, [Guelph], 22 March 1917; Report of the OAC for 1928, in Ontario, *Sessional Papers*, 1928, #21, 51; *The OAC Review*, June 1920, 521-522; Midsummer 1945, 459-460; RE1 MAC A0017, box 2, file 1926-27, E. Nichol to O. Cruikshank, Toronto, 27 April 1927.

137   Report of the OAC for 1930, in Ontario, *Sessional Papers*, 1930, #21, 41-42. In addition, nine students had taken the Optional course, sixty-five the public school classes, and nineteen the two-week Special course.

138   *The OAC Review*, February 1928, 209.

139   *The OAC Review*, February 1920, 306.

140   *The OAC Review*, October 1950, 62.

141   *Calendar*, 1921-1922, 86.

142   *The OAC Review*, March 1931, 400.

143   RE1 MAC A0017, box 9, file 1920–30, [O. Cruikshank] to M.D. Allen, [Guelph], 18 June 1929.

144   *The OAC Review*, May 1920, 477; June 1929, 488; June 1930, 599.

145   R. Wagner, "Libranni, 1914-1969," unpublished report, 1.

146   *The OAC Review*, January 1926, 219. In 1937 there was a brief experiment with mixed tables in Creelman, but it was soon discontinued; see *ibid.*, January 1938,

212, 215-216; February 1938, 309-310. Otherwise the girls sat at assigned tables mixing first- and second-year students; *ibid.*, October 1935, 23. See also, *ibid.*, November 1933, 100.

147   *The OAC Review*, October 1920, 81.

148   R. Wagner, "Libranni, 1914–1929," 2; *Year Book*, 1918, 44; Ross and Crowley, *College on the Hill*, 101.

149   RE1 MAC A0017, box 6, file 1920–29, O. Cruikshank to G.I. Christie, Guelph, 16 April 1929.

150   *Year Book*, 1923, 55; *The OAC Review*, October 1935, 24; *ibid.*, December 1935, 148-150.

151   *The OAC Review*, March 1919, 334-336.

152   RE1 MAC A0014, box 2, file on World War One, M.U. Watson to W.A. Wilson, [Guelph], 23 February 1918.

153   *The OAC Review*, December 1933, 175; McKillop, *Matters of the Mind*, 362-363, 437, 439.

154   Annual Report of the OAC and Experimental Farm for 1929, in Ontario, *Sessional Papers*, #21, 9; *ibid.*, for 1936, in Ontario, *Sessional Papers*, #21, 26; McKillop, *Matters of the Mind*, 425. The numbers cited in fact add up to 249 students; the error is in the original.

155   RE1 MAC A0017, box 6, file 1920–29, J.B. Reynolds to O. Cruikshank, Guelph Bay, Ont., 13 August 1925; *ibid.*, [Cruikshank] to Reynolds, [Guelph], 21 August 1925; *The OAC Review*, September 1930, 12; November 1931, 196.

156   *The OAC Review*, September 1931, 47; February 1932, 416; October 1931, 123.

157   RE1 MAC A0017, box 3, file 1931–34, [O. Cruikshank] to H. Millar, [Guelph], 3 October 1932.

158   RE1 MAC A0017, box 7, file 1937–43, G.I. Christie to O. Cruikshank, Guelph, 16 March 1938; *ibid.*, Cruikshank to Christie, 18 March 1938; *ibid.*, file 1932–34, Summary of appropriation, staff and attendance, 1919–1934.

159   REI MAC A0017, box 7, file 1935–36, [O. Cruikshank] to G.I. Christie, [Guelph], 11 May 1935; *ibid.*, M.C. Kay et al. to Christie, Guelph, 4 June 1935; *ibid.*, Christie to Kay, 6 June 1935.

160   RE1 MAC A0017, box 7, file 1932–34, [O. Cruikshank] to G.I. Christie, [Guelph], 6 July 1932.

161   *The OAC Review*, April-May, 1934, 417-420, 436; RE1 MAC A0017, box 1 file 1931–36, A. Ross to Judge R.S. Hosking, [Guelph], 25 September 1934; *ibid.*, box 17, file 1920–42, [O. Cruikshank] to N. Hutchinson, [Guelph], 28 March 1928. On the rise of the child study movement in 1930s Canada, see V. Strong Boag, "Intruders in the

Nursery," in J. Parr, ed., *Childhood and Family in Canadian History* (Toronto: McClelland and Stewart, 1982), 160-178.

162   RE1 MAC A0017, box 7, file 1935-36, O. Cruikshank to G.I. Christie, Guelph, 29 February 1936; *ibid.*, box 8, file 1935-42, Cruikshank to O. McConkey, 1 February 1935; *ibid.*, McConkey to Cruikshank, 4 February 1935; *ibid.*, box 8, file 1935–42, 2 November 1938; *ibid.*, "R" to McConkey, [Guelph], 25 November 1938 and enclosure. On the eugenics movement in Canada, see A. McLaren, *Our Own Master Race: Eugenics in Canada, 1885–1945* (Toronto: Oxford University Press, 1990).

163   *The OAC Review*, November 1936, 121.

164   *Year Book*, 1930, 66; *The OAC Review*, March 1937, 296-297; RE1 MAC A0017, box 7, file 1937-43, [O. Cruikshank] to G.I. Christie, [Guelph], 4 February 1937.

165   RE1 MAC A0017, box 7, file 1935–36, [O. Cruikshank] to G.I. Christie, [Guelph], 10 December 1935; *ibid.*, box 7, file 1932–34, 16 November 1932 and enclosure; *ibid.*, box 8, file 1935-42, G.W. Clark to Cruikshank, 15 September 1928.

166   RE1 MAC A0017, box 8, file 1929-31, memo for Professor Bell.

167   *Year Book*, 1931, 89.

168   *The OAC Review*, May 1931, 383-384.

169   RE1 MAC A0017, box 8, file 1935–42, Result of questionnaire given to ninety-six junior students at Macdonald Institute, November 1937.

170   McKillop, *Matters of the Mind*, 421.

171   *The OAC Review*, November 1937, 95; Summer 1938, 482-483. See also, RE1 MAC A0017, [O. Cruikshank] to V. Timmins, [Guelph], 28 February 1939; *ibid.*, box 7, file 1937-43, [Cruikshank] to G.I. Christie, Guelph, 8 November 1939.

172   RE1 MAC A0017, box 16, file 1937, M. McCready to G.I. Christie, Ste. Anne-de-Bellevue, Que., 13 March 1944; *ibid.*, M. Kay to McCready, [Guelph], 16 March 1944.

173   RE1 MAC A0017, box 5, file 1931; *ibid.*, box 6, file 1930–31, [O. Cruikshank] to G.I. Christie, [Guelph], 5 February 1931; *ibid.*, box 7, file 1935–36, 29 February 1936.

174   Sixteen planned to take a degree, thirteen were undecided, and twenty-two hoped to take a degree in the future; forty-six reported no plans to take a degree. See *The OAC Review*, December 1937, 153-155.

175   Annual Report of the OAC and Experimental Farm for 1935, in Ontario, *Sessional Papers*, #21, 88. See also, *ibid.*, for 1933, 132. Macdonald Institute began to adjust its curriculum to facilitate the transition from Guelph to Toronto; see RE1 MAC A0017, box 7, file 1935–36, G.I. Christie to C.C. Benson, Guelph, 7 March 1936; *ibid.*, [O. Cruikshank] to Christie, [Guelph], 5 March 1936.

176 University of Toronto Archives, Sidney Smith Papers, A68-0007-050, file 7, A. Fennell to S. Smith, Toronto, 20 May 1946; *ibid.*, a meeting of the representatives from Macdonald Institute and from the University of Toronto, 18 November 1936; RE1 MAC A0017, box 7, file 1935-36, G.I. Christie to O. Cruikshank, Guelph, 24 November 1936 and enclosure.

177 RE1 MAC A0017, box 3, file 1920–39, [O. Cruikshank] to T.H. Zavitz, [Guelph], 8 March 1938; *ibid.*, Cruikshank to A. Robson, 19 May 1939; *ibid.*, box 5, file 1931, [Cruikshank] to H.R. Fair, 17 November 1931; *ibid.*, box 5, file 1933–34, "R" to A.A. Morrison, 23 November 1934; *ibid.*, box 5, file 1936–37, [Cruikshank] to E.E. Held, 3 March 1937. For the early 1930s see the list of the 1931 graduates in *ibid.*, box 15, file 1931, list of graduates of Macdonald Institute, OAC, June 1931.

178 Annual Report of the OAC and Experimental Farm for 1929, in Ontario, *Sessional Papers*, #21, 43.

179 RE1 MAC A0017, box 5, file 1935, summary of December 1935 examination records.

180 See, for example, RE1 MAC A0017, box 8, file 1935–42, memo to OAC Review, [Guelph], 6 July 1938.

181 *The OAC Review*, July 1933, 476; Annual Report of the OAC and Experimental Farm for 1928, in Ontario, *Sessional Papers*, #30, 51; *ibid.*, for 1932, in #30, 182-183; *ibid.*, for 1933, in #30, 135.

182 R. Heap, "From the Science of Housekeeping to the Science of Nutrition: Pioneers in Canadian Nutrition and Dietetics at the University of Toronto's Faculty of Household Science," in E. Smyth, et al., *Challenging Professions: Historical and Contemporary Perspectives on Women's Professional Work* (Toronto: University of Toronto Press, 1999), 141-170.

183 RE1 MAC A0017, box 6, file 1920–29, [O. Cruikshank] to G.I. Christie, [Guelph], 17 December 1929.

184 RE1 MAC A0017, box 6, file 1920–29, [O. Cruikshank] to G.I. Christie, [Guelph], 14 Octber 1929; *ibid.*, box 6, file 1930–31, 15 December 1930. See, for example, Cruikshank's comments on Winnifred Schenck: "She is an enthusiastic, energetic teacher and gets good class-room results; but she is forever complaining in public, where she has no business to discuss college affairs, about the heavy programme and the lack of opportunity at Macdonald, and how overworked she is. When she is ordered to do extras such as articles for publication, such as special classes for two weeks students, she does it and does it well but one cannot depend on her to fill in and take hold when an emergency occurs."

185   University of Toronto Archives, S. Smith Papers, A68-0007-050, file 7, a meeting of representatives from Macdonald Institute and from the University of Toronto, 18 November 1936; RE1 MAC A0017, box 3, file 1935–37, [O. Cruikshank] to C.C. Benson, [Guelph], 27 July 1937; *ibid.*, RE1 MAC A0017, box 5, file 1935, [O. Cruikshank] to H.C. Hindmarsh, 13 November 1935.

186   *Guelph Mercury*, 10 May 1928, 1,8; *Calendar*, 1933–34, 113-4.

187   RE1 MAC A0017, box 14, file 1925, E.M. Chapman to O. Cruikshank, Toronto, 19 January 1925; *ibid.*, box 8, file 1932–34, A.E. Barber to Cruikshank, Guelph, 27 April 1932; *ibid.*, box 17, file 1920-44, [Cruikshank] to B.J. Sandy, 5 May 1937; *ibid.*, box 1, file 1931–36, [Cruikshank] to A.L. Laird, 5 May 1936; *Guelph Mercury*, 11 May 1938, 14.

188.   *The OAC Review*, June 1931, 454; April-May 1939, 429; RE1 MAC A0017, box 14, file 1927-28, 1927 Girls' Conference program and 1928 Girls' Conference program; *ibid.*, file 1926, 1926 Girls' Conference program.

189   *Ontario Farmer*, July 1932, 28, 31, 41.

190   RE1 MAC A0017, box 14, file 1925, [O. Cruikshank] to J.S. Martin, [Guelph], 24 February 1925.

191   RE1 MAC A0017, box 15, file 1931, [O. Cruikshank] to C.W. Buchanan, [Guelph], 5 March 1931.

192   See, for example, E. Chapman, "At Ontario's Farm and Home Week," *Ontario Farmer*, August 1932, 27, 29, 31, 41; *ibid.*, "Putting the Home in Farm and Home Week," July 1933, 25, 39.

193   RE1 MAC A0017, box 7, file 1935–36, G.I. Christie to O. Cruikshank, Guelph, 28 August 1936.

194   RE1 MAC A0017, box 6, file 1930–31, G.I. Christie to O. Cruikshank, Guelph, 17 September 1931; *ibid.*, 21 September 1931; *ibid.*, box 7, file 1935-36, 24 February 1936.

195   See, for example, RE1 MAC A0017, [O. Cruikshank] to C.E. Pickett, [Guelph], 22 October 1931.

196   RE1 MAC A0017, box 5, file 1936–37, Supervisor of Watson Hall to B.A. Blackwell, [Guelph], 19 February 1936.

197   *The OAC Review*, November 1929, 145; February 1930, 345, 350; March 1930, 404.

198   *The OAC Review*, March 1930, 404.

199   *Calendar*, 1932–33, 126.

200   *The OAC Review*, March 1930, 405-406; February 1936, 291; McKillop, *Matters of the Mind*, 414.

201   *The OAC Review*, February 1934, 272-273.

202   *The OAC Review*, December 1938, 174-175, 181-182; November 1940, 83.

203   *The OAC Review*, February 1935, 301, 304, 318-19; October 1936, 10-12. See also, *ibid.*, December 1936, 165.

204   *The OAC Review*, March 1930, 416-417; December 1930, 170; February 1931, 344.

205   *The OAC Review*, Summer 1935, 489.

206   RE1 MAC A0017, box 5, file 1938–39, C.J. to O. Cruikshank, Toronto, 10 January 1939.

207   *Libranni*, 1934, 80.

208   Ross and Crowley, *College on the Hill*, 101-102.

209   *The OAC Review*, March 1931, 400.

210   *The OAC Review*, April 1930, 488.

211   *The OAC Review*, May 1918, 437-438.

212   *The OAC Review*, September 1931, 40-42; October 1938, 56.

213   RE1 MAC A0017, box 1, file 1931–36, [O. Cruikshank] to M. McGregor, [Guelph], 8 March 1934. Photographs of the 1930 wrestling team make it clear that at least one person of colour had recently attended the OAC.

214   *The OAC Review*, February 1940, 286-306; Annual Report of the OAC and Experimental Farm for 1940, in Ontario, *Sessional Papers*, #21, 24; Annual Report of the Department of Agriculture for 1942, in Ontario, *Sessional Papers*, #21, 5; *ibid.*, for 1941, #21, 6.

215   *The OAC Review*, October 1940, 18-19; Annual Report of the OAC and Experimental Farm for 1940, in Ontario, *Sessional Papers*, #21, 23.

216   *The OAC Review*, Midsummer 1941, 485.

217   Annual Report of the OAC and Experimental Farm for 1944, in Ontario, *Sessional Papers*, #30, 6; RE1 UOG A1340020, 1989 interview with L. Brill.

218   UGA, RE1 MAC A0019, file 1946–49, President of OAC to L. McMechan, Guelph, 11 October 1945.

219   UTA, Sidney Smith Papers, A68-0007, box 19, file 5; *ibid.*, file 7. Dr. Smith later encouraged the president of the OAC to think of an independent university for the Guelph campus.

220   UTA, Sidney Smith Papers, A68-0007, box 19, file 7, Confidential Report of C.B. Arny to S. Smith, 24 June 1947.

221   *Ibid.*

222   UTA, Sidney Smith Papers, A68-0007, box 19, file 7, S. Smith to T.L. Kennedy, 18 February 1949.

223   *The OAC Review*, December 1944, 151-152; March 1945, 324-326, 340; Midsummer 1946, 449.

224   *The OAC Review*, April-May 1949, 416.

225   UTA, Sidney Smith Papers, A68-0007, box 19, file 7; UGA, RE1 A1340019, interview of D. Lindsley Walden, 14 April 1989.

226   "Our Heritage in Macdonald Institute," *Home and Country*, 33, #1 (Winter 1967), 16-17; "A Girl and Her Goals," *Home and Country*, 27, #3 (Fall 1961), 11-12; "The Girls' Conference," *Home and Country*, 22, #3 (Fall 1956), 8; *Home and Country*, 17, #1 (overseas tour issue), 12; "Dr. Margaret McCready Speaks," *Home and Country*, 16, #1 (Spring 1950), 13-14; *Home and Country*, 15, #1-2 (Summer 1949), 1; *Home and Country*, 14, #1-2 (Spring & Summer 1948); *Home and Country*, 10, #4 (Winter 1944-45).

227   Macdonald Institute *Calendar*, 1948–1949, 1. See also, *The OAC Review*, Midsummer 1949, 490-491.

228   Macdonald Institute *Calendar*, 1951–1952, 1.

229   UGA, RE1 MAC A0020, box 1, file 1949–55.

230   M.S. McCready, "Over the Years at Macdonald Institute," *Canadian Home Economics Journal*, 5, #4 (December 1955), 5.

231   UGA, RG1 MAC A0020, box 4, file 1953–54.

232   Annual Report of the Department of Agriculture, in Ontario, *Sessional Papers*, #21, 1954, 73-74; *The OAC Review*, Spring 1960, 23.

233   G.L. Duggan, "A Study of Some Aspects of Home Economics Education in Canadian Universities," *Canadian Home Economics Journal*, 2, #2 (June 1952), 12-15. See also, *ibid.*, 2, #4 (January 1953), 8; E.C. Rowles, "Are Our Universities and Colleges Offering Adequate Programs in Home Economics?," *Canadian Home Economics Journal*, 8, #4 (December, 1958), 9-10, 21; M. DuBois, "The Challenge of Home Economics Today," 9, #1-2 (March, June, 1959), 3-4, 26, 3-4, 22.

234   Ross and Crowley, *The College on the Hill*, 141.

235   Olive Wallace reported in *The OAC Review*, April 1956, 10, that an estimated 85 percent of dietitians married within five years of graduation, creating many openings for employment.

236   M.S. McCready, "The Days Ahead," *The OAC Review*, June 1955, 12.

237   Macdonald Institute *Calendar*, 1960–1961, 33.

238   O.A.C. and Macdonald Institute *News Bulletin*, 8 June 1959, 1-2; D.R. Baskerville, "A New Development at Macdonald Institute," *The OAC Review*, Summer 1959, 23; UGA, RE1 MAC A0020, box 1, file 1961–62.

239   UGA, RE1 MAC A0020, box 1, file 1961–62, "One Year Diploma Course," 20 November 1961; *Librani* 1963.

240 M.S. McCready, "Whither Home Economics?," *The OAC Review*, Spring 1957, 8-9.

241 E.M. Curran and D.R. Baskerville, "Satisfying Homemaking: One Homemaker Meets Today's Challenge to Homemaking," *The OAC Review*, Winter 1956, 12-13. See also, "Satisfying Homemaking: Another Homemaker Meets Today's Challenge to Homemaking," *ibid.*, Spring, 1957, 12-13.

242 See, for example, L.M. Poole, "Canadian Association of Consumers," *The OAC Review*, Summer 1957, 15, 31.

243 *Macdonald Institute Alumnae News*, February 1962, 13.

244 M.S. McCready, "Over the Years at Macdonald Institute," *Canadian Home Economics Journal*, 5, #4 (December 1955), 6-7; *The OAC Review*, October 1951, 7; March 1952, 282-284; Winter 1957, 22-23, 31. A fadeometer tested colour fastness of textile material; a launderometer tested the washability of a fabric and the effects of soaps and synthetic detergents.

245 *Ibid.*

246 *Canadian Home Economics Journal*, 13, #1 (March 1963), 13; UGA, RE1 MAC A0020, box 1, file 1949-61, recruitment pamphlet [1961]. UBC had the second largest program with 195 degree students and 30 education students; Manitoba was third, and Laval was fourth.

247 *The OAC Review*, January 1954, 182; *Ontarion*, 1 February 1961, 3.

248 Mabel Sanderson carried out graduate work at Purdue in the mid-1950s, while Mary Singer went to Ohio State University. Sanderson was promoted to full professor on her return.

249 UGA, RE1 MAC A0020, box 5, file 1961, Macdonald Faculty 1961; *Macdonald Institute and Family and Consumer Studies Alumni Newsletter*, Summer 1978, 4; Ross and Crowley, *College on the Hill*, 146.

250 Ross and Crowley, *College on the Hill*, 150.

251 *The OAC Review*, Spring 1954, 314, 318, 322; UGA, RE1 MAC A0020, box 6, file 1954-65, M. McCready to C.H. Bailey, [Guelph], 18 October 1954; *ibid.*, to A.C. Goodings, 18 October 1954; *ibid.*, box 8, file 1953–54, 1907–1966 Graduate Studies of Macdonald Institute Graduates.

252 *Macdonald Institute Alumnae News*, February 1962.

253 *Librani 1947*, 2.

254 *The OAC Review*, Winter 1955, 13.

255 *The OAC Review*, October 1949, 30; October 1953, 23.

256 *The OAC Review*, Winter 1957, 6; *Ontarion*, 19 October 1960, 1.

257   *The OAC Review*, March 1949, 324; Summer 1959, 6.

258   *The OAC Review*, November 1951, 140.

259   *Calendar, 1950-1951*, 4; *Calendar, 1954-55*, 17; *Ontarion*, 31 January 1963, 1.

260   *Ontarion*, 19 October 1960, 1-2.

261   *Ontarion*, 2 March 1960, 4.

262   *Calendar, 1957–1958*, 20; *Calendar, 1961–62*, 15.

263   *The OAC Review*, December 1950, 154; *Ontarion*, 19 November 1952, 5.

264   *The OAC Review*, February 1952, 252.

265   *The OAC Review*, December 1946, 163; December 1948, 144; January 1948, 222.

266   M.L. Adams, *The Trouble with Normal: Postwar Youth and the Making of Heterosexuality* (Toronto: University of Toronto Press, 1997).

267   *The OAC Review*, October 1951, 38. See also, *ibid.*, November 1949, 117; February 1950, 311; Midsummer 1950, 495; January 1952, 186; March 1952, 322, 328; November 1952, 87.

268   *The OAC Review*, March 1949, 309-310; *Ontarion*, 6 February 1957; UGA, RE1 MAC A0020, box 2, file 1950-55, M. McCready to S. Margolius, [Guelph], 15 September 1955. In 1959 there were six married students, out of a total of 212; UGA, RE1, MAC A0020, box 4, file 1951-63.

269   *The OAC Review*, October 1950, 57.

270   *The OAC Review*, October 1946, 1, 20, 38, 54; October 1953, 38-39.

271   *Ontarion*, 9 February 1955, 4.

272   *The OAC Review*, November 1946, 109.

273   *The OAC Review*, February 1948, 292-293; Midsummer 1951, 403, 412.

274   *Ontarion*, 5 November 1955, 1-2; 24 October 1956, 1; 31 October 1956, 1; UGA, RE1 MAC A0020, box 4, file 1953-54; *ibid.*, file 1955.

275   M.S. McCready, "Over the Years at Macdonald Institute," *Canadian Home Economics Journal*, 5, #4 (December 1955), 7.

276   "Manhattan Diary," *Ontarion*, 26 September 1956; UGA, RE1 Mac A0020, box 2, file 1954-57.

277   D.R. Baskerville, "Home Economics? A Home Economist Challenges Her Profession," *The OAC Review*, Fall 1958, 8-9, 30-31.

278   D.R. Murray, *Hatching the Cowbird's Egg: The Creation of the University of Guelph* (Guelph: University of Guelph, 1989), 15.

279   UGA, XR1 MS A559, F.W.I.O. Macdonald Institute Expansion Presentation to the Department of Agriculture, April 1964.

280   Murray, *Hatching*, 65.

281 D.R. Baskerville, "Home Economics? A Home Economist Challenges Her Profession," *The OAC Review*, Fall 1958, 8-9, 30-31.

282 Baskerville, "Home Economics?," *The O.A.C. Review*, Fall 1958, 8-9, 30-31.

283 A. Prentice, et al., *Canadian Women: A History* (Toronto: Harcourt Bruce Canada, 1988), 289-294, 319-324; *1970-71 Canada Year Book* (Ottawa: Statistics Canada, 1971), 221.

284 UGA, RE1 MAC A014185, box 015C, food study group file, E. Thompson to M. McCready, 13 September 1966.

285 *Canadian Home Economics Journal*, July 1969, 15.

286 UGA, RE1 MAC A014206, box 002A, McCready file 1964–68, Report of Special Meeting, 28 May 1965.

287 UGA, RE1 UOG A1317138, UofG President (Winegard), Correspondence with Dean, Macdonald Institute, 1966–67, B.C. Matthews to M. McCready, 29 August 1966.

288 UGA, RE1 MAC A014183, box 015A, file 1964–65; *ibid.*, A014206, box 002A McCready, file 1964-65; *Ontarion*, 14 January 1965, 10.

289 UGA, RE1 MAC A014206, box 002A, McCready, file 1964–65, staff meeting of 16 September 1964.

290 UGA, RE1 MAC A014183, box 015A, McCready, Senate Executive Committee, 1964–65; *ibid.*, A014184, box 015B, McCready, Senate, 1964-66, Macdonald Institute Report to Senate, December 1964.

291 UGA, RE1 MAC A0020, box 6, file 1954–65, M. McCready to C. Black, [Guelph], 10 April 1963; McCready to M.A. Rollins, [Guelph], 30 April 1963; *Ontarion*, 28 January 1965, 4.

292 UGA, RE1 MAC A014183, box 015A, McCready, Senate Executive Committee, 1964–65, minutes, 8 December 1965.

293 UGA, RE1 MAC A014184, Senate minutes, 13 December 1965.

294 UGA, RE1 MAC A1317/66, Macdonald Institute Brief, 1966.

295 *Ibid.*, unsigned minute [by J.D. MacLachlan].

296 J.M. Wardlaw, "History College of Family and Consumer Studies 1968–1978", 2.

297 UGA, RE1 MAC A014205, box 001F, "Academic Brief: Macdonald Institute and School of Hotel and Food Administration," 28 June 1968 [henceforth "Academic Brief"].

298 *Ibid.*, 2.

299 *Ibid.*, 35-36.

300 UGA, RE1 MAC A014183, box 015A, Senate Executive Committee 1964–65.

301 UGA, MAC RE1 A014163, box 0009H, *Canadian Hotel Review and Restaurant*, 15 April 1963.

302 E.M. Legacey, "The Development of HAFA and Macdonald Institute," 4-5.

303   UGA, MAC RE1 A014182, box 014F, study committee on food management file, M.S. McCready to M. Sanderson and O. Wallace, [Guelph], 16 March 1965.

304   *Ibid.*, 5-7.

305   University of Guelph, *Calendar, 1969–70*, 14.

306   UGA, RE1 MAC A014206, box 002A, McCready, file 1964-68, staff meeting of 7 September 1965; *ibid.*, 28 March 1968; *Ontarion*, 9 November 1967.

307   University of Guelph, *Calendar, 1970–71*, 21.

308   University of Guelph, *Calendar, 1968–69*, 30-31.

309   University of Guelph, *Calendar, 1968–69*, 268-295.

310   *Macdonald Institute and Family and Consumer Studies Alumni News*, Summer 1978, 20.

311   *Macdonald Institute Alumnae News*, Fall 1968, 13.

312   *Macdonald Institute Alumnae News*, Spring 1970, 5; *ibid.*, Fall 1969, 1; *ibid.*, Winter 1971, 4; *Macdonald Institute Family and Consumer Studies Alumni News* [hereafter *MacFACS Alumni News*], 17, #2 (Summer 1978), 23.

313   *MacFACS Alumni News*, 13, #3 (Fall 1973), 1.

314   *MacFACS Alumni News*, 17, #2 (Summer 1978), 22.

315   *MacFACS Alumni News*, 13, #1 (1973), 3.

316   *MacFACS Alumni News*, 15, #1 (Spring 1972), 7.

317   *MacFACS Alumni News*, 18, #1 (Spring 1979), 2.

318   *Macdonald Institute Alumnae News*, Winter 1971, 3, 5; interview of G. Morgan, Guelph, 17 and 25 September 2001; interview of R. Barham, Guelph, 20 September 2001.

319   *Macdonald Institute Alumnae News*, 12, #2-3 (1972), 12; *ibid.*, 11, #4 (1971), 7.

320   *MacFACS Alumni News*, 12, #4 (1972), 7.

321   *MacFACS Alumni News*, 13, #1 (1973), 4, 6-7.

322   *Macdonald Institute Alumnae News*, Winter 1971, 4.

323   *MacFACS Alumni News*, 12, #4 (1972), 4; *ibid.*, 16, #2 (1977), 6.

324   *MacFACS Alumni News*, 13, #1 (1973), 5, 7-8.

325   *MacFACS Alumni News*, 1980 alumni weekend supplement, 2.

326   *Macdonald Institute Alumnae News*, Summer 1971, 6.

327   *Macdonald Institute Alumnae News*, 11, #4 (1971), 6; *ibid.*, 12, #2-3 (1972), 12; *MacFACS Alumni News*, 12, #4 (1972), 1-2; *ibid.*, 17, #2 (Summer 1978), 21; *ibid.*, 14, #3 (1974), 3; *ibid.*, 16, #1 (1977), 2.

328   *MacFACS Alumni News*, 16, #3 (1977), 3.

329   *Guelph University News Bulletin*, 10 January 1985, 1-2.

330   *At Guelph*, 12 July 2000, 8; 25 March 1992.

Index